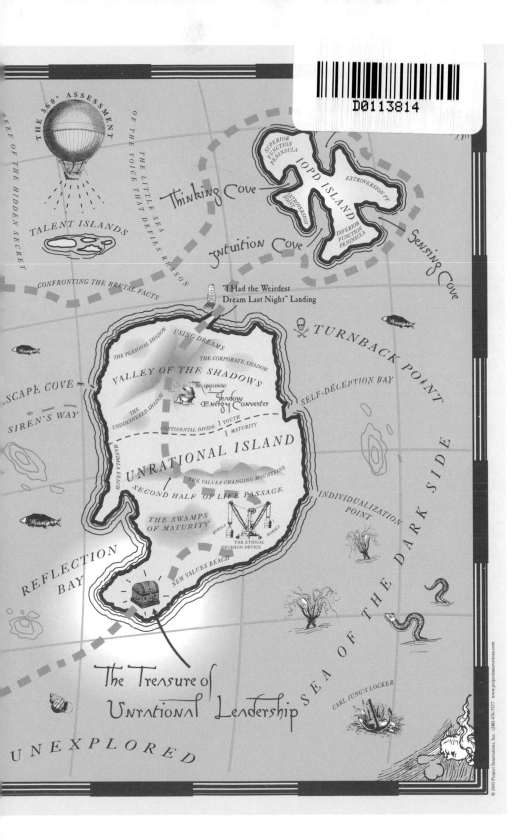

THE
SEARCH FOR
Un Rational
LEADERSHIP

Chris,

Enjoy the Search!

Charlie

THE
SEARCH FOR
Un Rational
LEADERSHIP

Using rational *and*
irrational *methods*
to change your life

Charles Fleetham

Right Brain Books LLC

Right Brain Books LLC
22000 Springbrook Ave., Suite 106
Farmington Hills, MI 48336
Tel: 248-476-7577 Fax: 248-476-2515

Library of Congress Control Number: 2004099768

Fleetham, Charles B. (Charles Blake), 1953—
    The Search for Unrational Leadership™ / Charles Fleetham.—1st ed.
    Includes bibliographical references and index.
    ISBN 0-9763868-0-1 (hardcover: alk. Paper)
    ISBN 0-9763868-1-X (paperback: alk. Paper)

Editing: **Lisa Burdige & Anna Raleigh**
Copyediting: **Beverly Church**
Text Design/Lay-out: **Sans Serif Inc.**
Manufacturing: **Cushing-Malloy, Inc.**
Map/Logo: **Bidlack Creative Group**
Fairytale Illustrations: **Simon Breslav**

Printed in the United States of America

For
Pauline Napier

To
Derek Fleetham and Chelsea Fleetham

Contents

Acknowledgements

When I started the predecessor of *The Search for Unrational Leadership*™ in 1991, I imagined that I would write a book, send it to a publisher, and wait for the good news about my best seller. The journey to complete this book opened my eyes. It took a team to find the treasure of Unrational Leadership™. I would like to acknowledge the following people for their feedback, inspiration, and work on this project: Kathy Anderson, Linda Anger, Rick Arons, Chris Bidlack, Simon Breslav, Vivian Bradbury, Lisa Burdige, Beverly Church, Jeffrey Duvall, David Fleetham, Gary Fujita, Pat DiGiovanni, John Giannini, Dick Hinshon, Lewis Jones, Rich Kingston, John Leigh, ML Liebler, Mary Moultrup, Rich Pierson, Ken Pool, Tom Power, Anna Raleigh, Andi Schuldt, Alicia Shankland, Melody Shoemaker, Joey Silvian, Jo Anna Trierweiler, and Mary Trybus.

And, I would also like to thank the following people for their special contributions to the book:

- Debbie Pezon for all the love and care she put into preparing this manuscript
- Ken Collard, Chuck Daniels, Russ Gronevelt, Kim Lehrman, Don Trim, and Teresa Weed Newman for sharing their heroic stories
- Asya Raines for her unflagging enthusiastic support
- And to Steve Deckrow for being the first to believe

> "If everything on earth was rational, nothing would ever happen."
>
> FYODOR DOSTOEVSKY

Introduction

T his book is about a new leadership process that I have developed called Unrational Leadership™. In the following pages I describe the process and show you how to use it. It is the only leadership process that consciously incorporates the unconscious into the workplace. I have designed the book as a guided adventure—*The Search for Unrational Leadership*™. The search follows the map included in this book. I wrote this book for any person who has ever faced a difficult problem or cataclysmic change. During the writing, I sat an imaginary leader on my shoulder and envisioned what he or she needed to build a more harmonious and successful organization. Organizations rule our world and our fate rests in the unconscious of their leaders.

What is Unrational Leadership™?

Unrational Leadership™ is leadership that uses both rational and irrational methods to achieve a desired outcome. Don't let the word "irrational" turn you off! I know that irrationality implies mental unsoundness or the inability to reason. **Unrational Leadership™ does not overthrow reason!** This book is about balance. Unrational Leadership™ **balances** reason with small, manageable doses of irrationality. In fact, Unrational Leadership™ inoculates and protects you against the plagues of irrationality that sweep through organizations just as an injection of a tiny piece of virus creates antibodies that protect you from a full-blown disease.

I define "unrational" as that which is not rational—either in perception or reality. I developed the term "unrational" to avoid some of the overwhelming cultural prejudice against the word "irrational." Unrational Leadership™ is the marriage of traditional rational thinking and the irrational, intuitive mind, that part of our self that emerges in our dreams, that hidden self that can sense when we walk into a room that someone sitting at the table is going to be a friend or a lifelong foe. I am writing about unsealing that intuitive self that has been buried for centuries. I want to bring it to the surface and use it to solve the huge challenges in front of us.

To be irrational is not something we normally aspire toward. Leaders have a difficult time calling on their intuitive side. They have been trained to avoid this incredible source of energy. In our organizations, we have swallowed a myth: *If we can measure it, we can manage it.* It has dominated our society since the Scientific Revolution, when men first imagined that nature could be understood and tamed. The myth turns rationality into a compliment and twists irrationality into an accusation.

All modern leaders use rational methods based on drawing logical conclusions from observable data. Examples of rational methods include time management, project management, the scientific method, and the five pillars of modern management: Plan, Organize, Direct, Monitor, and Control. These left-brain processes imply the withdrawal of emotions and intuition from decision-making. These techniques control the way things are *supposed* to work in business, government, religious, non-profit, educational and even criminal organizations.

Our organizations are formally ruled by rationality but informally ruled by irrationality. Whether they know it or not, leaders also use irrational methods to get things done. These methods are based on the general principle of **seeing around corners to arrive at conclusions that cannot be factually proven.** Interpreting your dreams, visualizing the future, following your gut, listening to your heart, going with the flow, and praying are positive irrational methods. But, let's not forget the destructive irrational behaviors in our portfolios: victimizing scapegoats, projecting faults on our competitors and scaring the hell out of people. Unconsciousness is the parent of these right-brain behaviors and sometimes, they unwittingly dominate our agendas.

How is Unrational Leadership™ Different?

The primary difference between Unrational Leadership™ and current management thinking is that Unrational Leadership™ accepts irrational methods as routine practice **without sacrificing reason.** Rationality is used throughout the process to assimilate and interpret irrational data: dreams, fantasies, fairy tales, symbols, and feelings. Unrational Leadership™ releases Mr. and Mrs. Irrational, those wild and unpredictable twins from the basement closet that they have been forced to occupy since the dawn of the Age of Reason. Unlike the rational leader who says he relies on reason alone for making decisions, the unrational leader is much more honest. He says: "We divide our world into rational and irrational halves. We embrace the rational half and run away from the irrational side like scared rabbits." The unrational leader doesn't pretend that he is or should be or can become Mr. Spock of Star Trek fame. He carefully and consciously uses his God-given ability to see around corners and uses the information to make better decisions.

Rationalism has been Taken Too Far

Rationalism, our greatest strength for 500 years, is turning into a weakness. Now, the only way our civilization can sustain itself is by tapping our irrational mind. Our forefathers planted the Age of Reason in our land and used the fruits to build a great nation. We have the world's strongest military, best education, most productive farmers, most-admired political system and on and on. But our way of life is endangered—not by loose morals, not by rapacious capitalists, not even by the terrorists. Our world is threatened by the same rational methods that we used to build it. We have taken rationalism too far and this great strength is turning into a glaring weakness.

Here are 15 examples of the decline of rationalism: Five each from national, organizational, and personal perspectives. Each example features a rational goal, pursued with rational methods, that has yielded an unintended and potentially disastrous consequence. As you read the list, focus your attention on the unintended consequence. When we recognize them and try to correct them, we usually say either people are making bad decisions or we haven't perfected the technology. What we don't say is that the method we used to achieve the goal—rationalism—is the problem.

The National Decline of Rationalism

1. The more we educate our kids about safe sex, the more they experiment with sex (and they are doing it earlier, too).
2. The more we adopt timesaving technology, the more we work and the harder we work.
3. The more we protect ourselves from terrorism, the more insecure we become.
4. The more computer systems we build to provide instantaneous information about publicly traded companies, the more companies have been able to defraud and swindle employees, investors and banks out of billions of dollars.

5. The more we automate our infrastructure, the less control we seem to have when something goes wrong (like a blackout).

The Organizational Decline of Rationalism

1. The more we talk about corporate ethics, the more cynical we become about the conversation (yeah right, here we go again).
2. The more efficient we become (to compete with foreign producers), the more production we outsource offshore.
3. The more we try to change our organizations, the more our middle management resists (despite the factual demonstration of the overwhelming need to change in order to survive).
4. The more programs we institute to ensure diversity (and fairness), the more complaints we get about unfair practices.
5. The more our capability expands to visualize and prepare for the future, the more we focus on short-term decisions and results (the next quarterly report).

The Personal Decline of Rationalism

1. The more I look to outside experts and authorities for moral guidance, the more I am betrayed.
2. The more I try to organize and balance my life, the less time I have for my family and myself.
3. The more wisdom I gain through life experience, the more society seems to reject my wisdom in favor of youth.
4. The more I seek and follow my creative passion, the more trouble I create in the rest of my life.
5. The more I am bombarded by information, the less I can absorb and use to make decisions.

More Rationalism is not the Answer

These unintended consequences are the result of excessive rationalism, and they can't be fixed with more rationalism. A classic example of unintended consequences is occurring in the Great Lakes. Governments opened up the Great Lakes to ocean freighters to strengthen the economy. These freighters have dumped new and invasive species into the waters. The result is the destruction of natural fisheries. Unrational Leadership™ would have alerted leaders to the negative consequences of their decisions and would have inspired them to find more creative solutions for growing the economy. (See Chapter One for more discussion on saving the Great Lakes.)

Unintended consequences breed problems that defy reason. **Problems that defy reason have irrational foundations based on unconscious drives.** These problems can't be solved with a spreadsheet, with a policy, with a plan, with a study, with new technology or with a great and powerful leader. They need solutions that defy reason. In my two decades as a management consultant, I have met thousands of people who have wrestled with problems that defy reason. As a company president, a son and a father, I also have run into my share of dilemmas. Great conflicts, sweeping changes, and foreboding futures assault us whether or not we're ready for them. At such times, our culture and education tell us to be rational. But reason and logic are increasingly failing us—no matter how much we plan, weigh pros and cons, and consult experts. We can't make decisions without producing unintended negative consequences! Our collective inability to solve these problems frustrates us immensely. We feel exhausted and overwhelmed, fighting the nagging feeling that we're looking for the answers in all the wrong places.

Big Results from Tapping the Unconscious!

The key to becoming an unrational leader is tapping your unconscious for information and energy. During this odyssey, you will learn how to dive into your unconscious, collect images, intuitions, and feelings, and use them to make practical decisions that will lead to achieving rational goals. *Figure A* shows how you move into your unconscious and emerge with better decisions. I want to emphasize the practicality of my methods. Although innovative for the organizational world, they are proven techniques (some of them ancient) that knowingly employ your unconscious. As you move through the book, you will be challenged and sometimes even jarred out of your comfort zone. As a leader, you know that the price of change is discomfort.

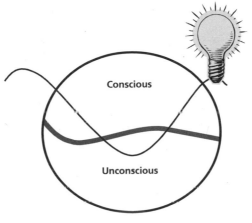

Figure A

Our culture doesn't train leaders to use their unconscious; we train them to avoid it. In order to become an accomplished unrational leader, you will need to develop a new way of looking at yourself and the world. Ironically, the higher you are in the organization, the more difficult this task may be because you have spent your career being right. In your zeal to learn the rules and win the game, you may have drowned your inner voice and stifled your creative energy. In a sense, you condemned yourself to competence. Working with your unconscious will open up new fields of uncertainty. But this uncertainty is needed to open your personality and help you breathe new life into your organization. If you complete this search for Unrational Leadership,™ you will develop your leadership strengths and:

- Understand the limits of rational thinking

- Learn the five principles for solving our most complex problems

- Find your deepest and most powerful inner voice

- Discover the magical path for growing your personality

- Unseal the mysteries in your dreams and change your life

- Lead yourself and your organization to success

If You want to Become an Unrational Leader, Take the Inner Journey

This book calls you to take an inner heroic journey. A good life has two heroic journeys. One journey is external; the other one is internal. The outside journey comes first. It is that great rags-to-riches story of the young hero striving against challenges great and small to reach the top of the heap. If you have worked your way through college, raised a family, turned around a losing proposition, rescued something or someone, pulled up stakes and moved across the world, or chased a childhood dream, you have made an outer heroic journey.

The inner journey generally starts after the age of 25 and continues for the rest of your life. It is the story of finding meaning in life and deciding what legacy you want to leave after you die. Can you think of a better way to demonstrate a heroic journey than a fairy tale? Accordingly, in Chapter Four, you will meet TrueHeart, a heroic knight who makes the inner journey in a five-part tale. These tales, strategically placed in the midst of rational text, will light a fire in your unconscious. But, when you first enter TrueHeart's world, you may feel lost or confused. You may have trouble remembering the names of the characters or getting the plot. This is completely normal! All heroes must get lost (if not in the woods, then in a story). Don't worry, as you wander, your unconscious will find the right path for you.

When I ask people if they consider themselves to be heroes, more than half tell me something like: "I'm not a hero. I am just doing my job." Anyone can become a hero! The heroic journey sits in our unconscious. It is like the mothering instinct. When my wife went into the hospital to have our daughter, she went into the delivery room and emerged as Chelsea's mother. From that moment, I watched a series of extraordinary changes unfold within her. She could tell the difference between a hungry cry, a sick cry, and a whining cry. She knew how long to feed Chelsea and when Chelsea needed to sleep. What really amazed me is that she received absolutely no training in motherhood. The complete program emerged from her, as if a software application had been turned on in her unconscious. The inner heroic journey is software with integrity, action, courage, love, and vision.

Like any life-altering journey, the quest for Unrational Leadership™ is not short. Have you ever taken calculus? Imagine trying to learn it in a weekend or with a series of one-minute checklists. If you really want to learn calculus, you have to change how you think about math. You might say you have to change your personality. This adventure is no less difficult. It has to cook. It takes most people a year or more to overthrow the god of rationalism. It can take even longer to learn how to listen to and trust the unconscious.

The Map to Unrational Leadership™

Every hero needs a map for guidance through trials and tribulations, and you have been given the Map to Unrational Leadership™. Don't lose the map! It leads you to the treasure and reveals the secret passwords required to unearth it. To whet your appetite for the journey, here is short preview of some of the places that you will visit:

Comfortopia—This is your current home and whether or not you like it you are probably comfortable in this place. What makes you so comfortable is your belief that rationality is the best method for managing your life and your organization. Here's your chance to shake this conditioning and jump into the wild blue unconscious sea.

The Good Ship Ego—This is the captain of your personality and will be responsible for your safety and completing the voyage. You must have a strong ego in order to deal with the unconscious forces that will be unleashed on this journey. A strong ego has two hallmarks: It has adapted to daily life and it has the courage to change. This is a journey for people who want to be winners. During the first leg of your journey, you will get several opportunities to strengthen your ego before landing on Unrational Island.

The Colossus of Rationality—The Colossus of Rhodes was a 104-foot statue of Helios at the entrance to the harbor of Rhodes and was considered one of the seven wonders of the ancient world. Ironically, an earthquake toppled it at its knee, its weakest point. The Colossus of Rationality represents the fact that Rationality is the most powerful god in our culture as Helios, the Sun god, was the most powerful god in Rhodes. The Colossus stands in the center of the map, guarded by two sirens, who beckon weary and frightened searchers to halt their journey.

IOPD Island—IOPD (The Individual and Organizational Path to Discovery™) Island is somewhat like Isle Royale, a national park dedicated to wildlife preservation in the middle of Lake Superior's cold pristine waters. As on Isle Royale, the only human residents on IOPD are the rangers, but in this case they are psychologists and philosophers who study the nature of personality. As you approach the island you will notice that it is shrouded in mysterious clouds— a permanent condition that symbolizes the fact that we can't ever completely know ourselves or anyone else.

Unrational Island—This island is the dark place, the land of the unconscious, filled with fairy tale characters, long winding journeys, challenges that must be met with courage, and of course, the Treasure of Unrational Leadership™. When you land on Unrational Island, your unconscious will present you with a series of dreams that will open your trap door. On this strange island, outer voices don't have as much power as they do in Comfortopia. As you make your way south to the treasure, the inner whisper is most important. Tomorrow's leader must find the strength to grow his personality by facing difficult inner truths and exploring the unconscious. Like the knight in the fairy tale, he must take the last journey left in the Modern Age—the journey into the self.

Carl Jung's Locker—I can't write another word without acknowledging Carl Jung's influence on this book. Carl Jung was a Swiss psychiatrist and contemporary of Sigmund Freud. Jung anchored his theory of personality growth on the premise that wisdom ultimately comes from a positive confrontation with the unconscious. As you pass by Carl Jung's Locker, also remember that Unrational Leadership™ is more than a restatement of Jung's theories. It goes past Jung and puts his theories to practical use in today's fast and furious world.

The Unrational Leadership™ Effectiveness Survey

William Edwards Deming, the father of manufacturing quality, said that it was not possible to measure quality. It is possible to measure the consistency of the processes prior to finishing production, but ultimately, the incredibly fickle human determines what is and what is not quality. Walk into any art museum and you will quickly wonder how the curator determines quality, especially if you see a 12 × 12 black painting with a single blue swirl in the middle. Similarly, in *The Search for Unrational Leadership™*, whether or not you become an unrational leader will be based on how well you see around corners and arrive at **quality** decisions. History will measure you by your results, not at the moment of your decision.

However, just as Deming's methods ensure consistent processes and provide pretty good clues about the quality of a final product, Unrational Leadership™ has assessment tools to help you measure your progress. In Appendix A, you will find the Unrational Leadership™ Effectiveness Survey. This survey is based on the principles and skills that you will learn in this book. Start this journey by assessing yourself, and then distribute the survey to six people. You have our permission to make copies of the survey for this purpose. Promise them that you can tolerate negative feedback! A year after leaving Comfortopia, return to the original respondents and resurvey them. The results will give you good clues on your progress.

Will You Answer the Call?

All heroic journeys start with a call. The world we live in is submerged in irrationality. We are swimming along day-to-day imagining that we control our universe through the conscious part of our personality, but the unconscious calls the shots. Your conscious mind is like the tip of the iceberg and the majority of the iceberg lies hidden below the surface of the water. This underwater mass is what sinks ships and strikes fear in a sailor's heart. It is the number one force to be reckoned with in the future and it is so frightening to our rational world because we can't really see or measure it. The conscious part of our personality that we bring to work is only a fraction of the energy that we can deliver to an organization. Most of the energy we bring comes from the unconscious and we don't understand it at all.

Business leaders struggle daily to find problems, dissect them and then deliver answers. This traditional process will no longer work by itself. Within our organizations we have this incredible untapped energy in our unconscious and it doesn't work very well with goals, checklists, plans and directed behavior. It needs to be opened up so that it can inspire us. If a leader knows how to tap this force, it becomes much, much easier to solve the big problems.

The unrational leader knows that the secret to success will come from personality. As an unrational leader you can expand your personality because you are on speaking terms with your unconscious. Personality gives you the strength to make tough moral decisions. Personality gives you the energy to change yourself. It provides the courage to walk into the fire when other leaders send in consultants or lawyers. It opens the hidden treasures of creativity. And it delivers the insight you need to find your true vision.

Will you answer the call?

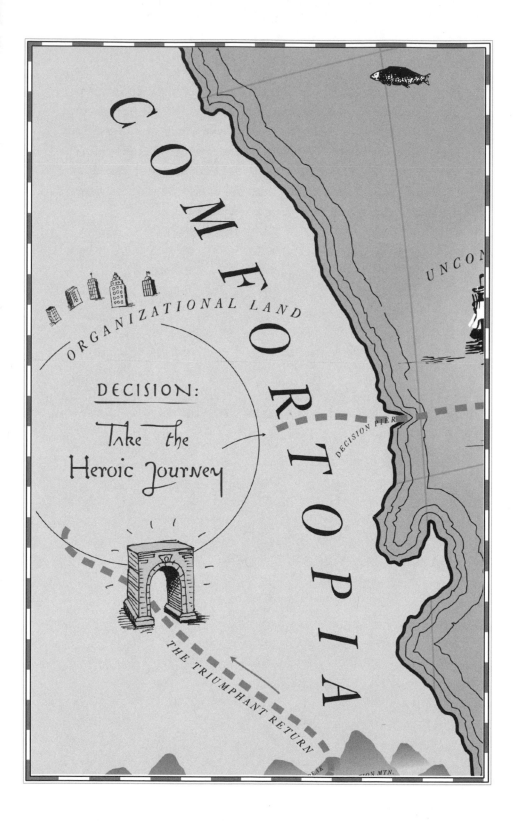

1 The Principles of Unrational Leadership™

In this post 9/11 world, when someone asks me for my perspective on the business climate in the Midwest, I sum it up in two words: **fear and ignorance.** Throughout Michigan or when I travel to Ohio or Illinois, I hear fears about terrorism, blackouts, the threats posed by China, India, and Mexico, the retreat of manufacturing, rising interest rates, rising gas prices, slow growth, the war in Iraq, and the declining quality of life. Sometimes I hear that a structural change has occurred in the global economy and that for the first time since the Great Depression, the Midwest is in deep trouble. I **never** hear that these problems are related to the decline of rationalism. People don't want to know what is really happening here. They are waiting for the good times to return. They are stuck in Comfortopia.

The Journey Begins and Ends in Comfortopia

The search for Unrational Leadership™ begins in Comfortopia, the largest and easternmost province of the mind. After completing their search, unrational leaders return to Comfortopia and work with rational leaders to achieve good ends. However, these unrational leaders must guard their visionary powers. It is easy to lose your vision in Comfortopia! On most mornings, a gentle blanket of fog rolls in from the sea, obscuring all prominent features except the Colossus of Rationality.

As rationalists, Comfortopians spend much of their time looking for rules and following them. With their passion for structure and predictability, Comfortopians are quite productive. Unfortunately, some leaders go overboard in regards to rules, and their driving principle becomes: "Don't rock the boat!" Comfortopia is filled with businesses, governments, schools, churches, mosques, temples, and criminal organizations. Most of these organizations (except those that are led by unrational leaders) have one thing in common: They avoid solving problems that defy reason. These problems are given to large non-profit organizations.

Leaving Comfortopia Takes Courage

You can't force anyone to leave Comfortopia. Everyone leaves the place in his or her own time. This is not a task of getting buy-in or assigning an action item or putting a note in your planner to leave Comfortopia after lunch on Tuesday. It takes lots of courage to jump (as you will undoubtedly discover). You probably know or even work for leaders who aren't ready for an inner heroic journey. They may be afraid to look within, or they think that they know everything. Watch out or you might become one of the following leaders!

- **The "What, Me Worry?" Leader** doesn't hear a call to become a hero and won't listen for one. He says: "I am okay with myself. I don't see anything that needs to be changed inside of me. I deliver results—that's my job. I don't have time to bother with thoughts about personality. By the way, did you see the Lions last night?" These leaders are my golf buddies and can make great clients when they want to take an outer heroic journey—in other words, accomplish a great project. But they need to know that the unconscious is always with them and is something that must be dealt with.

- **The "It Ain't Me Babe" Leader** hears a call to action but refuses to look at his own role in the solution. This leader hires me to change his employees. He focuses on changing everyone except the most important person—himself. Here is an example: The president of a Michigan based machine tooling company called a meeting to address the company's red ink. He said: "We all have to work as a team. We have to try to work together. Today, I terminated four people. If all you want to do is complain, come into my office and tell me that you don't like it here. From now on, everyone is going to cooperate and support each other. Any questions?"

- **The "I Believe in Magic" Leader** is overwhelmed by unconscious fantasies and doesn't know it. He secretly believes in magic. He buys company stock when everyone is selling their shares. Ironically, the unrational leader is less prone to magical thinking because he digests his fantasies as they emerge from his unconscious. Magical thinkers believe their own lies! For example, the president of a company had lost customers, market share, revenue, and key employees. At the annual sales meeting, he briefly touched on the company's difficulties and then gave a rousing but delusional speech that skirted the problem that pressed on everyone's heart: Will I have a job next week? "I Believe in Magic" leaders hire me to change them, but they refuse to admit it.

The Call to Action is Your Signal to Leave

If you want deep change, if you want to solve tough problems, if you want to become an unrational leader, you have to truly leave Comfortopia. The call to action is your signal to depart. It is an inner urge that just won't go away or an external pressure that keeps pushing. A call to action implies weight, courage, and significant change. It can even be divinely inspired. For example, the Bible describes how Moses received his calling at the burning bush when Jehovah spoke to him and told him to bring the children of Israel out of Egypt. Most calls, even divine ones, are not greeted with open arms. According to the biblical story, Moses was not overjoyed to receive his call to action. He asked Jehovah to justify the call! In his book *Callings*, Gregg Levoy describes how he began hearing a calling to become a freelance writer. Levoy wrestled for years with an inner voice that urged him to leave a successful career as a newspaper reporter. Here is what he wrote about his call:

> A calling requires action, decision making, change. We may break a stick in half to symbolize our intention to break with a tradition or a person, but unless we also put our asses on the line and concretize that break with real action, the power of our resolution can erode into wishful thinking. Breaking a stick is not breaking with tradition but a demonstration of intent. Although intent is powerful, we still need to follow through with time spent at the grindstone. We still need to work with the back and legs and voice.

The Day I Heard a Call to Action

I was thirty-eight and the manager of a good-sized management consulting practice. I worked for a fast-growing information technology firm and had built the practice myself by selling software, training, and process reengineering services. I was a seller-doer type of leader. I sold projects, assigned staff to run them, made sure the projects were headed in the right direction, and then turned to the next sale. I ran lots of projects simultaneously and expected a lot from my staff and myself. During job interviews, I said that my ideal employee was a self-starter with passionate commitment to the client, an unrelenting focus on completing projects on time and under budget, and a talent for selling new business.

I really wanted people to be like me. I had learned consulting by getting thrown into pools filled with sharks. I had spent five years learning the trade on the job and had not received a single day of training. I thought nothing of dropping a new employee off at an assembly plant and telling him to call me if he had any problems. I worked long hours, 80 to 100 hours per week. When I joined the president of my company at 10 pm on a Sunday night to prepare for the week ahead, I wanted to see my supervisors working alongside of me. When I sold projects, I estimated expenses for plane flights, and then asked my staff to drive to project sites to shave costs. Of course, I wanted them to drive on Sunday nights—as I had done when I had started consulting.

Trouble started at the end of my first year as a manager. One of my prize recruits left for a competitor and on the way out he told my president that I was the problem. I told my president that my prize recruit didn't have the right stuff. He responded by telling me to think about adjusting my style. But he warned me: "Don't change your work ethic for your employees." So, I tried to change my style. I asked my people about their weekends. I tried to listen more carefully. I met with the employees and asked them what I could do to improve, but one by one, people walked out the door. When the fourth person left, I asked him why he didn't tell me his problems before he gave notice. He replied that he didn't want to get fired before he was ready to go. When the sixth person left my group with more complaints about me, I knew something had to be done.

I hired a facilitator to meet with my group. She passed out file cards and asked each person to write their problems on the cards. I participated and recorded my problem: "My people are not dedicated to growing the business." The facilitator took all of the cards, transcribed them, and presented them to me later. Ten people worked for me so I expected about 20 problems. The facilitator gave me a list of 140. I was shocked, but I was stubborn. I wasn't ready to leave Comfortopia. I suspected that 80 percent of the problems were petty complaints that had nothing to do with getting projects done or growing the business.

We met every two weeks and worked through the list. I successfully addressed issues regarding travel advances, purchasing the right software for the job, preparing better estimates, and I even sent a couple of folks to training. These efforts stemmed the tide of departures, but I felt like I was holding back the flood. After three months of work, we neared the bottom of the list of 140 problems and landed on: "Management treats employees unprofessionally." This one hurt the most. If nothing else, I considered myself scrupulous in my communications—I didn't swear, pound tables, or joke about sex.

"What is this complaint about?" I asked the facilitator in front of my team.

"At a staff meeting a year ago, you told Dave that he was acting like a clerk with the client because he had prepared some overblown and useless reports for him."

"I called Dave a clerk?" I couldn't believe it. I never ran down my staff in public. "Unfortunately, Dave is not here to tell us the truth. As you know, he left the firm last year."

"Maybe the rest of the team can help," said the facilitator. "How many of you remember Charlie making that statement to Dave?" I shook my head in disbelief. Who would remember such a trivial comment? Then, I watched eight people raise their hands one by one. Each one looked at me and told me with their eyes that I had hurt Dave. I was mortified and astounded at their memories.

Suddenly, I realized that I had the wrong vision of a leader. It turned inside out in a moment. My job wasn't throwing projects at people and criticizing them when they didn't fulfill my expectations.

My job was making their work easier and more rewarding so they could produce more for the company. At that moment, I heard my call to action and that afternoon, I started my search for Unrational Leadership™.

The Five Principles of Unrational Leadership™

Eighteen months after I stood on Decision Pier (the Comfortopian jump off point on the Map to Unrational Leadership™), I left the fast growing technology firm and opened my own consulting business. I left with a feeling of pride. My early experiments in Unrational Leadership™ had worked. In those last 18 months, I did not lose one soul. I left with a determination to find a new way of leadership that would work from the inside out and that would tap the deepest levels of the personality. It took me eight years of research, trial and error, and more than a little heartbreak to identify the following Five Principles of Unrational Leadership™:

1. **Start all problem solving by taking personal responsibility:** Unrational leaders always assume personal responsibility by asking: "What is my role in creating this problem?" Rational leaders talk about it, but they try like hell to wiggle away from it because their personalities aren't always strong enough to bear the responsibility. The unrational leader doesn't say something like: "Our intelligence community gave us bad information when we made that case for war. It's not my fault." The unrational leader doesn't take more than 100 words to respond to a simple question: "You voted for the resolution to go to war. Do you bear responsibility for the results?"

2. **Aim at increasing energy, not just efficiency:** The rational leader almost always looks for ways to improve efficiency, a process that works well with machines. It doesn't work with human beings if you want creativity and enthusiasm. Have

you ever seen a machine smile? The unrational leader works at releasing unconscious energy in his staff because it fuels personality growth, the ultimate source of creativity and profit.

3. **Confront and partner with the unconscious:** The unrational leader walks into the fire of the unconscious and wrestles with it until he achieves a partnership. He knows that all significant change must address the unconscious. When he sees rational leaders pretending that newsletters, corporate e-mails, and HR departments can address the impact of organizational change, he knows they are on a collision course with failure.

4. **Creativity drives change:** Everyone agrees that creativity is good, but the unrational leader understands that creativity is needed most during the journey. Rational leaders like to use creativity to start things, but it has just as much value in the middle of a project when the plan has to be thrown away. Rational leaders respond to troubles by putting on blinders and talking about discipline and focus. What they need is planned chaos. Depicting powerful ideas and emotions through drawing and writing poetry has helped my clients gain a fresh perspective on their conflicts and has given them the energy needed to move in new directions.

5. **Look two generations behind and two generations ahead:** Rational leaders like to focus on the business at hand, and that is not a bad thing if they can also think about the future and the role the past has in creating it. The unrational leader asks questions like:

   - What work did my grandparents leave undone?
   - What do I want my great-grandkids to say about my decisions?
   - What problems can I solve for them with the decisions that I am making right now?

Unrational Leadership™ Solves Real Problems

It should be clear that the unrational leader is also a competent rational leader. He chooses to apply Unrational Leadership™ principles because he knows from practical experience that rational approaches will not reliably produce results. The unrational leader doesn't tap the unconscious because it's cool, because he is in group therapy, or because he started doing yoga. He taps the unconscious because he wants to succeed. To demonstrate the Five Principles of Unrational Leadership™, I present three realistic problems and strategies for resolving them. In Appendix B, you will find a set of tables that contrast detailed rational and unrational solutions for these problems. I suggest you wait until you finish this search before reviewing Appendix B, as it outlines techniques presented throughout the book.

Saving the Great Lakes

This problem concerns two countries, several native tribes, millions of people and the greatest fresh water ecosystem in the world. Currently, overdevelopment, pollution, invasive species, climatic change, and water withdrawals from other regions of the country threaten the Great Lakes. Although many groups have been formed to watch over the lakes, no single group has the authority to ensure that the lakes survive as a viable source for drinking water, fishing, recreation, and travel. For example, a comprehensive process to assess and monitor the health of the lakes does not exist. Invasive species are wiping out the fish; mercury continues to accumulate in the wildlife; farm and industry pollutants continue to pour into the water; and development eats up more and more shoreline. Although many helpful programs exist, there is no strategic approach for saving the Great Lakes.

Strategy for Saving the Great Lakes:
Confront and Partner with the Unconscious

The critical challenge in a project like saving the Great Lakes is getting the important constituencies on the same page at the same time. This level of unity generally occurs only when there is a crisis, as when the Cuyahoga River caught on fire or Lake Erie almost died. In so-called normal times, the times when the crisis is building, rational leaders try to build consensus through education, communication, political deals, etc. These consensus-building efforts take a long time (if they work at all) on problems that defy reason because the rational leader ignores the unconscious drives, fantasies, emotions that fragment and derail unified approaches. In other words, he only works with the tip of the iceberg. To shorten the problem solving cycle, the unrational leader concentrates on partnering with the unconscious energy. Then, he or she educates the participants about the power of the unconscious and helps them prepare plans to address the inevitable resistance that will emerge as a plan unfolds. The rational leader will often resist this strategy, saying: "It takes too much time." But, in the long run, confronting and integrating the unconscious fragments saves time and dramatically increases the chances of success. Remember: When the unconscious drives emerge early, the group can deal with them. When they emerge late in the process, they are viewed as betrayals.

A Tired Information Technology Company

An information technology company has an old and entrenched management team that has failed to groom the next generation for corporate leadership. This management team doesn't have energy for mentoring or coaching. In the past five years, turnover has risen to triple the industry average and several key leaders have joined competitors or formed their own companies. Formerly, the marketplace used the company as the benchmark, but the firm's reputation is declining. In the last two years, layoffs reduced the staff by 25 percent. The management team changes the organization annually and some people have worked for five managers in five years. The management team wants to sell the company, but global competition (especially from India) is driving valuation prices into the cellar.

Strategy for Rousing a Tired Company: Increase Energy (Not Just Efficiency)

The unrational leader sees this problem as **an energy shortage** and taps the unconscious for energy. The rational leader plans to accomplish the job with hard facts and disciplined planning. In the process he plays to the logical, analytical strength of his management team. He doesn't know that rationality is wearing out in Comfortopia. He also doesn't know that when his personality wears out, it turns into a weakness. A strategic plan will be created, but this tired management team will not implement it effectively. Then, they will place the responsibility for failure on the shoulders of the next generation. They will say: "They don't have the same fires that we had when we were young."

A CEO's First Failure

This struggling manufacturing company went through two CEOs in five years, so the Board exhausted itself in hiring the third, a rising star in the sector with an unblemished resume. She sold the Board on her ability to turn around the company in one year. She started the transition quickly by bringing in her own management team. At the six-month mark, she confidently told the Board that the turnaround was in sight. But, by the end of the first year, not a single indicator had improved on the company's balanced scorecard. Under intense questioning, the CEO admitted she had underestimated the depth of the problem, and predicted the light at the end of tunnel was only six months away. After the CEO left the meeting, the Chairman of the Board (COB) revealed that he had reports that the CEO had lost the confidence of her management team and that she frequently blew up at meetings. In his view, she had made two gross hiring mistakes, one in Sales, the other in Engineering. The Board concluded its meeting by agreeing that it did not want to bring in another CEO.

Strategy for Dealing with CEO Failure: Take Personal Responsibility

In general, the more successful a rational leader is, the less likely she is to question herself when a significant failure occurs in her organization. During the past decade, we watched the directors of large corporations sit passively as CEOs ran their companies into the ground and cost investors billions of dollars. In this case of the CEO's First Failure, the directors will turn their guns on the CEO and begin a series of rational defensive actions. But the COB pursues a strategy of personal responsibility by asking: "What role have we played in this drama in view of the fact that we have repeated it twice in the last five years?" And he doesn't stop at the tip of the iceberg; he goes below the surface and asks everyone to look how his or her unconscious contributed to the problem.

Unrational Leadership™ has Powerful Personal and Professional Benefits

At the close of the Introduction, I asked you if you would answer the call. I hope I have given you enough information to inspire you to leave Comfortopia. But the decision is never easy. Like all heroes in the face of danger, you are alone. You sense the turbulence underneath the placid waters of the sea before you. You don't need to have a famous person to tell you to do this. Please, don't look for numbers to influence your decision. You don't need to know how many people have gone before you, how many succeeded, how many turned back, or how many got lost. These numbers won't say anything about the dimensions of **your personality**. As Plato said: "A good decision is based on knowledge and not on numbers." People ask me: "Why should I make this journey? Tell me again what I will get!" Here are my responses.

- The search will increase your personal energy and improve your health. In other words, you will become happier. It takes a lot of energy to maintain the wall between your conscious and unconscious and when you begin walking through it, you release positive energy.
- You will make it easier for your organization to succeed. If you unseal your unconscious, your team members will start their own heroic journeys. This is the nature of the relationship between the leader and the follower. Do you want more creativity, energy, wisdom, courage, and vision in your organization? Here is what one of my team members wrote about her experience with my company a few years after I left Comfortopia:

> There is not just one experience that I can pick from my years at Project Innovations. What motivates me the most is a sense of accomplishment at the end of the day and the feeling that if I ask others for help, that I won't get NO for an answer. It will be: "Sure, what can I do for you?" I have gained more confidence in myself than I ever thought possible. I don't know where I would be today if it weren't for Project Innovations.

- By making this search, I lightened the burden for my children and their children and their children. (If you don't have children, you reduce the burden for the children that you do know.) The burden contains the unconscious failings that are unwittingly passed from one generation to the next. For example, if I am willing to reduce my tendency to negatively stereotype people from other cultures, I lighten the load for my kids.[1]

- If not you, then who else? You are one of the most highly educated, most wealthy, most secure individuals on this planet. If you don't decide to take on the challenge of confronting and partnering with the unconscious, who will? Certainly not the addicts, not the poor and starving, the war torn, and not the refugees. We have climbed Maslow's Ladder of Self-Actualization and it is our job to take the industrialized world to the next level of personality development—one step beyond its sole reliance on rationality to govern and manage itself.

Take a Secret with You

When a hero leaves home, he or she often takes a magic talisman. It might be a rock, a handkerchief, or a picture. On this inner journey, I want you to take a secret with you. When my clients enroll in our company's eight-month guided search for the inner hero, I start the first session of our program by asking everyone to take out a piece of paper and record a personal secret. It should be a significant secret, something with a little darkness. I don't want to know your secret and I don't want you to share it with anyone else. Perhaps, you think you don't have any secrets? Think a little harder. Hasn't anyone ever trusted you with a secret? Surely, there is something in your life that you don't want anyone else to know about. After you record your secret, think about the treasure that you want to find on this search. Underneath the secret, describe your treasure. Please fold the secret and put in a safe place in your wallet or purse. If you can carry this secret, you can find the treasure.

Now, you have left Comfortopia.

Note

1. When I was 12, I moved to New York and was bussed to an integrated school. I remember my Dad telling a friend: "Charlie doesn't mind going to school with black people." My Dad had never given me any reason to care. He had done some work on himself.

> ## Important Concepts for the Unrational Leader
>
> - The journey begins and ends in Comfortopia.
> - Leaving Comfortopia takes courage.
> - The Call to Action is your signal to leave Comfortopia.
> - There are Five Principles of Unrational Leadership™.
> - Unrational Leadership™ has powerful personal and professional benefits.

2 A Sailor's Guide to Really Leaving Comfortopia

The purpose of this chapter is to help you absolutely, positively
sail away from Comfortopia. Set your course in a northeast-
erly direction on the Route of the Great Adventure (see the
Map to Unrational Leadership™). Get ready to tie yourself to the
mast as you navigate the many temptations in this great sea of the
unconscious. The first temptation is to hug the coastline. After rid-
ing the bounding main for a few uncomfortable leagues, many leaders turn starboard and reenter Comfortopia under the cover of
darkness.

I once had a client who wanted to know what his people really
thought of him. I interviewed and surveyed his team, who saw this
man as a powerful mixture of executive talent and personal immatu-
rity. He tended to put people down at meetings and elevated himself
at every turn. When I shared the team's feedback, my client shook
his head in self-recrimination and swore that he would change his
style. We established a plan to help him become a collaborative

leader who interacted with his staff on a basis of equality and mutual respect. The plan had three components:

1. He would meet one-on-one with each of his direct reports and ask two questions: What do I do that makes your job easier? What do I do that makes your job more difficult?
2. I would attend some staff meetings and signal him when he started his put-downs.
3. We would hold a team building off-site, offering his people an opportunity to deliver face-to-face feedback about his leadership behavior.

My client eagerly committed to these tasks and informed his team that he was on the path to becoming a great executive. For a few weeks, he gave his people images of an involved, caring, changed executive. But, as he conducted his few one-on-one meetings, he began to hear things about himself that made him uncomfortable. I encouraged him to stay the course, but he said that he didn't have time. He missed his deadlines. To get the action item off his plate, he stood up at a staff meeting, declared the effort a rousing success and thanked everyone for his or her honest participation. Within the month, he resumed his aggressive behavior, reserving his sharpest needles for the executives who had been most honest with him in the one-on-one meetings. As you can imagine, his team lost faith in my ability to effect real change, and my effectiveness was quickly diminished. I learned a most valuable lesson: Talk is cheap when the topic is leaving Comfortopia.

You have to Engage Your Entire Personality to Make the Voyage

On the Map to Unrational Leadership™ four ships lay in the Comfortopian waters. These ships are symbols for the parts of your personality that you will ride on this journey, and they are named:

Talents, Unconscious, Ego, and SS Creative. Most leadership development programs focus on identifying your talents and shaping your ego to meet the needs of your business. A few programs help leaders tap their creative energy through the arts, e.g. drama, poetry and drawing. One of my consultant friends tapped the creative energy in a team of Ford executives by challenging them to cook a seven-course meal for themselves and their partners. The dinner was an unqualified success. But only the rarest program, like this search for Unrational Leadership™, asks the leader to look inside his or her unconscious and partner with it.

You can't complete the inner heroic journey with only a portion of your personality. It takes a fleet to find the treasure. Lots of leaders tell me that they already know themselves and that they only need a little nip and tuck to become great executives. This is like saying you can be a great teacher without asking your students what they want to learn or that you can be an effective parent without listening to your children. These nip and tuck leaders are leery of their creative side and are spooked by the thought of diving into their unconscious. However, these are the two ships that must be sailed in order to truly change. We have to get over our fear of coloring outside the lines! To this end, what follows is a series of practical steps for engaging your whole personality on this search.

The Journey Starts with Identifying Your Talents

The first ship in the harbor is the *Talents*. Identifying your talents is key to a successful journey. I believe that we are all born with a set of talents and that these talents can be developed through education, trial and error, and hard work. This quest works best when you have an opportunity to do what you do best everyday. A great source for understanding the role of talent in management and leadership is the book, *First, Break All the Rules* by Marcus Buckingham and Jerry Coffman. I have given this book to many of my clients and have received many thanks in return. Buckingham and Coffman do an excellent job of covering the subject, and they give the reader tips on how to identify talent and how to interview for talent.

I started my career as a civil servant in the US Army. I was an equipment specialist and had to work with mountains and mountains of weapon system data. I had to apply computers, maintenance manuals, parts catalogs, procurement specifications, engineering drawings and reliability data to a wide array of problems. Most of my work occurred in an office, far away from the field. Unfortunately, I lacked talents for absorbing details and for visualizing how components of a machine worked together. The work was interesting but frustrating because it didn't tap my core talents, so after five years I left the Army to become a consultant. It took only a month as a consultant for me to know that I had found my chosen career. It thoroughly engaged my talents for conceptual thinking, writing, and teaching.

Stay Connected to Your Unconscious

If the Map to Unrational Leadership™ was true to the scale of the personality, the *Unconscious* would look like a cruiser and the *Ego* would look like a tugboat. First, let's talk about the tugboat. The role of the tugboat is to guide the bigger ship. The tugboat can function if both ships are in open water and **if they are connected.** If the tugboat gets separated from the cruiser, it loses its ability to function. The tugboat limps back to shore and rusts away. These are the leaders who cling to the way things have always been done. Our rationalists tell us that we need to change our leadership paradigm. But I think we need to reconnect leaders with their unconscious.

The leader cannot grow without integrating the unconscious. This is the great challenge of the modern organization. Recently, a young leader told me that he had programmed his feelings. "I only feel what I want to feel," he declared. Largely influenced by books that push mind control, he believed that he had overpowered his inner demons. I told him to call me when his unconscious knocked him over and left it at that.

Our unconscious mind is the mysterious sum of the thoughts, memories, impulses, and feelings that are not present in our conscious. It has a tremendous influence on our emotions and behavior. Most leaders don't want to talk about the unconscious and its impact on leadership. Some of this reluctance stems from the popularity of Sigmund Freud's thinking about the unconscious. He called it the subconscious, and to this day, most people use this term when describing this unknown part of our personality. Freud subordinated the subconscious to the ego and filled it like a basement with lots of junk, worn out memories, and frightening urges. There was little room in his psychology for partnering with the subconscious.[1] He thought that we needed to dominate it, and this philosophy permeates organizational life to this day. One of the major aims of this book is to rehabilitate the unconscious and show how it can be trusted to help the unrational leader grow himself and his organization. There are at least three powerful reasons for partnering with the unconscious:

1. **If we don't pay attention to our unconscious, it can sabotage our plans for change by erupting when we least expect it.** We have all experienced a Freudian slip. But sometimes this slip turns into a freefall. For example, I have participated and even led teambuilding workshops (before I developed Unrational Leadership™) that ignored the unconscious. In these workshops the participants tell intimate stories and reveal their deepest aspirations. Then, they swear to trust each other and treat each other with mutual respect. When they return to their workplace, they quietly begin to knife each other in the back. They use their new knowledge as a competitive advantage. This is why some people hate teambuilding workshops.

2. **Our unconscious provides the energy that we need to break free from Comfortopia and to sail past the Colossus of Rationality.** The next chapter will describe the Colossus

and the perils that it presents to the leader who seeks deep change.

3. **Our unconscious gives us critical guidance**. Granted, sometimes the inner voice will run contrary to every rational principle. For example, in a college interview for software developers, your unconscious might whisper through your gut: "Hire that young man with the long orange hair and the lip ring. He can unlock the inspiration for your next great product."

Consultants like to tell golf stories. Like many dedicated golfers, I have tried a host of putting techniques, including different putters, stances, grips, concentration and relaxation gimmicks. Not surprisingly, with all this rational engineering, my putting still stunk. I remember discussing this curse with my golf buddy Brian, the guy who watched me get my first and only hole-in-one. It was a fine Saturday, but already ruined by a series of three putt greens, and Brian said: "Charlie, I can tell you one thing and it's pretty technical, so listen closely: You've got a lot of crap between your ears. If you would get rid of some of it, you'd be a pretty good putter."

As I walked to the next green, it was all too easy for me to identify the crap. It was all the rational thoughts, worries, projections, calculations, advice, and warnings that I brought to every putt.

Taking my friend's advice to heart, I stood over my ball and imagined a trap door in my mind. I opened it and all the crap fell out. Then, I envisioned a stream of bright unconscious energy moving from my mind and into my putting stroke. A miracle occurred. For the next nine greens, I sunk every single putt—long, short, uphill or down. They dropped into the holes like strangers in a strange land. During the run, I knew every putt would land in the hole—just knew it. Since that day, my putting has improved and whenever I give myself too many conscious instructions, I remember to let go of the crap and ask my unconscious to takeover.

I hope that my golf story advanced my cause to rehabilitate the unconscious. Perhaps, you are wondering when and how to tap it. I like daily contact with my unconscious. I ask it to give me data about my problems. Sometimes, I learn amazing things about myself. Sometimes, I am left confused by symbols and feelings that I don't understand. But I always feel more balanced for making the effort. Throughout this book, I will present a variety of techniques for tapping your unconscious. Here are three baby steps to get you started:

1. **Every day for the next 21 days, write one paragraph about some aspect of your leadership process that you want to improve.** For example, let's say that you find it difficult to communicate your vision. In your daily paragraph, write about your vision for your organization ten years hence. Each day, get more and more concrete about the vision. As you write these paragraphs, let your emotions and feelings flow into your fingers. Try not to filter any images. Try not to judge your writing. The more you write, the more you tap your unconscious for energy and inspiration.

2. **Before your next staff meeting, criticize your leadership style.** Try this exercise to prevent your unconscious from sabotaging you. Put yourself in front of a mirror. Imagine the worst critic on your team. Pretend you are the critic. Highlight every flaw. Expose every cover up. Unearth every inconsistency. Show no mercy. Continue your criticism until you smile and realize that in this meeting, you will be able to deal with rejection.

3. **Find a picture of a personal hero and place that picture on your desk.** Whenever you face an important decision, ask the face in the picture for input. Don't ask for the decision. You shouldn't relinquish your ego to your intuition so easily. Take the advice as another dataset for you to consider as you make your decision.

Dialogue: A Group Process for Tapping the Unconscious

Leaders tell me: "I have practiced your techniques for tapping the unconscious and have found them useful. How can I get my team in on the action? I can't force them to keep a journal or talk to a picture!" Yes, it is true that you can't reliably force people to have a positive interaction with their unconscious. It is much easier to scare the hell out of them!

All seriousness aside, there is a safe way for groups to tap their unconscious. It is known as dialogue, and it's a valuable tool for the unrational leader. [2] A dialogue is an alternative process for conducting a meeting. Imagine a typical meeting. Someone raises an issue; people present facts and opinions (usually as truth). They debate the pros and cons, and the boss makes, confirms, or delays a decision. Oftentimes a decision is made with the approval of the group. But after the meeting, group members begin to consciously or unconsciously work against the decision that they just supported. **The typical meeting process avoids dealing with unconscious opposition that emerges after the decision**. A dialogue is a conversational process that teases out unconscious assumptions and fears before you invest in the action plan.

Once, a client who ran a large company asked me to work with his troubled and fragmented leadership team to create a powerful and sustainable strategic plan. They had so many strategies they didn't know which way was up. I sold them on trying the dialogue process. At the first dialogue, 15 of us sat around a huge table, and I started the dialogue by showing them a rock and introduced the process as follows:

> This is a Magic Rock from the bottom of the Ganges River. When you hold the Magic Rock, deep wisdom emerges from the recesses of your unconscious. Today, you will participate in a ritual conversation of making meaning. You will not create a list of action items. You have already made enough of them

and you still don't use them. Some of you will say: 'Charlie but we don't have accountability and this is why we never follow through.' I say, 'You don't have enough meaning.' And meaning is the only thing you will produce today. There is one important rule: You can't talk if you don't have the Magic Rock. No interruptions for clarifying questions. No debates. No give and take or pro and con. You all have diplomatic immunity in this circle, regardless of your position on the organizational chart. The holders of the Magic Rock can speak as long as they want, and when they are done, they can give it to anyone signaling for it. Now let's check in. I want everyone to hold the Magic Rock and give us a sentence or two on how you are feeling.

After this passionate explanation, I presented the dialogue topic: "What is your ethical responsibility to this company?" I wanted these leaders to wrestle with their responsibility to the company, to their departments, and to their team members. It's a tough question, and at first, the group greeted it with silence. As they began to speak, I could almost see the unconscious hopes, fears, and images of success and failure arise and place themselves in the middle of our circle. At the end of 90 minutes, I asked them what meaning they had drawn from the dialogue and most of them said something like: "Now, I know that we are all in the same boat."

Week after week, I started the dialogue with the same question about ethical responsibility. I asked this question about ethics to shift the team from **doing** to **reflecting.** I knew that their strategy would become clear after they had swept away their unconscious guilt. Erroneous and loosely held opinions faded away. One leader said: "This process allowed everyone to tap their unconscious whether they talked or not. Even if you just listened, your creative energy increased." Deep passions were shared about lack of follow through and perceived betrayals. Finally, the group centered on a single ethical responsibility: *To lead this company to the next level.*

This deep and commonly held value stimulated the development of a unified strategic plan within a month, an incredibly short time for any company of size.

The dialogue works because it taps the unconscious through ritual. When people sit in an open circle and pass around a mystical object like a rock from the bottom of a sacred river, they connect to an ancient decision-making process, a way of working in a group that sits deep in their unconscious. Carl Jung said that we have a 200,000-year-old man inside of us, and if we can touch this man symbolically, we release unconscious energy. In dialogues, this energy can settle into silence so profound that you can see thoughts emerging into your mind or hear someone breathing across the room. A participant once told me: "Charlie, this is the first time in years that I have felt people really listen to me. So many of our meetings are nothing but quiet surrenders. Dialogue transforms a meeting into a ceremony."

Your Ego should be the Strong Commander

The good ship *Ego* is the commander of your fleet. Like a tugboat, it leads the unconscious, marshals your talents, and unleashes your creativity (to be discussed shortly). The ego is the part of our personality that experiences the world through the senses and directs waking activities. A healthy ego is a necessity, not a luxury, if you want to find the treasure on this search. It takes a strong ego[3] to manage your day-to-day business and simultaneously withstand the rigors of tapping and assimilating unconscious energy.

Beware of people who tell you to lose your ego entirely. You will be accused of egotistic behavior on this journey. The further you sail from Comfortopia, the more unease you will create in your organization. Your personality growth will threaten some Comfortopians. It makes them look at themselves more closely than they would like to. Some will ask: "What is he doing? Who does he think he is? Does he think he can make his own law? He must have a huge ego."

Respond positively by addressing their fears and reassuring them that there is a place for them in your bold vision—**but you do not stop sailing.**

People often confuse a healthy ego with an inflated ego. While the former is essential for personality growth, the latter can alienate the leader from his staff. People with inflated egos blow up their personality with a lot of hot air. They stretch the skin of their personality, especially under pressure. Worse yet, the inflated ego is too weak to stay connected to the unconscious. The following questions can help you to discover whether or not you have an inflated ego. They are tough questions. Take some time to think about them.

1. When things go wrong, does a hypercritical and almost god-like inner voice attack you?
2. Do you work harder than almost anyone you know to stay on top? Do you need the biggest house, the most expensive dining room table, the thinnest wife, and the most luxurious cars to feel good about yourself?
3. Do you have trouble talking about your childhood, trouble accessing the memories?
4. Do you need other people to say that you are good to really feel good about your performance?
5. Do you find it difficult to trust God?

How to Strengthen Your Ego

Your responses to these questions may give you clues about the health of your ego. Let me say this: If you feel bad about yourself, get some help from a trusted professional. In my programs on Unrational Leadership™, I have helped some clients decide to see a therapist. Reading this book is not an alternative to therapy if that is what you need to become healthy. The good news is that your unconscious has natural healing energies that can build your ego. If you find that your ego lacks the necessary strength, your journey may be longer but no less rewarding.

Here are ten practical suggestions for strengthening your ego.

1. Become the president of a volunteer organization.
2. Create your own list: My Secret Ingredients to a Successful Life.
3. Read the biographies of five successful people and figure out how they succeeded. (I chose Sir Frances Drake, Ulysses S. Grant, Carl Jung, Queen Elizabeth I, and Henry Ford.)
4. Take a long trip to a place that you have always wanted to visit—but have avoided due to lack of energy, time, or confidence.
5. Identify a skill that intimidates you and learn how to do it until you can cope with your fears most of the time. (I chose public speaking.)
6. Create your own prayers and discipline yourself to pray daily.
7. Add three new friends to your network.
8. Fall in love—again.
9. Look ahead ten years from today and write a detailed description of your life.
10. Become a mentor to a younger person.

Find a Creative Practice to Energize Your Journey

The fourth principle of Unrational Leadership™ is: Creativity drives change. In this search, you can practice this principle by exploring your natural creativity. What's creativity? You are the ultimate judge. If you are a professional actress, you might get creative juice from learning how to make furniture. If you are a college professor, you might enjoy building trails for the US Forest Service. If you are a therapist, you might like working the corner at the local racetrack. If it juices you—if it awakens something new within you—then you are on the right path.

When I teach Unrational Leadership™, I always include a creative element in the program. I have hired artists, poets, singers, and actresses to teach Comfortopian émigrés how to tap their right brains. I have used Legos, Play-Doh, and collages to awaken the lost children in my students. They watch in wonder as works of art emerge from their personalities. Invariably, these searchers begin the program very skeptical about spending any time on creativity. The most common phrases I hear are: "I am not a creative person," or "My company would never let me do that back at the office." Of course, these words stun me, for if they are not creating solutions to problems, what are they doing at work? As I gently unlock the creative energy in the searchers and help them leave Comfortopia, their attitudes transform. Here is one of my favorite reviews of how I use creativity in my workshops:

> It does seem strange, to walk into a meeting and be confronted with piles of Legos, boxes of Play-Doh (with or without sparkles). To be asked to draw a picture of a complex business problem with finger paints! And it doesn't end there. In the membership exercises, you might tell stories about your ancestors, or partner with other people in the room while blindfolded. But by the end of the meeting, we accomplished an amazing feat: A group of 45 people—working together— wrote a partnering agreement. Before then, I had difficulty writing a simple product description with just five people.

Many years ago, sometime after I had left Comfortopia but long before I had found the treasure, I took my family on a cruise around Hawaii. One night I walked into the entertainment lounge and found my son Derek, singing karaoke. He was young and could barely read the words, let alone carry a tune. As I listened to him sing, with a mixture of pleasure and embarrassment, I waited for one of the other adults (who could presumably sing) to rescue him. No one stepped up and my little boy kept singing and singing, unaware of how terrible he sounded. After five or six songs, I got up the courage to sing.

As I approached the microphone, I envisioned Miss Hunter near the stage. She was the perky choir teacher from Jefferson Elementary School who had humiliated me by failing to pick me for the "All Kids Choir" after my dismal rendition of *God Bless America*. It was the last time I had sung in public, and when I saw her face again in Hawaii, my knees shook. I stumbled through *New York, New York*, hoping that this song of my youthful home would inspire a miracle. When I collapsed in utter relief, I told my daughter: "I sounded like a frog getting dissected without anesthesia."

Looking back, I think the image of the frog inspired me to learn how to sing. When I returned to Michigan, I engaged a voice teacher, and started to unlock the very deep and hidden creativity of a singer. During my first year, I referred to the "Do-Re-Me" scale as a song. Mastering it became my first challenge. After eighteen months, my teacher threw me into a recital, and I sang *C'est Moi*, from Camelot, the powerful and robust song that introduces Lancelot into the action. Before my performance, I told the audience that my goal was to suck less every day, but when I stepped off the stage, they sincerely applauded. Over the years, I have continued to engage a voice teacher and annually, I participate in a recital. In *my* search for Unrational Leadership™, singing has become my *SS Creative*.

Your First Monster can be a Secret Desire to Fail

After you have assembled your fleet and you are aware of the need to energize your entire personality, you immediately run into an obstacle. This is the way of a hero. He needs to run into a monster to test his strength. This monster is called the Reef of Hidden Secrets and it runs north to south on the Map to Unrational Leadership™, just east of the four ships. At the close of Chapter One, I asked you to record and hide a true secret. This task prepared you to look deeper into your personality and ask: "Am I hiding any secrets from myself?" If you don't ask this question, you are liable to run your personality into the reef. You might even sink the fleet. There are an infinite number of secrets hidden in our unconscious, but the one that I see most often is an unconscious desire to fail. This secret, nurtured by avoidance, influences our decisions and makes us do dumb things. Our friends, our family, our co-workers, even our competitors, wonder why we are making such obvious mistakes, but we don't see anything.

When we secretly want to fail, our unconscious seeks a meaningful catastrophe, an Enron of the personality that will require every ounce of heroic energy to overcome. In other words, we want to fail because we want to experience a deeper heroic journey. This happens frequently to people who work their entire lives to achieve success and stun everyone by throwing it away for a tawdry affair or lying on their resume. Once I had a client who was a true master of the universe. He had pulled himself up from the Midwest working class to the commander's seat of a billion-dollar company. When his company hit hard times, he asked me to help him turn it around. After working with him for a couple of weeks I told him: "Most CEOs fail because they secretly want to." He had made a series of poor decisions. If you examined any one of them, each was a simple mistake, but if you took them altogether, it was clear that he repeatedly sabotaged himself. He looked at me as if I was crazy and replied that he never entertained the thought of failure. I smiled and I said: "Just because you don't entertain it, doesn't mean you don't want it."

The Unrational Leader at Work

How can you prevent a hidden secret from overwhelming you? You need to learn and practice the Five Principles of Unrational

Leadership™. This discipline will help you unearth hidden secrets by opening your personality. Also, it will give you the courage to keep searching. To help you become a practicing unrational leader, I have inserted a section entitled: "The Unrational Leader at Work" at the end of many chapters in this book. These sections present practical situations and challenge you to think like an unrational leader. Here is your first case:

> You are the Director of Public Works for a large city. Due to budget cuts, you have to lay off about 10 percent of your staff. The affected employees are in their late '30s and early '40s and lack college degrees. Your region is in a recession. Jobs are tough to find. Your department is like a close-knit family. The staff is demoralized about the losses and feels betrayed by the city administration. How can you help your department endure this change without reducing the quantity and quality of services that you provide?

1. **Start all problem solving by taking personal responsibility:** You should prepare a presentation in which you admit that you, as a leader, take significant responsibility for the layoffs. Although your actions are precipitated by the city and in some ways dictated by union contracts, you, as the leader, have agreed to accept and implement these decisions. You decide to hold small group meetings with each section in your department. You give them one consistent message: "I can't guarantee you a job, but I can guarantee you that I will fight as hard as I can to preserve your job. I will challenge my managers to fight with me for you."

2. **Aim at increasing energy not just efficiency:** You meet with your management team and ask them what activities give the employees the most energy. You direct management to talk with employees and ask: "What gives you the most en-

ergy in your work? What takes away energy in your work?" You help your management team reduce the activities that de-energize your employees and match your employees to energizing activities.

3. **Confront and partner with the unconscious:** Before you sleep, you document your vision for the organization. You do this for at least 21 days and nurture positive energy for the future. You bring a picture of your great grandmother to your office and ask her: "What would you do about this problem?"

4. **Creativity drives change:** You reserve enough money in the budget to fund teams that will compete in local and regional maintenance and public service competitions. The top employees stay on their toes. You initiate a series of barbecues for your employees and citizens. Your employees give facility tours to the citizens. During the tours, your employees show off photo collages and drawings that you have asked them to create for the occasion. To top it off, you hire a local poet to start an after-hours poetry group. You pay her through an "Art in the Workplace" block grant.

5. **Look two generations behind and two generations ahead:** You form a cross-functional team of volunteers to prepare a history of the department. After completing and distributing the book, you conduct a series of dialogues throughout the department that ask: "What meaning can we make from this suffering?" You take notes during the dialogues and the comments inspire you to launch a department-wide vision and strategic planning process with the following theme: "What kind of city do we see in 50 years and what is our department's role in creating it?"

Notes

1. Carl Jung liked to call the subconscious, the "unconscious." He believed that the ego rises from the unconscious and that the unconscious is a vast store of positive and negative opportunity.

2. See Peter Senge's *The Fifth Discipline* for a more extensive discussion on the dialogue process.

3. When I interviewed for my first consulting job, I couldn't hide my nascent ego. I carried samples of my work products—a report, a technical guide and a newspaper article. I wanted 'the man' to see that I was a producer. As the interview unfolded, I flaunted my writing like a used car salesman. About a year after he hired me, I asked him what he saw in me in the interview and he replied: "You showed me that you had an ego that wouldn't quit."

Important Concepts for the Unrational Leader

- After you leave Comfortopia, don't hug the coastline!
- You have to engage your entire personality to make the voyage.
- Stay connected to your unconscious.
- Your ego should be the strong commander.
- Find a creative practice to energize your journey.
- Your first monster can be a secret, unconscious desire to fail.

THE ROUTE OF THE GREAT ADVENTURE

THE REEF OF THE HIDDEN SECRET

TALENT IS

NTS

SIREN'S WAY

ESCA

SIREN'S W

THE COLOSSUS OF RATIONALITY

ST   NT

SF   NF

COPYRIGHT 2001 BY PROJECT INNOVATIONS

"Cogito ergo sum."

RENE DESCARTES

3 The Colossus of Rationality

From the moment he leaves Comfortopia, our hero hears the seductive voices from the Sirens guarding the Colossus of Rationality. Modeled from the ancient Colossus of Rhodes, this Colossus represents our culture's unquestioning faith that all problems can and should be solved with reason. While the sight of the Colossus of Rationality reassures loyal Comfortopians, for the aspiring and sea-bound unrational leader it is an ominous obstacle.

It rises awesome and geometrically perfect from the sparkling unconscious waters, protected by Sirens. The Sirens live on small rocky islands around the Colossus and sing an irresistible song that lures mariners to their journey's end on the rocks surrounding their islands. The Sirens use the traveler's instinctive fear of the unknown and an infatuation with rational arguments to divert our hero from his quest. Even when the banks of Comfortopia become memories in distant sunsets, the Sirens will still tease him.

The Colossus is an All-Too-Familiar Trap

The ancient Colossus of Rhodes is an apt metaphor for our unwavering devotion to rationality. The citizens of the ancient Greek city of Rhodes built their Colossus in 282 B.C. to commemorate the military victory over the Antigonids of Macedonia, and to honor their sun god Helios. It was an ancient technological marvel: A hollow bronze structure with a framework of iron and stone, towering 110 feet on top of an impressive marble pedestal. One of the Seven Wonders of the World, it stirred awe and fear throughout the Mediterranean. The Rhodeans believed the bronze giant would ensure their wealth and military dominance. However, only 50 years later an earthquake brought down the Colossus. It broke at the knee—its weakest point. Eight centuries later, Arabs invaded Rhodes and sold the remains of the statue for scrap metal to a Syrian who used 900 camels to carry it off—a tragic yet fitting end for a weak-kneed god. Will our own Colossus suffer the same fate?

As a consultant, I see the same pattern over and over with leaders and their organizations. A crisis creeps into their business and after much stalling and many meetings, weeping and gnashing of teeth, the leadership agrees: "Yes, we have a crisis." Then, after more stalling and meetings, heroic energy bursts through, and the leadership decides: "We will change." They make strategies, appoint champions, alter processes, sell divisions, consolidate resources, and align performance incentives—in short—they actually leave Comfortopia. Things go well for a while, and the change effort spurs important decisions and reorganizations. Some of these changes are significant. Suppliers are terminated and a vice president from the old guard is removed. Then, mysteriously, just as the workforce begins to believe that leadership is finally serious, the change effort stalls. Leaders who resisted the effort get promoted. The consultants get fired. The reorganizations get reevaluated. The CEO announces, that for the sake of efficiency, the change effort has been renamed and successfully integrated into that holy document known as the

"Strategic Plan." This surrender, cast as a victory speech, is the signal that the Colossus has claimed one more victim.

The tragedy in this all-too-familiar story is that the leadership actually left Comfortopia. They saw the crisis before it consumed them, and they mounted a serious campaign. But they made one critical error that our hero won't make. They ignored the power of the Colossus. They left with the conviction that they would do whatever it takes to succeed, but when faced with the sacrifice of their dearest rational principles, they meekly succumbed to the Sirens. Even though the Sirens sing old songs, they endow the notes with unconscious promises. They offer a haven from hard decisions, comfort for the morally conflicted, and simple solutions to complex problems. Below, you will find four of the most popular songs performed by those beguiling warblers. If you are singing them to yourself, hearing them as a chorus from your team, paying yet another band of consultants to entertain you, you can be sure that you are steaming for the Colossus.[1] Be forewarned: When you dock there, all real change stops.

Colossus Hit #1: If You Can Measure It, You Can Manage It. *This all-time number one hit can be used to stop almost any significant change. It paralyzes any change that is centered on resolving a problem that can't be measured. How much does conflict cost? How much does honesty weigh? (I wonder if anyone ever asked the leaders of Enron this question?)*

Colossus Hit #2: The Only Thing That Counts Is The Bottom Line. *This song, most popular in Wall Street, warns sailors not to make any decisions that might compromise their financials. Most changes require trade offs, short-term reductions in profit in return for long-term gains.*

Colossus Hit #3: You Must Hold People Accountable For Results. *This song has a subtle magic. It is true that good leaders hold their people accountable for results. However, during significant change, roles and responsibilities must shift and a certain amount* *of chaos infects the organization. Leaders who don't really want to change use this song to maintain organizations that don't work.*

Colossus Hit #4: If You Manage By Facts, Your Business Will Run Itself. *This song became very popular in the 1980s when American manufacturers spent millions (or maybe billions) trying to copy Japanese management processes. As a resident of Michigan and an ex-consultant in the automotive sector, I am sad to report that two decades of implementing Japanese methods has not done the trick. Ford and GM are still struggling for survival.*

The Colossus is a Symbol of Our Unquestioning Allegiance to Rationality

In our culture we unknowingly endow rationality with extraordinary power. We insist on making decisions with reason, logic or scientific knowledge, without the interference of emotion or prejudice. Even though we may think it's as natural as breathing or smelling, the concept of separating reason and emotion, rational and irrational, is relatively new. Although rationality traces its roots to the works of ancient Greek philosophers (who certainly frequented the Island of Rhodes), its first modern champion was Rene Descartes, the famous seventeenth century French philosopher and scientist. At the time of the Protestant Revolution, discovery of the New World, and raging debates about the nature of the solar system, Descartes grew weary of disagreements and skepticism and set out to create a new method to study life and the universe, a method that created certainties and left no room for doubt.

The first certainty on which Descartes founded his method was his famous dictum: *Cogito ergo sum*—I think, therefore I am. With painful simplicity he reasoned that his own ability to doubt the opinions of his predecessors proved his existence as well as the existence of God. Who else but God, Descartes reasoned, could place such ideas as perfection and unity in the mind of an imperfect human? From these propositions, he leapt to a grand and fateful conclusion that mind *was* the soul—that invisible and immaterial divine spirit that separated humans from animals. Feelings, emotions, and intuitions, on the other hand, were material substances in our bodies, very much like blood or lymph. They occasionally acted up—mostly in dangerous and counter-productive ways. When these disturbances occurred, the mind could and should control its passions. Descartes put the mind on a divine pedestal, branded emotions as base and animalistic and banned them to the shadows.

Descartes believed mathematics was the most pure tool of reason and should form the basis for all learning. He held that all ideas must be clearly and distinctly observed before they may be accepted as truth, that each inquiry must be reduced to small, manageable pieces, and that all possible facts should be included to guarantee reliable results. Each newly established certainty could be used to create yet new certainties, the body of knowledge thus expanded. These principles became the foundation of the Colossus of Rationality and led to some debilitating unintended consequences: Our withering and mind numbing specialization; our obsession with meaningless measurements; and our religious focus on immediate, tangible results from any initiative. All these excesses and much more can be traced directly to Descartes' ideas.

Descartes himself did not rely on reason alone. The unconscious cannot be vanquished. The more we avoid it, the more it wreaks havoc in our world. **Ironically, he claimed that his method came to him in a dream.** He often neglected experiments and arrived at many erroneous scientific conclusions. For example, he believed water that had been boiled froze more quickly than water that hadn't. Of course, this claim is wrong and could have been easily disproved with experimentation. He did not believe in the existence of a vacuum outside of Earth's atmosphere and assumed that the universe was filled with matter, which due to some initial motion, had settled into a system of vortices, which carried the sun, the stars, the planets and comets in their paths. Although many of Descartes' scientific pronouncements have long been discarded, we still cling to the colossal idea that the mind is superior and reason is the best way to solve all problems. Because his philosophical principles served us so well in establishing science and industry, we hoped it would teach us how to manage our societies. We were wrong.

We are all Cartesians, Now![2]

Descartes' philosophies can appear in the voices of your colleagues, industry experts, supervisors, even well meaning friends and family. They will try to trap you by promising you control and seducing you with rationality. They will remind you of all your accomplishments, the wealth and honors you have gained by planning and executing in a rational way. And, they will promise even more success if you only would continue to worship sweet reason.

Rationality is the foundation of the current leadership development genre. The genre is fixed on the promise that you can fly through the hurricanes of business, government, and life with logic, fact, and numbers as your guides. If a new methodology is based on rationality and dressed in efficiency, it is enough to seduce leaders. They shout for innovation, but they are only really satisfied with more of the same. One of the leading consultants on time management is Stephen Covey, author of *The 7 Habits of Highly Effective People*, a book that took the business world by storm in 1989. At the time, I was working as a consultant at the Ford Motor Company, which sent thousands of employees to Covey's workshops. I watched the newly indoctrinated automotive professionals struggle to pack 16 hours into 12-hour days while spouting Covey mantras and toting Franklin Planners like Bibles. More than a few of these converts would whisper ironically (for it was counterculture to oppose Covey): "I'd love to follow Covey, but I need a time management course to do it!"

Most business consultants spout change but they don't want their clients to leave Comfortopia. They write about inner journeys but stop at the door to the unconscious. They ignore its overwhelming power. This explains why so many people like Covey's work but have so much difficulty implementing it in their lives. They run into unconscious obstacles that they can't manage. The unconscious can thwart the best schedules, mission statements, and core values. When "rational" voices promise you a "common sense technique" that will improve efficiency in your organization, listen for the honey in their voices. Listen to it for too long, and your efforts to change may perish on the rocks.

Our fascination with technology demonstrates how deeply we have bought into Descartes' religion. Reason tells us that computers, cell phones, and PDAs should strengthen our self-control, lessen stress, save time, and make us more secure. But how liberating has all this technology really been? As a teenager in the '60s, I thought my father, a chemical engineer for Mobil Oil, was a slave to his job. Daily, he commuted to New York City on the train. I remember whining: "I never want to do what you do!"

In her recent book, *The Overworked American*, Juliet B. Schor estimates that the average American worker is now on the job an extra month each year, compared to the average worker in 1969. The income of the average American is 65 times greater than the average worker in the rest of the world, but Americans work harder than workers in any other industrialized nation. Flashback to my hapless father staring into the angry eyes of his spoiled son . . . he never brought work home at night, never received a fax on a Sunday, and never checked his email on vacation. And without these productivity-enhancing tools, every summer he squeezed in a four-week vacation! Why do we still believe that technology can free up leisure time?

One of the most frustrating things is to watch large-scale change efforts leave Comfortopia knowing that they are doomed to failure because they refuse to address their rational foundation. Modern education is famous for initiatives that foundered on the Colossus and the "No Child Left Behind" Movement is the latest example.

In the name of child development it uses standardized tests as weapons to force teachers and students to narrow their learning to memorizing facts and formulas. These tests qualify students for promotion, set funding levels, and shape curriculums. Instead of helping students create innovative learning projects, teachers are forced to turn classrooms into test-prep factories where students learn to answer multiple-choice questions. To make time for coaching children on tests, valuable programs are cut, including literature, art, music, current events, and even science. The Sirens sing: "If it's not on the test, it doesn't matter!" Not surprisingly, most of the standardized tests don't measure deep thinking, only superficial knowledge of unrelated facts. They certainly don't explore the irrational side of our personalities. As a result, talented teachers flee the profession, students lose interest in learning or turn into grade-driven zombies. Puzzled parents stare into cryptic printouts of their children's test scores that tell them nothing about their education. [3]

Forty years ago, a different educational reform movement lost its way. In the '50s and '60s, teachers and researchers realized that children learned the most when engaged in real-life projects, where they worked together, with support and guidance of knowledgeable teachers. Instead of treating students as empty, quiet receptacles for pouring in facts, they treated them as personalities with variable learning styles and motives.[4]

This reform failed to spread nationwide. Many principals, school board members, corporate leaders, and even parents heard the Sirens singing that the reform was too radical, would cost too much money, and would take control out of their hands and leave too much of it to the teachers and students. Traditionalists dismissed the new methods as soft nonsense, ignoring the sound research and proven success behind them. Although their own school memories may have been marked with anxiety and boredom, they believed that the system itself was fine—after all, it produced them and they had become successful and productive. The conviction grew that the 3R's (Reading, Riting, and Rithmetic) were just fine, thank you. After two decades, the reforms stalled and in the '90s the "No Child Left Behind" Movement emerged. Comfortopia! Full speed ahead!

When Your Cheerleaders Turn into Sirens

The Sirens instill the fear of everything that's different and smacks of irrationality. If beguiling you with the promise of control and efficiency fails to dash your adventure on the rocks in front of the Colossus, they ignite your natural fear of the unknown. "You don't have enough time," they warn as you change careers. "The odds are against you," they remind as you make a bold investment. "Everyone will oppose you, ridicule you, desert you," they threaten as you prepare a controversial proposal. "You will have to work hard and give up things you love," they caution as you decide to change your leadership style.

The Sirens often emerge in people who should be your biggest cheerleaders. I will never forget the afternoon that I introduced a fellow organizational development consultant to my concept of Unrational Leadership™. Before I could finish my last sentence, he declared: "No one will ever get it." I also remember when I told a co-worker at the US Army that I wanted to leave the civil service and work in the private sector. We called him the "Major." He was a decorated veteran from Vietnam, a man with fierce and hard eyes.

"How old are you?" he asked.

"Thirty-three," I replied.

"You're washed up, Charlie. Forget about leaving. No one will want you now."

In Chapter One, I described my departure from Comfortopia when I finally understood that I had to focus on my people and help them succeed. It didn't take much time for tensions to arise between my boss and me. He had taught me the consulting game, and I looked up to him as a father, but he didn't want me to change. As I tried to adjust my leadership style, he demanded that I keep my consultants billable virtually 100 percent of the time. He resisted requests for allotting on-the-job training time to new consultants. He didn't want to send them to school to learn software programs. He insisted that we hold staff meetings in the evenings. And he began to criticize me. He accused me of breaking the rules, of betraying all the opportunity he had given me and, even worse, setting a bad example for the younger consultants. I was the fallen star, and he withdrew his approval. When I refused to stop my search for Unrational Leadership™, he removed me as a manager and put me in charge of selling training services—the kiss of death in any information technology consulting firm.

The Unrational Leader at Work

How can we resist these modern Sirens? When his ship was about to pass the legendary Sirens, Odysseus had his sailors stuff their ears with wax, but he had himself tied to the mast for he wanted to hear the Sirens' beautiful voices. The Sirens sang when they approached, their words even more enticing than the melody. They claimed that they could give knowledge to every man who came to them—along with ripe wisdom and a quickening of the spirit. Odysseus' heart ran with longing but the ropes held him and his ship quickly sailed to safer waters.

Tie yourself to the mast and imagine that you are the president of an engineering services company with offices clustered in a declining region of the country. Core industries have been leaving the region for several years, and although your company has compensated for the downturn by developing new clients, it has stopped growing. Your intuition tells you that your company is on a burning platform, but your management team believes that an economic upturn is near. (Are the Sirens singing to you?) You decide on an expansion strategy and declare your intention to open branch offices in more prosperous parts of the country. Your management team is lukewarm regarding your bold decision but agrees to support you. Within a year of launching your strategy, you hear complaints that the expansion is costing too much money and diverting attention from your core clients. What can you do about these Sirens?

Apply the Five Principles of Unrational Leadership™!

1. **Start all problem solving by taking personal responsibility:** Did you really leave Comfortopia? Did you assign your top people to open the branch offices or did you hold back the "A" Team to mollify the naysayers? Have you spent personal time in the branch offices or have you kept your heart in Comfortopia?

2. **Aim at increasing energy, not just efficiency:** If you are only measuring efficiencies, you are getting a one sided-picture. Major expansions almost always negatively impact efficiency and costs in the short run. Have you tried measuring how much energy the strategy has released in the organization? Are you measuring the eagerness of your up-and-coming stars to open new territories? Are you accounting for the energy that new customers have brought into the organization? Are you measuring the lack of support from key managers and taking appropriate follow up action?

3. **Confront and partner with the unconscious:** Rituals help you confront and partner with the unconscious. Helpful rituals include: Setting aside time for prayer or meditation, maintaining a daily journal of your experiences, or conducting a monthly dialogue with your management team. Recommended topic: How is this expansion an ethical decision for our company?

4. **Creativity drives change:** You can spark creativity by facilitating a series of workshops in which you present the expansion as a heroic journey. Prior to the workshops, draw a picture of the company's heroic journey. Present your picture and ask your troops to draw their own heroic journeys. Form teams and have them synthesize the individual

pictures. Mount the final drawings on walls throughout the company—especially in the expansion offices.

5. **Look two generations behind and two generations ahead:** Form a team of corporate elders. Ask them to star in a video in which they tell stories about the company's history. These stories should cover favorite legends, corporate triumphs, and individual heroics. The elders should move throughout the company, showing the video and helping employees understand the strong and resilient roots in the corporation.

Final Words of Wisdom

In your search for Unrational Leadership™ you will never quite get out of the danger zone. The songs of the Sirens will always be present, although they might change their tune as you enter different stages of life. Ultimately, you will need a song of your own that will overpower the Sirens. Homer tells us that the Argonauts escaped the Sirens because Orpheus heard their song and immediately realized the peril they were in. He took out his lyre and sang a song so clear and ringing that it drowned the sound of those lovely fatal voices. Ernest Hemingway defined courage as grace under pressure. Keep your courage close to you on this journey and discover your clear, ringing voice. This inner voice rises from your unconscious and gives you courage. You will further "tune" this voice in the Little Sea of the Voice That Defies Reason, but before you sail there, it's time for you to tap your unconscious by discovering how a young knight transforms himself into a TrueHeart.

Notes

1. After years of consulting, I have become convinced that most leaders hire consultants to help them **avoid** change. The last thing most rational leaders want to hear is that they need to personally change.

2. We have lived on a steady diet of Descartes' philosophies for so long that we no longer recognize the source or the symptoms of our malady.

3. I remember one parent teacher conference, where a high school teacher greeted me with a spreadsheet of more than forty grades. When she finished reviewing my daughter's grades, I asked her: "Is she learning anything?" She looked at me like I asked her the most ridiculous question.

4. In high school in 1966, I had a biology teacher, Mr. Davis, who treated students as personalities. He is the only teacher who I can still see in my mind's eye. He taught me how to learn in my own best way. Not surprisingly, the high school fired him after one year.

Important Concepts for the Unrational Leader

- You must sail past the Colossus to become an unrational leader.

- The Colossus is an all-too-FAMILIAR TRAP.

- The Colossus is a symbol of our unquestioning allegiance to rationality.

- We are all followers of Rene Descartes (even if we don't know it).

- The Sirens seduce us with fear of the unknown.

4 Rationality's Last Stand

O nce upon a time, there lived a King, renowned for his rationality, who ruled a large and prosperous Kingdom. His family included the Queen, the Crown Prince, the Prince, and the Princess. In his sunny life, the only shadow was cast by memories of Moira, his twin sister. After gaining the throne as a young man, the King and Moira had a terrible fight, and the King had exiled her to the Dark Forest. No one thought about Moira anymore except the King. He spent nights worrying that she would return and claim her share of the Kingdom. His worries thickened into a recurring nightmare about a giant serpent that chased him across a kitchen.

"What does this dream mean?"

"It's indigestion and nothing more," the Queen replied sharply.

One Christmas, as many lords and ladies sat in the Great Hall drinking and making merry, a winter storm assaulted the castle. But, inside the castle there was only warmth and security. The great King relaxed on his golden throne, surrounded by his family.

In the midst of the revelry, the Young Knight (who secretly loved the Princess) asked the King to share the secrets of his success.

"The Nine Habits," replied the King firmly. "The prophet Covey, long live his memory, brought us seven habits and my mother, God rest her soul, gave me the Ninth—*Neither ask nor give any quarter to your enemies.*"

At the mention of the Ninth Habit, memories turned to the Court Fool, who had lost his head on Christmas Eve for joking about the King's manliness. The Fool's head stood guard above the castle gates as a reminder of the power of the Ninth Habit.

Suddenly, the night watchman burst into the Great Hall.

"What brings you, good watchman?" asked the King.

"Your majesty, an army masses at the castle gates under the cover of the storm. Their ambassador petitions you with this gift." The watchman handed the King a bejeweled chest. The King opened it and a snake darted out. The Queen and the Princess screamed. The Crown Prince and the Prince rose with their swords, but their powerful blows missed their marks. The snake slithered into the shadows of the Great Hall.

"The serpent is from Moira," the King whispered. No one in the room saw him shudder.

Let's Give Her the Ninth!

The King quickly convened his War Council.

"Give her the Ninth Habit!" The Young Knight shouted to resounding cheers.

"Brave men," pleaded the Princess, "the Young Knight, however brave, speaks without reason. Your anger is mother to blood and sorrow. Let us seek first to understand the mystery in this message."

"Sweet daughter, you underestimate Moira's power," said the King. "She has created many spells of doom and destruction in the shadows of the Dark Forest."

"The Princess speaks wisely," countered Rich in Wisdom, the King's aging counselor and court magician. "An irrational woman has attacked us and we talk as men crazed. You can't kill the irrational with anger alone. Let us serve this bitter kitten a little magic in return." The King refused to listen to his faithful magician.

"The Young Knight is right," he declared. "Let's give her the Ninth!"

The War Turns the Wrong Way

While preparing for battle, the Crown Prince beseeched the King for command of the Army. He was the Kingdom's best warrior and most ardent follower of the Nine Habits. The next morning he paraded out of the city as the King's champion and confronted the enemy. Moira quickly defeated him.

Upon hearing the news, the Young Knight begged the King: "Oh Great King, unleash my sword and allow me to avenge the Crown Prince."

"Young Knight, we need an experienced warrior. Put first things first and learn from men how to wage war," replied the King.

The King's second son, the Prince, was the next to take up

the challenge. He was the Queen's favorite. She cried for him to reconsider his decision.

"I will avenge my brother," he declared. And the next morning, the Prince and his troops galloped into the battlefield to the sounds of men cheering and ladies swooning. Yet, Moira quickly dispatched him.

On the third day of Moira's siege, the King forbade all visitors to enter the Great Hall. But, the Young Knight disobeyed the King and snuck into the King's fearsome presence.

"Good King, I am your secret weapon," whispered the Young Knight as he knelt before the tired man.

"Why do you insist on getting yourself killed?" asked the King.

"A voice calls me to the battle. I know it defies all reason, but it clearly says **'You can save the Kingdom.'**"

"So, follow your voice and give your life without reason," replied the dejected King.

"And so I will become your champion," declared the Young Knight.

For Whom Do You Search?

Only the Princess appeared at the City Gate to say good-bye to the Young Knight as he set off on his quest. He rode a donkey—for he was too poor to buy a horse and no one would lend him one.

He entered the woods near the castle to find Moira's black horde. Even though he had been in the woods a thousand times, he quickly became lost. He wandered for hours in the snow, and even the donkey left him. Hungry and cold, he stumbled onto a woodcutter's hut. He built a roaring fire and soon fell asleep. When he awoke, he saw a snake curled near the fire.

"For whom do you search?" asked the Snake.

Surprised by a talking snake, the Young Knight sat up and reached for his sword.

"I wouldn't do that if I were you," warned the Snake, nodding toward the weapon. "I can get to you a lot faster than you can get to me. I ask you again—for whom do you search?"

"I might as well tell you, Snake, for I am lost and no one else will help me. I am the champion of the Princess, and I am hunting for Moira, our King's evil twin sister. She has defeated the Crown Prince and Prince. Soon, she will overcome the whole Kingdom unless I can stop her."

"And, what will you do with her when you find her?" the Snake asked.

"I'll give her the Ninth Habit, of course. I may die in the process, but I will be remembered forever as the Kingdom's Savior."

"I see. You seem like a nice young man. Have you ever killed a snake before?"

"No, I haven't. And I must confess that I don't even like to catch them. They scare me a little."

"Then, I think I can help you," hissed the Snake. "Bend your ear to my forked tongue, and I will tell you how to save the Kingdom."

The Young Knight Turns into a TrueHeart

The next day, the Young Knight found his way back to the castle and went directly to the Princess' chambers. Based on the snake's advice, they hatched a plan to save the Kingdom.

"Oh Young Knight! Such hopeful tidings you bring this New Year's Eve. A Young Knight you are no longer. Now, you are my TrueHeart." With these words she renamed the Young Knight as TrueHeart. Then, she kissed him deeply, and imprinted her love upon his soul.

A few hours later, the young lovers crept into the Great Hall.

"Father, we have come to share good tidings," said the Princess, gently clasping her father's hand. "The Young Knight succeeded in his quest and has become my TrueHeart. Listen to his news."

"Sire, unseal your grief this dark evening," TrueHeart said. "Your sons are kept alive in careful spells by Moira. To break the spells, you must come with us into the woods tonight. There we will meet a magic snake."

"Are you crazy?" bellowed the King. "A magic snake?"

"I swear on the Nine Habits, my Lord," said TrueHeart. "The snake in the chest can talk!"

"A talking snake? You are a fool!" said the King. "I rue the day I swore to your father that I would raise you as my own."

"Stay your anger, I beg of you. The snake said you would not believe me. So he told me to tell this story:

> Once upon a time there was a King who hired a clever tailor to make him the most beautiful clothes in the world. And the tailor wove the King a most excellent suit. When the King put on the suit and proudly paraded before his people, they hid their laughter. The tailor had fooled the King. His clothes were not clothes at all and the King was naked. But no one was willing to relieve the King of his shame—neither his nobles nor his ministers. Only one child spoke out and shouted: "The King's not wearing any clothes!"

"Daughter," said the enraged King, "If I see you again with this fool, both of you will lose your heads. Be gone from my sight."

A Rational Fact Not Explained

On New Year's morning, the King saw that Moira's army had emerged from the woods and had gathered in front of the castle. Since becoming a man, the King had prided himself on his ability to make rational decisions. But, on this New Year's morn, he saw only fog. "Should I sue for peace? Should I keep fighting? Should I talk to her?"

Sometimes, the simplest ideas are the most difficult to absorb, especially for a man condemned to being right for so many years. He just couldn't imagine talking to his sister. He couldn't sue for peace. He had to do what made him feel most comfortable. He put on his armor and set off for the battlefield. His army cheered his arrival. His white charger smashed against Moira's army. Rejuvenated by the King, the army forced Moira into a slow withdrawal that became a steady retreat into the woods.

The King, searching for Moira, heard her rallying her knights for a last stand. "Men of the Dark Forest, we are saved by courage," she cried. "Saved by courage!" The words fed only hatred in the King and he charged at her, eager to remove her head.

From the castle walls, the Princess shivered as she watched the action near the edge of the woods. Looking into the crowd of mayhem, she spotted TrueHeart charging on his donkey between the King and Moira.

"TrueHeart! TrueHeart, turn back," she shouted hopelessly.

Then silence everywhere. Men, horses, cries, the Princess and the weapons—all stilled as if sleeping. TrueHeart opened his eyes and found himself sprawled on the ground near Moira. She lay on the bloody snow, struggling for breath. She motioned for him.

"Come here and remove my armor," she told him. "I need to

breathe." TrueHeart unbuckled her breastplate and eased it off her chest. Her beauty was more striking than he had imagined.

"Who are you?" she asked.

"I was called the Young Knight but the Princess has named me TrueHeart."

"TrueHeart, for what do you search?" she asked, with a shallow breath.

"For peace. I tried to stop your brother from killing you," he said, pointing to the unconscious King. "He is most unreasonable when angry. Your snake told me that you had merely bewitched the Crown Prince and the Prince."

"You did stop him from killing me. Thank you. But in the meantime I cast a sleeping spell that cursed my brother and his entire Kingdom to an eternity of dreams." She whispered the spell with labored breaths.

> In the shadows, Courage hides.
> Ready to draw me from evil's side,
> And with Courage's help I shall be strong,
> To banish all that do me wrong.
> Send them away, send them to dream,
> Never again to plot and scheme.

"Does the Princess dream this sleep?" asked TrueHeart.

"Yes. It appears only you were spared, a rational fact I cannot explain."

TrueHeart Receives a Sacred Quest

TrueHeart reflected on his fortune. What would come next?

"Can you reverse the spell?"

"I know it not."

"Then, what should we do?"

Moira responded with a quizzical look. "My teacher always said that transformation begins with the weak."

"What is your teacher's name?"

"Brigid." Moira smiled at the sound of her name.

She grabbed TrueHeart and pulled him close enough to stare fiercely into his eyes. "I give you this sacred challenge. Go to the Dark Forest. Learn the secrets of Unrational Leadership™ from Brigid and return to rescue us all."

"What is Unrational Leadership™?" TrueHeart asked. "I only know the Nine Habits."

"The Nine Habits have fallen."

"How can I betray my King?"

"How can you not?" she replied, waving at the sleeping castle. "You are the Kingdom's only hope. Go find Brigid in the Dark Forest. Swear on your love for the Princess that you will perform this sacred quest. Swear it now, TrueHeart."

"I swear it before God."

"Good. A brave man still lives."

"What will happen to you?"

"God will help me now."

TrueHeart began to weep.

She placed a finger on his lips. "No tears or questions, my hero to be. Go and find the new path. Rationality has made its Last Stand."

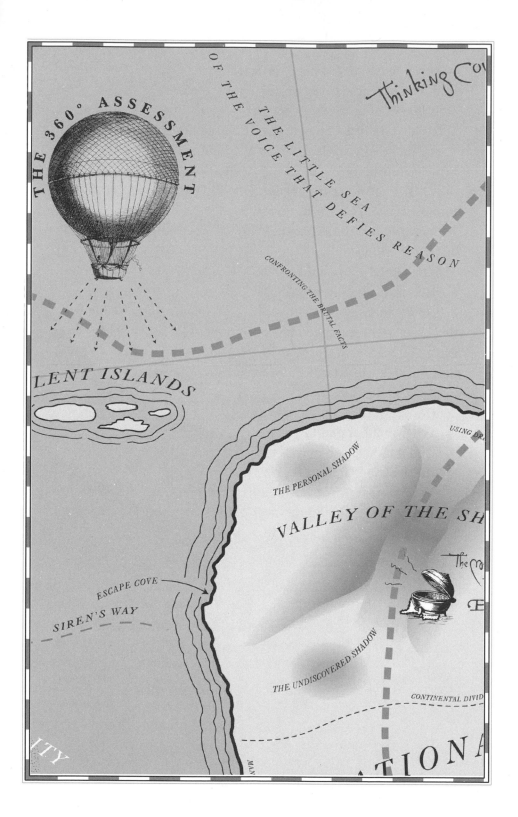

The Little Sea of the Voice That Defies Reason

Have you noticed the Little Sea of the Voice that Defies Reason on the Map to Unrational Leadership™? It is an expanse of placid waters north of Unrational Island. While crossing this little sea, you will learn more about your unconscious and how it can help or hurt you in your role as a leader. In the Introduction, I wrote that Unrational Leadership™ was the marriage of traditional rational thinking and the irrational intuitive mind, that part of our self that comes out at night. In Chapter One, I defined the Five Principles of Unrational Leadership™ and introduced the third principle: Confront and partner with your unconscious. In Chapter Two, I invited you to step aboard the *Unconscious*, one of the ships at your command on this heroic journey. I gave you some baby steps for tapping unconscious energy. Then, I talked about the Reef of Hidden Secrets and how some leaders tend to nurse a secret desire to fail.

This chapter begins with stories of leaders who ignored their unconscious and paid a steep price. The sad thing is that these leaders were dreamers who had the courage to leave Comfortopia. In the early stages of their heroic journeys they found good fortune, energized the hidden potential in their teams, and easily sailed past the Colossus of Rationality. But in the middle stages of their journeys, as is always the case, another monster appeared to test them. This monster emerged from the depths of their personalities. Although the monster can be terrifying, it is actually an honor to see it because it only emerges when the hero's ego is strong enough to confront it. These heroes faced a choice to partner with their unconscious or to succumb to it. You wouldn't know it from reading the business press, but the most catastrophic leadership failures occur when leaders surrender to the unconscious part of their personalities. If you have ever followed a leader whose character failed him just as he grabbed the brass ring, you have seen this tragic surrender.

Ultimately, this chapter offers a deeper exploration of the third principle of Unrational Leadership™: Confront and partner with your unconscious. Understanding and practicing this third principle is the most difficult task for the rational leader, so I am devoting an entire chapter to the topic. The rational leader has been trained to avoid his unconscious, especially in the workplace. When it arises, as it does in any heroic journey, he has to do something with it. What should he do with this unconscious energy? Pretend it doesn't exist? Drink it away with his friends? Put huge bonuses into his bank account? Or turn the screws of efficiency on his organization? In this chapter, you will learn how to recognize the voice of your unconscious and you will learn a set of powerful techniques for partnering with it. As you learn how to dance with your unconscious, you may question your sanity or at least, you will question my sanity. But take heart. This is a natural consequence of the heroic journey. As you break free from your rational confines, your unconscious thrusts itself into your life. Will you flee from it, push it down, feed it to your dark side, or befriend this voice that defies reason and gain the treasure of great leadership?

The Case of the Missing President

Some leaders sail into the Little Sea of the Voice that Defies Reason and are never heard from again. Sam left Comfortopia when his mother retired and left him a small telecommunications company in northern Illinois. From the moment he took the corner office, Sam supercharged the sleepy company with energy and vision. He wanted to take the company from $10 million gross revenues to $500 million in five years. He brought on new shareholders, developed a formal strategic plan, instituted a management development program, implemented cross-functional process improvement teams, and hired new talent for critical positions—including Paula, a young and vivacious Marketing Vice President. He even hired an actress to teach the sales staff how to apply acting skills to large account acquisition. As an unrational leader in the making, he strengthened the company's ego, leveraged its talents, and injected creativity into the organization.

Sam was 45. His wife worked in the Accounting Department and his daughter interned in the Information Technology Group. He played golf every Saturday with the same foursome at the only country club in town and spent Sunday mornings in church. He had been married 24 years and the thought of having an affair had never occurred to him—until he met Paula. Everyone saw it coming except Sam. He approved an oversized Marketing Plan from Paula and the two of them began working late into the evenings. She passionately shared his vision for the company, and she became his listening ear when he complained that his management team "just didn't get his vision". He experienced strange feelings. He began to fantasize about her. At first, he was too busy pursuing his corporate vision to notice the attraction, but then he found himself creating special assignments for Paula in order to provide a reason to work with her. When he finally recognized his sexual urges, he went through a long cycle of backing away from and moving towards the relationship, until the two of them attended a Mergers and Acquisition Conference in San Francisco.

After he committed adultery, the door to his unconscious opened and visited him with plagues of guilt, anger, and fantasy. He lost his bearings and withdrew from his routine. He quit his weekly golf match. Complicating matters, Paula began to spread her wings beyond the Marketing Department and tried to fix Operations. She didn't know what she was doing, and Sam had to protect her from his team. A whisper campaign ignited, and Sam became paranoid. Sometimes, he exploded at meetings, and he quit talking openly to his staff. He swore to the Board that his relationship with Paula was purely business (as he kept having intercourse with her). Soon thereafter, his wife asked him for a divorce.

I am not going to tell you that Sam lost the company or that the company stopped growing. Although these outcomes are common in these situations, Sam had a knack for making good deals and for finding hard-nosed people with a single-minded focus on the bottom line. Yes, Sam won the battle, but he's losing the war. His family doesn't trust him; his reputation has been tarnished in the industry; and many of the idealistic men and women that he hired to expand the company have quietly left for other pastures. And, as you might expect, the relationship with Paula ended when Sam realized that he had to choose between her and the company. But, more than all of this, Sam lost a big piece of his personality and until he brings it back to the surface, he's doomed to wander the mysterious waters in the Little Sea of the Voice that Defies Reason.

The Case of the Sunken Company

If you are up on your ancient history, you remember the dot.com bubble at the end of the last century. Do you remember when Yahoo's stock was worth more than General Motors? When the upstart AOL swallowed Time Warner? Or, when every ninth person in Santa Clara County, California was worth a million dollars? In hindsight, the bubble represented a massive migration from Comfortopia as our nation embraced the Internet Revolution. Companies worth no more than the fancy bindings on their business plans garnered millions of investor dollars and loosed a horde of buccaneers. Some of these companies made it past the Colossus of Rationality, and a few even made it all the way back to Comfortopia. But many sank into the cold waters of Chapter Eleven. This is the story of one of those shipwrecks.

Four bright software geeks had developed propriety software for managing e-marketing campaigns. They founded ABC.com and wrote a great business plan. Their first round of venture capital funding was successful, and after buying the requisite BMWs, they built a hip organization in San Francisco. Doug, the young and hard-charging president, heard about me from one of his investors and hired me to provide a fresh and objective perspective on his company. He said: "You know something about this crazy business. I want you to help us take this thing to the next level." Doug believed that he had empowered his handpicked management team and that he had transformed them into super achievers. He told me his guiding mantra: "One vision, one team, one company."

Using *Diagnosing Organizational Culture* by Roger Harrison and Herb Stokes, a reputable cultural assessment tool, I surveyed a statistically significant sample of his company, including the management team. The results, corroborated through one-on-one interviews and focus groups, showed that Doug ruled his company with fear and intimidation and abused his power to build personal advantages for himself and his brother (the Marketing and Sales VP). I suspected that the company had grown way too fast for Doug and the thought of losing his chance for a multi-million dollar payoff scared the pants off him. He reacted to his fears by turning into a tyrant and concentrating control instead of spreading it around. I prepared myself to present the results to him and his team. I had wanted to talk to him privately but he said that whatever I had to say to him I should say to the whole team because they had an open, team-based culture.

When I presented the results from the interviews and the cultural assessment tool, I told Sam and his management team that the company was sick and that if they didn't address it, the company would not survive the next growth phase. I said that their business model required lots of decentralized management and that the more the team centralized control, the less responsive it would be to the marketplace. I did not say that Doug was fully responsible for the malaise, but my meaning was clear.

He fought every one of my points. He challenged my competency, the culture assessment instrument, the size and quality of the sample, and the findings from the focus group. He implied that I had misled them with leading negative questions. Then, he challenged his management team to support my conclusion that the company was sick. The team greeted his request with wise silence, until the courageous Operations Manager spoke. She picked her words carefully and said that even if the results were untrue, they represented a powerful perception that needed to be corrected. Doug quickly agreed with her. Then, he announced that he would personally look into the assessment results and report back to the team at **a time of his choosing**. He got up and left the meeting without another word.

The next time I heard of Doug's company was from a law firm specializing in bankruptcy. They wanted to know what I was willing to accept from Doug's company for my fees—a nickel on the dollar or a chance for a dime on the dollar if it ever emerged from Chapter 11. Doug had misspent his investment capital and lied about the business plan. I accepted the nickels and chalked up the $10,000 loss as another testament to the power of the unconscious.

When the unconscious fires burn, leaders walk into the fire or build a thick firewall. In *The Case of the Missing President*, Sam opened the barn door to his unconscious desires and had a life-altering affair with Paula. In *The Case of the Sunken Company*, Doug poured concrete over his inner terrors and painted the cement with a rosy picture of his tyrannical leadership style.

A Special Case: The Fortune 500 Executive

Sam and Doug talked like Masters of the Universe, but they were small company guys and they confronted their unconscious in simple, small company ways. Sam let the energy overwhelm him and Doug suppressed it. But, what about leaders of big companies? What do they do when their unconscious wakes up and barks? Flight or fight options are not usually available to the Fortune 500 executive. If he or she wants to survive in the rarified air of Mahogany Row, he or she cannot afford any extreme behaviors. Take Ford Motor Company for example—the competition for a Vice President position is truly global and the leader who aspires to this role can't sit still for a moment. There are always competitors in the wings, not to mention the stress of overseeing a global operation, and maintaining the image of a progressive, thoughtful, innovative, motivational, visionary, and above all else, results oriented leader. Clearly, the Fortune 500 executive who wants to succeed has to deal very carefully with an internal voice that defies reason.

Although most top-flight executives reach middle management by making things happen, they don't get from the middle to the top by producing results. In fact, many of them don't spend enough time in one job to create any results that one could assign to them. Top executives earn their next promotion in meetings with other executives through good acting and excellent communications. They must show the well-oiled pose of the accomplished leader and communicate a thorough mastery of their business without dominating the agenda. In these meetings, winning arguments openly is a death sentence. The successful executive must wait patiently to make an insightful comment, to propose a daring innovation, to ask a question that takes the group into a quiet moment of self-reflection. And then, he or she must report performance results without self-promotion or avoiding any brutal realities buried in the numbers. They must always be ready; they can never be surprised.

These people are truly the crème de la crème of the business world and whenever I work with them, I am awed by their band-width. But, I am also amazed by the price they willingly pay for their success. They can't blow their cover. They can't be honest with each other—in other words, they can't be real. I remember debriefing a Fortune 500 female executive about a program that we had delivered on gender diversity. In a series of workshops, we had facilitated some dialogues on the topic of what it meant to be a man or woman in her company. I will never forget what she said: "I am grateful for your efforts because you proved that it is possible to create an honest conversation between a group of executives, but I am saddened because I don't think it can happen again."

In some cases, I have been struck by the almost inhuman quality of high-level executive conversation and decision-making. Some of them remind me of alligators lying in the shadows waiting for unsuspecting prey. They live behind reptilian masks. They wait for weakness and pounce on it without revealing anything more than the power of their personality. They can stop million-dollar projects with a single question and derail a young manager's drive to the top with subtle yet timely public criticism. **These executives have learned how to convert their unconscious energy into their shadows.** They know how to terrify people without being terrifying; they know how to disrobe someone without touching them. They patrol the shores of Comfortopia and only allow the chosen few to leave. But ironically, even though they live and act like Kings and Queens, they have unwittingly condemned their personalities to swimming restlessly in dark waters.

Detecting a Confrontation with Your Unconscious

As these stories show, a confrontation with the unconscious is a wrestling match between the ego and a powerful drive that emerges unbidden from the unconscious. Some leaders experience it as a depression; others experience it as a call to change their lives; and others experience it as a powerful explosion of energy. Regardless of the experience, when it occurs you will feel as if an alien force has invaded your consciousness. Here are five signs that a confrontation has come upon you:

1. You find yourself repeatedly breaking your own hard-and-fast rules.
2. You repeatedly question the structure of your life and/or your organization.
3. You find yourself with almost no energy or with tremendous energy that stops you from sleeping.
4. You experience unexpectedly strong feelings at the strangest times.
5. You find yourself wiling away your days in fantasies.

You may have experienced some of these signs when you were about to leave Comfortopia. Nevertheless, there is a crucial difference between your initial call to action and this passage. The call to action is often external. It may be caused by a financial or personal crisis that pushes the individual to seek a different path. It is possible to ignore or postpone answering the call, or to take a safe detour. In the Little Sea, you steam into your own fears, desires, and obsessions. If you ignore them, they will overwhelm you and sabotage all your rational efforts to succeed. The trick is to figure out how to partner with your unconscious without losing your ability to think and act rationally. In the rest of the chapter, I present four processes for partnering with your unconscious:

1. **Drawing Mandalas**—an ancient, creative technique for integrating negative, chaotic feelings.
2. **Finding a Sponsor**—forging a relationship with a wise counselor who has successfully made the inner heroic journey.

3. **Honoring the Inner Voice**—listening to your inner voice and allowing it to work in your life.
4. **Reconnecting with Your Ancestors**—searching for a connection to an ancestor and using that connection for inspiration that defies reason.

Partner with Your Unconscious by Drawing Mandalas

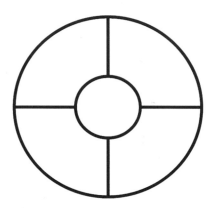

Basic Mandala Structure

Derived from a Sanskrit word, mandala means "magic circle" in Hindu. The structure of the mandala is a circle divided into quarters with a centering circle. It is the naturally occurring structure that our personality uses to integrate chaos into order. Drawing mandalas helps you reduce inner conflict and the sense of irrationality that haunts you during a confrontation with your unconscious. Mandalas have been used across centuries and cultures in spiritual rituals and in decorative architecture. The Tibetans use the mandala as a meditation object, viewing the mandala as an imaginary palace contemplated in meditation. On the next page is a mandala that I created during a period of confusion and doubt about my business. This image helped me understand how to integrate the services provided by my company and sparked the emergence of Unrational Leadership™.

Delving into the history of magic circles in her book *Creating Mandalas*, Susanne F. Fincher points to natural science as a starting place for understanding the power of mandalas and why the human psyche is predisposed to this arrangement of circles. Fincher points out that we grow as a round egg in a round womb that is pushed by circular muscles through a tubular canal, out a circular opening onto a circular planet in a circular orbit around a circular sun in a galaxy full of circular planets and circular stars. We think we are standing still yet the planet on which we stand is spinning, and our bodies are quietly and subtly in continuous circular movement.

Look around and you will see mandalas—in the stained-glass windows and mosaics of churches, the layout of cities such as old

Boston, and the structural form of many buildings around the globe. Individual designs vary, but most have the classic mandala characteristics: a center, cardinal points, and some form of symmetry. Some are very simple, such as the Chinese T'ai Chi symbol, which represents the universe as the mingling of opposites. Others are amazingly complex, such as Native American and Tibetan sand paintings. The Great Seal of the United States of America, the two circular forms found on the back of a one-dollar bill, is a mandala laden with mystical symbolism. Small children draw mandalas spontaneously, and it is no accident that many adults "doodle" by drawing circles and spirals.

In his travels Carl Jung observed that most cultures use the mandala in one form or another and speculated that it was a universal symbol for integration. When he was thirty-eight, he began creating spontaneous mandala drawings. He had resigned from what he felt was an unfulfilling and empty academic career to focus on private practice and delve deeply into his experience of depression. In his autobiography,[1] Jung wrote: " . . . I sketched every morning in a notebook a small circular drawing, a mandala, which seemed to correspond to my inner situation at the time. . . . Only gradually did I discover what the mandala is . . . the self, the wholeness of the personality, which if all goes well is harmonious . . . " Over a long period in which Jung discovered and articulated the psychological concept of self, his depression lifted. Based on his personal success, Jung introduced mandala work to his clients.

Creating your own mandala may begin with highly patterned wheels, but the intent is to represent the issues and symbols in your mind. I suggest you fill your mandala with representations of your thoughts and emotions. Are you worried about how missing a project deadline will affect job security? Depressed about the changes in your company? Mourning the loss of a loved one? Dreaming of changing your life? Give each emotion, each incident or issue a face or a shape in your mandala. You might make one mandala representing your immediate experience, and another representing the most favorable outcome. If you're thinking that there is no artist inside you, if pencils or inks are unwieldy, foreign objects in your hands, try a different medium like rubber stamps, or finding pictures and words in magazines that speak to you, and arrange them inside your "magic circle". The imagery summoned from your deepest self is more important than the means used to portray its significance. Here are some guidelines, for creating mandalas:

1. Suspend your inner judge. There is no right or wrong mandala.
2. Before you start, close your eyes and see what fills your mind.
3. Draw a circle freehand, with a compass, or trace a plate.
4. Fill the circle with your visions, or let your inner hand move your pencil.
5. Identify the top of your mandala by placing a "T" wherever it belongs.
6. Date and title your work.

Partner with Your Unconscious by Finding a Sponsor

The word "sponsor" comes from the Latin "surety" and expresses the relationship between a learner and a person who has solemnly promised to undertake certain advisory responsibilities. In the search for Unrational Leadership™, a sponsor can teach you how to work with your unconscious, a skill that you will not learn in school, business, or government. Many sponsors prefer to call themselves therapists or analysts, but in my case, I was lucky to find a person who insisted on rejecting these labels for our relationship. Her name is Pauline Napier, and I dedicated this book to her in gratitude for her sponsorship. Pauline is a licensed Jungian analyst trained in Switzerland by members of Carl Jung's first circle. She is a former elementary school teacher and an inspiration for successful people across the country. More importantly, she possesses the life-affirming energy and the fierce honesty that are so essential for a sponsor.

I will never forget the first time that I met her. Her attitude was: "The world can and really might end in 30 seconds, but until that happens, let's see what we can do about this life." I had developed a leadership-training program based on Jung's concept of archetypes. At that point, I had not read Jung's work or seriously studied his ideas. I had picked up the idea of archetypes from an excellent book by Robert Moore entitled *King, Warrior, Magician, Lover*. Given her background in Carl Jung, I wanted to know what Pauline thought of the training manual that I had sent her.

"What do you think an archetype is?" she asked me after I described my program.

"It is like operational software. Archetypes lie deep within our personalities and drive our behavior. We can change the software, but only with very careful instructions," I replied confidently.

"And you think you can teach people how to do this?"

"Of course. Didn't you read my training manual?"

"You're either a fool or a very dangerous man," she replied fiercely. I wish I could convey the seriousness in her voice, the implicit warning, a verbal tick from the clock that shows the world is only seven seconds away from nuclear destruction. She said: "Archetypes are powerful beyond my comprehension, beyond even Jung's comprehension! They originate in the unconscious and if you don't understand the unconscious, you have no hope of helping leaders really develop their personalities." She certainly got my attention, and soon I felt like the Sorcerer's apprentice[2] in *Fantasia*.

"Charlie, how are you going to help businessmen when you encourage them to believe their own fantasy that they can control the world and everyone in it, including their own unconscious? The unconscious exists outside of your ego and will do what it must do to survive. It will not be fenced in. It will not be programmed. It is the atmosphere of life. If you can't breathe, how can you lead?"

With whatever degree of humility that I could muster at that time, I asked her to teach me how to work with my unconscious and that is how our relationship began.

People ask me: "What is the difference between an executive coach and a sponsor?" Most executive coaches are goal-oriented behaviorists, i.e. rationalists of the mind. They help their clients define their goals/problems and take appropriate actions. They might also do a personality assessment or even include some cognitive therapy if they are clinical psychologists. What they hardly ever do is help a

Leadership Element	Executive Coach	Sponsor
Articulating values, core ideology and mission	Helps executive identify strongly held personal values and inject them into corporate ideology by working with executive team and culture.	Helps executive identify personal and corporate shadow and helps executive see how these shadows play out in organizational ideology.
Setting goals and holding the organization accountable for achieving them	Helps sort through conflicting goals, using core ideology as foundation for prioritization.	Helps differentiate personal goals from organizational goals, using personality growth as foundation for prioritization.
Solving problems that defy reason	Advises formation of problem solving teams and associated tracking mechanisms.	Teaches executive how to tap the unconscious.
Inspiring the company with inclusive, empowering style	Using multi source instruments and feedback helps identify and correct non-productive behaviors.	Helps identify weak side of personality and shows how it can be expressed more positively.
Creating and communicating powerful vision and strategies	Encourages reflective and creative thinking to identify visions and strategies.	Encourages recording and analysis of dreams to inspire energy and symbolic thinking.

client partner with his or her unconscious. They can't—because they haven't done it themselves. In my company, any employee can form a relationship with a sponsor, a.k.a. Jungian analyst, and the company will pay for associated travel and consulting fees.

Many readers have retained or will retain executive coaches. I am not discouraging these relationships. I had a marketing coach for a year and learned a lot from him. But I also needed a deeper experience that related to growing my personality. If you want to find a sponsor, I suggest you start by contacting your local Jungian Society (most of them have websites) or by talking to a respected elder. The table on the previous page outlines the fundamentally different approaches between the typical executive coach and a sponsor.

Partnering with Your Unconscious by Honoring Your Inner Voice

In our daily grind, the easiest voices to hear come from the outside, from the family, the community, the church, the government, or the media. These voices speak to us at the same time, making it difficult to hear ourselves. Some people live and die under the spell of these external voices. They have been fooled into accepting society's babble as their own song. They habitually turn their ears to the outside and listen for the answer to these questions: "What is right? What should I do? Who should I fear? What is wrong with me? What will the future bring?" If their unconscious intrudes with unwanted answers in the form of dreams, nagging intuitions, or fantasies, they run away from these sources of individuality. Without original energy or thoughts, they become the lost sheep—ripe and ready for shearing.

Here is a story that my father told me that helped me understand the power of the inner voice. I heard it as a boy, but it forever challenged me to discover and honor my own inner voice. My Grandpa Charlie (my namesack) was my grandmother's second husband, and although he was not blood kin, the familial bond between us was as strong as steel. Grandpa Charlie was a life-long dirt farmer in mid-Michigan, and he was tough and independent. His attitude was this: Are you sick? Milk the cows anyway. Had too much to drink the night before? Go out in the snow and shovel coal into the furnace anyway. He hated doctors. So when he became seriously ill in 1963, he resisted all pleas to go to a hospital. He didn't want any doctoring, any heroic measures. He was 84 and wanted to finish life on his own terms. And what he wanted most was to die in his farmhouse.

My grandpa had no interest in organized religion, but my grandma was a dedicated Christian. She loved Charlie and truly believed that he was destined for Hell. Over the years, he defied her attempts to convert him, preferring his own way. As he lay dying in his bed in February of 1963, my kind and ever so patient grandma begged him to accept Jesus as his savior. She even asked her reverend to visit, and together the two pleaded and prayed for hours for my grandpa to become a Christian. But Grandpa Charlie[3] resisted to the end. In his final minutes, he stirred and his eyes blinked once before he declared loud and strong: "I believe in nature." Then he closed his lips, his eyes, and died.

Charlie Fleetham and his Grandfather, Charles Gragg

Partner with Your Unconscious by Reconnecting with Your Ancestors

The fourth partnering technique is reconnecting with your ancestors. This advice is not about channeling or participating in a séance. It is about grounding yourself in the memories and deeds of your ancestors. Their stories will give you strength to move forward against the long odds, against the outer voices that say: "You're not the one. You're nothing special." (If you are an orphan, try to find a dead hero and learn everything you can about this person.) Whether it is your ancestor or a hero, your task is the same: Create stories and use them to embrace your inner voice, (instead of running away from it). Whenever I ask people at my workshops to dig into their roots, this is what I observe: 1) about half of the people have very little knowledge of their ancestors and 2) the process of learning about them almost always makes them feel better about their own lives. The following exercise will help you reconnect with your ancestors:

1. Make a list of five ancestors, such as your great grandparents, grandparents, uncles, aunts, parents or step-relatives. If you don't know your ancestors, think about elders that have helped you or that you have admired, such as teachers, foster parents, religious leaders, coaches or managers.

2. Select two people from your list and record one of their heroic deeds. Tell their deeds as short stories.

3. Spend a few minutes reflecting on the lives of these ancestors and answer the following questions:

   • What was the challenge before this person?
   • How did they confront their unconscious in their heroic adventure?
   • What monsters did they face and what allies did they earn?
   • What did they gain and what did they give up?

- Imagine they are talking to you. What are they saying to you about your own journey?

The ancestor that I needed to learn the most about was my father. He died in a tragic accident when I was 21. I had no doubts about his love and have many, many great memories to comfort me, but I knew very little about his life beyond his role as my father. He didn't talk much about himself and when he did, like most children, I took in only the headlines—if that. Not long after I turned 40, a powerful urge set upon me to learn more about him—an urge that I now recognize as an upwelling from my unconscious. Fortunately, as a management consultant, I have probably interviewed a thousand or more people, and I used this experience to contact a group of his friends and relations. On the phone I explained that I wanted to know who my father really was from a grown-up perspective.

These farmers and small town businessmen told me wonderful stories about my dad's heroics, his sense of humor and his ideals. Even though my dad had been dead for 20 years, they had protected that small candle of my father's life that burned in their minds. After I completed the interviews, I wrote a letter to my dad and told him what I had learned:

> Dear Dad,
>
> I have finished the interviews about you. The proud and gray elders have spoken. They loved you Dad—without hesitation or reservation—and while they talked in their parlors that the years have weathered into temples, I could hear your voice and see you as a young man living your life. The images of you were almost as clear as if I had found a reel of home movies. Here are a few of the scenes that touched me:
>
> - I learned that on Friday nights you walked a mile up a farm lane to your grandpa's house and spent the weekends with him talking late into the night of your dreams of the future.

- I learned that you loved how Grandpa Charlie claimed you as 'his son'.
- I learned that you took a bus to Detroit on your first night in the Navy in 1944.
- I learned that you liked women and they liked you, but the first woman that you wanted to marry refused your hand (and is unmarried still).
- I learned that as a kid, you did your best friend's math homework while he fished and 30 years later, you told him that you were coming home to fish with him again.
- Everyone talked about your brilliance, but everyone also loved to tell the story of the fire you started in the college Chemistry Lab. Fortunately, you transformed this passion into a degree in Chemical Engineering and became the first college graduate in the family.

Dad, your friends honored me simply because I am your son. Thanks.

George H. Fleetham

Writing this kind of letter to an ancestor is a classic Unrational Leadership™ process because it helps you release buried emotions and integrate them into consciousness. Whenever clients tell me they are struggling with the death of a loved one, I suggest that they write a letter of thanks to this person. My letter (and interviews) helped me paint a new set of images about my father. In writing it, I closed a door of doubt about him; I now could see the way I was connected to him. I could see the "him" in me. We are not simply a product of the here and now, but rather an end product of our ancestors, their experiences and their own personality types. By getting in touch with my father, I discovered a deeper understanding of myself, and ultimately became a stronger and more confident leader.

Confronting the Unconscious is a Heroic Act

A final warning about confronting your unconscious: Don't quit your job! When I got down on myself as a teenager, my mom told me to find some work because it would make me feel better. I scoffed at her then, but I have come to honor her wisdom. The unconscious overload will cause you to take your eye off the ball and make your routine seem as tasty as stale peanut butter and jelly sandwiches. During my most turbulent period, when my unconscious slithered like a snake in the tall grass, I called a staff meeting and told my team members that I wanted to change careers and that I was going to find someone to lead the company.

Even though I had enough money to stop working for several years, the idea was absurd for a couple of reasons. First, most of the business that my company generated came through me and without me the company wouldn't have much value. Secondly, I wasn't sure what I wanted to do. My mind crawled every which way. I entertained becoming a Jungian analyst, going back to school to get my MBA, taking my family to Hawaii to write a book or buying a completely different business where I could apply my ideas to production or retail. I spent about six months talking to people about different opportunities and I even asked my lawyers to prepare a stock purchase plan so my employees could buy me out.

But through this search process, I kept working, even though I ached for a drastic change. Yes, I kept doing agendas, facilitating meetings, coaching executives, preparing reports, making speeches, writing proposals, and hiring and firing people. The work anchored me to reality. I had seen too many friends stop working and lose themselves chasing pleasure, money or a fantasy. It was hard for me to concentrate, but I disciplined myself to keep working. My fantasies dropped away and on the other side of my confrontation, I discovered Unrational Leadership™.

If you have made it to the Little Sea of the Voice that Defies Reason, give yourself a pat on the back. You have come farther than most. You have worked hard and fought hard. You have achieved good things—maybe even great things. You have rewarded yourself, but you haven't forgotten the people who have helped you. You are becoming a hero, and like all heroes you have made mistakes. You have taken advantage of your people—not to mention yourself. You have made some bad decisions—decisions that cost people their jobs. And, with this guilt, this memory of failure, you have sailed on. In this respect I am no different, and when I get discouraged, I recall these inspiring words from Theodore Roosevelt:

> It is not the critic who counts; not the man who points out how the strong man stumbles, or where the doer of deeds could have done them better. The credit belongs to the man who is actually in the arena, whose face is marred by dust and sweat and blood, who strives valiantly; who errs and comes short again and again; because there is not effort without error and shortcomings; but who does actually strive to do the deed; who knows the great enthusiasm, the great devotion, who spends himself in a worthy cause, who at the best knows in the end the triumph of high achievement and who at the worst, if he fails, at least he fails while daring greatly. So that his place shall never be with those cold and timid souls who know neither victory nor defeat.

Note

1. Taken from *Memories, Dreams, Reflections.*
2. Although the Sorcerer's Apprentice comes to us from an ancient fairy tale, the most well know version is in Disney's *Fantasia*. A magician's assistant tries to imitate his master before he is ready. He casts a spell on a broom to fetch water for his chores, and the broom does fetch water—in the form of a flood. The apprentice tries to end the spell by chopping the broom in half with an axe, but that only results in two brooms gone awry and more water, water, water. Finally, when the apprentice is near drowning, the master calls the broom to a halt.
3. I was lucky to inherit some of the land that Grandpa farmed. Years ago, I retrieved a rock from an overgrown pile on the back 40, the same pile Grandpa used to drag stones to during plowing season. I keep this rock on the top of my fridge and some mornings, I hold it and it conjures up the memory of Grandpa Charlie nuzzling my cheek with his scratchy beard.

Important Concepts for the Unrational Leader

- The further you travel, the more likely it is that you will have to confront your unconscious.

- Leaders with the courage to leave Comfortopia most often fail because they won't partner with their unconscious.

- There are five signs that your unconscious is confronting you.

- There are tried and true methods for partnering with your unconscious.

- Confronting your unconscious is a heroic act.

> "You can't become a man through a woman's shadow."
>
> PAULINE NAPIER

6 Success Has a Single Father

"**B**rigid, I have been in the Dark Forest for exactly one year. Is it time to return to the castle? Have I learned enough about Unrational Leadership™ to break Moira's spell by kissing the Princess?" asked TrueHeart.

"A fairy tale ending to be sure," replied Brigid[1] teasingly.

"Isn't that what a hero is supposed to do?"

"And so young hero, what have you learned about Unrational Leadership™?" She sat like an ancient Venus on a stuffed throne. Her black magician's robe hid her slight frame. Around her lingered the scent of white lilies. She smiled as she watched TrueHeart's unlined, bright face puzzle the question. A low fire simmered in the hearth.

"Success has a single father," replied TrueHeart.

"And who is the father?"

"The leader's inner voice," replied TrueHeart. "Now—please tell me if a kiss will break Moira's spell. Didn't you teach her the magic words?"

"Patience, my boy. What is your inner voice saying to you today?"

"It says that my head is filled up and I can't take another thought. I need some love! Your Dark Forest is wondrous, but I am tired of its shadows. It's too dark. I want the Princess."

"Do you dream about her?"

"Every night I sweep aside the creeping vines that guard her door and step over sleeping chambermaids to her slumbering form. Her long red hair flows over her breasts, which rise and fall softly with her breath. Ever so gently, I place my warrior fingers on her forehead. Then, I bend over her and kiss her fluttering lips. Slowly, her copper eyes open and the fire raises between us."

"Cool down lad. Do you know that a great cook once discovered a food that vanquishes a woman's desire for lovemaking? It is known as a Wedding Cake!" TrueHeart frowned while Brigid cackled. A sorceress with a sense of humor, she reached across the room and touched his hand. "Have I been indelicate?" She seemed to enjoy his discomfort. "And, her father the King? Is he in your dreams? Will he forgive your conspiracy with Moira?"

"He raised me after my father died for him in battle," said TrueHeart defensively. "He will forgive me. After all, I am going to break the spell and rescue his Kingdom."

"TrueHeart, you have made great strides in this year. My God, most leaders don't even know that they have an inner voice. They listen to their ministers, their wives, even their enemies, but they don't listen to themselves. They secretly search for someone to tell them what to do."

"But when the King rode out to face Moira wasn't he listening to his inner voice? He seemed so sure of himself."

"No. Many years ago he replaced his own voice with the voice of the Nine Habits. Like so many rational leaders, he unknowingly betrayed himself and a rage filled him. To balance himself he had to give this rage to Moira and those around him." TrueHeart winced as the image of the Fool's head crossed into his mind.

"Brigid, how do you know when you've found your inner voice? The King thought he heard it. Moira thought she heard it when she attacked our Kingdom. And I think I hear it telling me to rescue the Princess. It's very confusing."

"Yes one voice tells a leader to vanquish his enemy, another tells him to negotiate for peace, and yet another tells him to run for his life."

"Brigid, people don't want to open their unconscious for this very reason. It creates too many choices. Following the Nine Habits is much simpler."

"It is a simple method, but it is meant for simple problems. The more difficult the problem, the more the leader needs Unrational Leadership™."

"Again I ask. How do you know when you've found your inner voice?"

"For a man, the secret rests in finding the voice of your inner father (a woman must find the voice of her inner mother). Your inner father is a strong but elusive creature and formed somewhat like the Sphinx. He has the backbone of your real father, the heart of your own unconscious, and the soul of God. This voice sits like a King in your unconscious and gives you the guidance you need for untying Gordian knots[2] and for tolerating the chaos of creation—that twilight time before a solution brings light."

"Whoa! That's a lot to swallow . . . practically speaking, I never knew my father, and my mother died during my birth."

"It is true that the orphan has a greater challenge in locating the inner father, yet other men can and do generously serve as symbolic fathers—like grandfathers, uncles, teachers, even Kings." She leaned into him and her voice softened. "But you are not an orphan TrueHeart."

"What?"

"Yes, your father lives."

"Where?"

"In a faraway land. He has been imprisoned by a most beautiful woman."

She turned to the bookshelves that lined the wall to the ceiling, pulled out a dusty volume and gave it to TrueHeart.

"The Further Adventures of an Innocent Woman," he muttered. The news that his father was alive stunned him. His imagination filled with long lost fantasies of meeting his father. Brigid told him to open the book and nervously he turned the thick leather cover to see a picture of a man standing on the top of a tall tower.

"Is that my father?"

"Yes, he lives in a dark fairy tale now."

"Why didn't you tell me this when I came here? I could have rescued him by now," TrueHeart said bitterly.

"Secrets have their own clocks."

"I must go to him," declared TrueHeart.

"Good, and when you rescue him, remember that a man who wants to listen to his inner father must find a way to stand

on the shoulders of his real father despite any weakness, sin, or betrayal. Do you understand me, TrueHeart?"

"When I find my father—no matter what happens, I must grow from him—not tear him apart."

"Yes, and if you succeed, you will have accomplished something that is truly heroic," said Brigid. Then, she gestured to the book. "The name of his mistress is Snow White. Don't be fooled by her. Evil often comes in pretty packages."

The Greatest Truths Can Come from the Weak

TrueHeart walked for weeks to the south. He had crossed six mountains and stood in front of a rushing river, the last barrier to his father. TrueHeart tied a rope around the three-legged dog that Brigid had forced upon him. "Yes, he will slow you down, but you must take Cedric,[3]" she insisted. "He was Moira's dog. Remember TrueHeart, the greatest truths can come from the weak."

TrueHeart stepped into the river and despite his best efforts, lost his footing and fell. As he tried to regain his balance, his hand smashed against a rock and he let go of the rope. The current quickly carried Cedric downstream. Without a thought, TrueHeart dove into the water and swam for Cedric. The dog thrashed his three legs, gasped for air and went under. TrueHeart redoubled his efforts, but couldn't find the dog. He surfaced, gulping for air and frantically searched the waters. Then, he heard a distant but familiar voice from the waters. He couldn't believe his ears! It seemed impossible, but when he placed the voice—he realized it was Moira.

"Dive here, TrueHeart, and you will save me," spoke the voice of Moira. TrueHeart plunged towards the voice and found the dog lying against some rocks on the bottom of the river.

Later, TrueHeart and Cedric rested in front of a warm fire in a cabin abandoned from another fairy tale. The dog began to speak in Moira's voice.

"TrueHeart before you meet your father, Brigid wants you to hear this story."

"Brigid? Moira? A talking dog? What black magic is this?"

"Your search will bring the understanding that you seek." Again the dog spoke as Moira.

"Just tell me what is going on!"

"My father died when I was 17. After a proper mourning, my brother prepared for the coronation by playing the wily rogue with his friends. After a feast and festivities that would make Bacchus blush, I stumbled upon him in his bedchambers and found him wrapped in the arms of a young man."

"How could this be anything more than drink and youth?" asked TrueHeart, defending his vision of the King's manliness.

"My sentiments exactly," replied the dog and Moira's voice echoed again in TrueHeart's ears. "Unfortunately, I was too young. My mother had raised me for the Religious Orders, and I couldn't tolerate the sight of my brother in a man's arms. I became hysterical and threatened to tell all unless he agreed to swear off this sin for life. My brother exploded in rage. I fled into my mother's arms and told her everything. In short order, my brother's lover found himself banished to the battlefront on a suicide mission and my brother found himself learning and following the Nine Habits as if his life depended on it—and it did. Most living are too young to remember my mother, but I saw her stare down demons in the castle graveyard. She was not above killing her own son."

"Soon after the turmoil, my mother died. After her death, her shadow stayed on my brother, but he knew it not. Upon his coronation, he took me aside and said he could not tolerate my betrayal. I was no longer his sister but his enemy. He banished me to the Dark Forest and as a warning he grabbed Cedric and slashed off his foreleg. He and I remember that awful day as if it were yesterday."

"And the King's lover? What happened to him?" asked True-Heart offhandedly.

"My mother's guard lured **your father** into an ambush and left him for dead. He would've died if Snow White had not saved him."

TrueHeart stood in shocked silence. "My father?" he finally asked, "That was my father?"

A Spell is Cast

The next day, TrueHeart and the dog arrived at Snow White's manor. The most beautiful woman in the world rushed through the doors to greet them.

"TrueHeart, you and your dog are most welcome to our home," she said with magical foreknowledge of his arrival. She hugged him tightly. He felt the soft comfort of her young breasts press into his weary bones and wanted to stay in that warm embrace for an eternity. "I am Snow White and these are my loyal servants, but you may have heard of them as the Seven Dwarfs." She winked at him and pulled him into the ivy-covered manor.

The Seven Dwarfs wore rose aprons and taffeta hats. They bowed slightly as TrueHeart passed. "I used to work for them," trilled Snow White, "but now they toil for me!" She winked again and again . . . or so it appeared. TrueHeart's heart melted into her eyes. She waltzed TrueHeart and Cedric through the Great Hall, down a long tunnel and then up a forbidding maze of winding staircases to their quarters in the West Tower. Opening the door, she said, "I am sure you want to freshen up before you meet your father. Please ring this bell if a need arises and one of my dwarfs will fulfill it immediately." She kissed him lightly on the lips and closed the door.

TrueHeart and Cedric entered an enormous bedchamber filled with sunshine, roses and the sound of birds singing. True-Heart sat on the bed while Cedric hopped to a corner and flopped on a pillow.

"How did she know I came to see my father?" TrueHeart wondered out loud.

"You have already lost yourself to her, haven't you?" asked Cedric.

"She is beautiful but her charms have no power over me. First, we will find my father and then we will go get the Princess."

"I respect your eagerness to meet your father, in light of what you have learned about him."

"Don't be absurd, Cedric. Nothing can keep me from meeting him. Brigid said I must learn to grow from him in order to find my inner father."

There was a knock on the door and Happy entered. "I came to tell of the wondrous ways of this manor," said the dwarf. He told of the daily feasts, tournaments, and balls staged by Snow White for her guests. Then, he lowered his voice and said: "Our mistress has only one rule: Absolutely no one is allowed in the manor basement."

A Legend in His Own Mind

Manor life suited TrueHeart. At first, he told himself that he needed to regain his strength before he met his father. But days turned into weeks and TrueHeart continued to immerse himself in Snow White's amusements. Weeks turned into months and he grew strong and fierce and became the champion of the manor. No one could defeat him. Months turned into years and he became a legend; women swooned at his feet. Paradoxically, TrueHeart never forgot his passion for meeting his father. He spoke about rescuing him at great length. But there was so much for a legendary warrior to do; he never seemed to have the time to complete his task. On the seventh year to the day of his arrival, he sat on his bed talking to Cedric.

"Snow White told me this evening that my father is busy with state affairs, often traveling as her ambassador. But I am not too concerned, she says . . . ."

Cedric interrupted him: "You talk big but don't deliver. Your father often comes to you when you are asleep or off hunting wild boar with the dwarfs."

"Have you told me this before?"

"Many times, TrueHeart."

"I have heard this before? How odd. I feel like I just learned it today. Tomorrow I am going to climb the steps of the tower." He yawned. "Even though the mere thought of that climb makes me tired. Did you know that according to legend "

Cedric interrupted him again, "The East Tower reaches to the sky. Yes, you've told me. Don't you think it's time to overcome your secret shame and meet your father?"

TrueHeart shook his head. "There is no shame. Don't worry, old pal. When the time is right, I will meet him."

Cedric didn't answer; he was already asleep.

The next morning, TrueHeart bolted up in bed as if he had been pierced with an arrow. "I had a dream," he gushed to Cedric. "I was talking with some men about warfare, and I was suddenly taken to a great battle, surrounded by swords crossing and men dying. My father was on the field with me. I had an intuition. I realized that only one man could survive the battle and I decided it had to be me—even though I knew that my father was on the field.

Like a snake, I slithered away from the action. I watched as enemies circled the men. They surrendered their swords without a fight. Out of the blue, the enemies asked the men if they wanted to be shaved. They brought them into a room filled with naked women. The women took off the men's clothing, shaved off all their hair and transformed them into women!"

"What is the dream saying to you?" asked Cedric.

"It shouts: 'TrueHeart, you have waited too long to find your father.'"

On his way to the East Tower, he ran into Snow White carrying a basket of flowers. A white dove was perched on her shoulder.

"My TrueHeart, where are you off to in such a hurry?" she trilled.

"I am off to see my father," he replied, barely slowing his pace.

"I see," she said. "I do hope he can see you today. He has been so busy. Your father is so wonderful! I have no idea what I would do without him. And from what I see, the son will someday best the father . . . in all ways," she added coyly, fluttering her eyelashes.

The King Tree Lives

TrueHeart climbed the endless steps of the East Tower. Round and round he trudged with no end in sight. He considered turning back, but each time he remembered the dream and pushed forward. Exhausted, he finally stood in front of the door to his father's room. Heart pounding as if he were going into battle, he knocked. A white-haired man, old before his time, opened the door.

"My son!" exclaimed the father, with outstretched arms. "Welcome to my home. I have wondered many times if you would have the strength to climb this tower. Snow White told me of your courage, but she never mentioned your strength. Is it possible she overlooked it?"

Instantly warmed by his father's open heart, TrueHeart embraced him. When he broke free and surveyed the room, he saw that it was piled with books, flasks, rusted old weapons

and cracked armor. In the center of the room TrueHeart noticed a painting depicting seven concentric circles. In the center circle water surrounded an ancient tree. The image grabbed his attention.

The old man followed his son's gaze. "It's the King Tree," he explained. "Do you know it?"

TrueHeart nodded. The tree lived in the main courtyard of the castle, planted by the ancients long before Covey arrived with his Seven Habits.

"It reminds me of my youth," his father explained. "It's a good task in the second half of life to find an image of one's youth and absorb it fully."

"You painted this?"

"It is the child of my imprisonment and finishing it has become my life's purpose," his father explained. "Come and sit, my son. This is a great blessing. Truly, God is good."

For many hours the father and son talked and shared their feelings. TrueHeart told his father of the King and Moira, Brigid and the Princess and the great quest for Unrational Leadership™. The man smiled at the stories of his old friend, the King, and he shook his head in sorrow when he heard of Moira's stormy revenge on Christmas night. Although he looked feeble, his voice was strong.

"When the Queen Mother had me thrown into that fierce battle, my doom was sealed, but Snow White discovered me and nursed me to health. Then, she brought me to the manor and I learned her ways."

"Father. Now that I have found you, I don't want to lose you and this energy that you have given me. Will you ride from this place with me?" asked TrueHeart passionately.

"Son, nothing would please me more, but I am bound to serve Snow White." Then he said quietly, as if the walls had ears, "Leave while you may." TrueHeart wanted to ask his father what bound him to Snow White, but the question emerged as a remark about the Prince who first rescued Snow White.

"I have often wondered about the original Prince."

"You mean the one who awakened her?" his father asked. "Oh, I replaced him. They fell apart very soon after they started living happily ever after. They argued over everything. Their final argument was about Snow White's stepmother. The wicked witch returned to Snow White one last time at the wedding. The handsome Prince wanted to send her back home or at worst throw her in the dungeon. But Snow White demanded a different ending."

"Did she win that argument?"

"Yes and then some," murmured the old man.

Standing on His Father's Shoulders

It was almost midnight when Cedric led TrueHeart down a dark passage into the forbidden basement.

"Take courage," said Cedric. The faint echo of Moira's voice in Cedric's words inspired TrueHeart.

Soon, they heard the sounds of a party. TrueHeart peered

through a crack in the wall and, in the dazzling light of a hundred torches, he saw a royal wedding. A roaring fire burned in front of the banquet. Musicians played while servants offered guests wine and food. Snow White glowed in her pink bridal gown. Her delicate hand rested on the ruffled sleeve of a man in the role of the Handsome Prince. TrueHeart recognized his father, and suddenly understood what bound him to the manor and its mistress.

"Snow White, your wicked stepmother has arrived," announced a footman.

"Ah, yes, send her in," commanded Snow White.

The wicked stepmother entered in a rustle of gowns and gasps. She was beautiful, tall and dressed lavishly in dark red. The music stopped. Two burly guards rushed up to her and forced her to sit on an uncomfortable wooden chair in the center of the banquet.

"Snow White! Where is the source of this rough play?" asked the stepmother. "I only came to wish you well!"

"And so you shall, stepmother," replied Snow White. "The Prince and I are nearly ready to commence our Wedding Waltz. Of course, you will need some lighter shoes to enjoy this waltz." Snow White gestured at her stepmother's black boots.

"Bring in the new shoes for my stepmother so she can dance with us," said Snow White, and Sleepy and Grumpy trudged to the fire and with large tongs removed a pair of red-hot iron shoes.

"Snow White, I never meant you any harm," pleaded the stepmother. "My only purpose was to bring you back home. I always knew you were the fairest of all."

"There is nothing like a mother's love, is there?" sneered Snow White.

"Help me, Handsome Prince! This evil comes in a pretty package." TrueHeart's father looked away, as the dwarfs drew near with the fiery shoes. "Fool," she spat at his father. "You cannot save yourself by serving this treacherous goddess."

The dwarfs placed the glowing shoes in front of the stepmother and the guards quickly strapped the struggling woman into the shoes.[4] Her flesh began to sizzle. Soon the music began and the bridal couple danced graceful circles around the stepmother's slumped, burning form.

True Heart watched the scene unfold as Cedric whispered: "Every month since the wedding, Snow White and your father marry again and dance while the stepmother burns in the red hot shoes."

"Tell Brigid that I found a way to stand on my father's shoulders," he said to Cedric. Then he charged into the center of the dance to save his father.

Notes

1. Brigid means, "exalted one" in Irish. Before becoming one of Ireland's greatest saints, she was a Celtic goddess and the traditional patroness of healing and poetry.
2. Greek mythology held that the person who untied the Gordian knot would rule Asia. According to legend, it remained untied until 333 B.C., when Alexander the Great cut through it with a sword.
3. The original Celtic meaning for Cedric is war leader—an apt name for Moira's favorite dog.
4. In one ending to *Snow White* (in Grimm's Fairy Tales), Snow White strapped her stepmother into burning shoes and killed her.

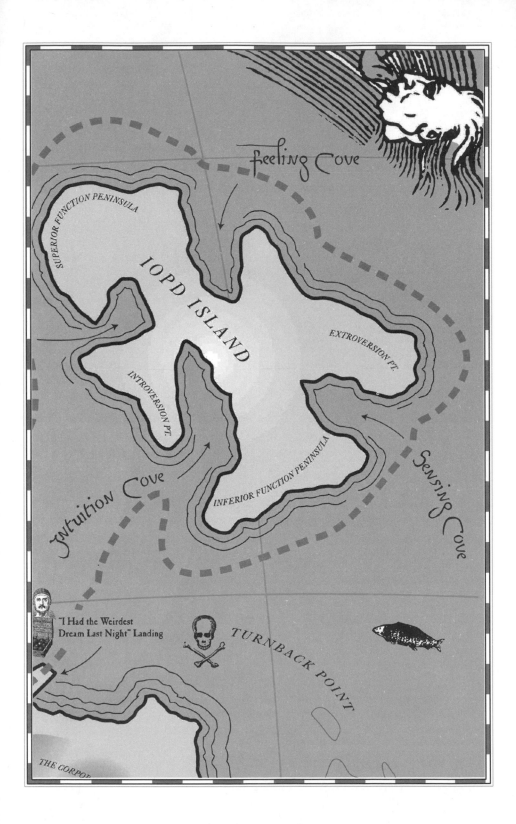

> "Old or young, we are all on our last cruise."
>
> ROBERT LOUIS STEVENSON

7 Cruising IOPD Island

We are now shifting to personality. Up to this juncture, I have focused on exploring the conscious/unconscious divide in the psyche. To the unrational leader the conscious symbolizes rationality, and the unconscious symbolizes irrationality. I have said repeatedly that leaders need to tap their unconscious in order to solve the most complex problems of the day. With this critical point in mind, in the next two chapters I present another way of looking at the challenge of integrating unconscious energy into the workplace. This perspective is based on personality theories developed by Dr. Carl Jung, the famous Swiss doctor and psychologist, who was born in 1875 and died in 1961.

The unrational leader is a student of personality, and this chapter is Personality 101. The next chapter takes a deeper dive and will show you how to **use** the Individual and Organizational Path to Discovery™ to achieve your desired outcomes. This chapter begins with a 30,000-foot look at how personality is shifting in our culture. This backdrop will hopefully energize you for a discussion of the structure of personality, including a guideline that will help you identify your dominant leadership style. Then, I will discuss the undeveloped sides of your personality, and show how they impact your performance. At the close of the chapter, the unrational leader goes to work on saving Michigan's faltering, post 9/11 economy with a personality based approach.

The Right-Brain Personality is on the Rise

In today's business world the strength of the collective personality is **shifting from the left-brain to the right-brain,** but we refuse to acknowledge it openly. Have you ever heard someone say: "I am too right-brained this morning. I have to get myself organized!" Our brain, like the rest of our body, consists of two halves, a left brain and a right brain. A fold that goes from the front to the back of our brain divides the halves. Both lobes are connected by a bundle of nerves at the base of the brain called the corpus collosum. Through a series of experiments with individuals who had their corpus collosum removed, Roger Sperry (Nobel Prize—1981), discovered that the two halves functioned independently. The left side favors the logical, sequential, rational, and analytical and allows verbal functioning. The right hemisphere is intuitive, holistic, creative, and tends to think systemically.

Since the Civil War and the onset of the modern industrial state, left-brained activities have dominated our culture. For the most part, we neglected the creative and holistic right brain, but we can't ignore it forever. The personality strives to balance extremes. When individuals or societies overdevelop one side of their personality and ignore or suppress the other side, sooner or later, the neglected part breaks through with a vengeance. In our case, it has taken centuries for the unstructured, non-logical, intuitive part of the personality to make its claim, but it is making it now and it is shaking the foundations of our world.

The Cult of Celebrity

The signs of intuition rising are everywhere, but there are two that stand out—the explosion of the celebrity culture and the rise of conservative idealism. Becoming a celebrity is largely an intuitive quest—being in the right place at the right time, having a feeling for what other people want, responding to a voice within that says: "Be this now." It is very difficult to engineer the quest for celebrity. As we all know, behind every celebrity there are hundreds of hungry would-be stars with more talent, credentials, and sweat in their portfolios. The universe seems to choose our celebrities, and this helps explain why so many people want to be one. If the universe blesses us, what else matters? Is it any wonder that the easiest route to stardom, the reality show, rules television? The impact of reality shows has been momentous. They have transformed the idea of working for success into performing for success.[1]

A few years ago, I learned firsthand the power of celebrity. After many years of marriage, I had gotten a divorce and had reentered the dating world. I attended a three-minute dating dinner, in which I had eight three-minute dates. At the end of the program, the owner of the dating firm asked me if I would allow myself to be interviewed by the local news about my experience. I agreed to do it and laughed to myself as the reporter tried to get me to admit how difficult it was "out there" for a single person. I didn't give the interview another thought, until the next morning when I received numerous phone calls and emails from friends who had seen me on the local news. Up to a year after the newscast, people mentioned it to me: "Hey, didn't I see you on the news about some dating program?" The thing that struck me the most about the process was that for years I have tried to get the media interested in my ideas about Unrational Leadership™, and I have spent thousands and thousands of dollars on public relations firms and advertising campaigns—with little positive result. Yet, one 90 second interview on the local news earned me a positive reputation as a man in the know about dating. (Seriously, this really happened to me.) Ironically, I didn't date anyone from the program. Again, the results were not important. What mattered was the media performance.

The Rise of Conservative Idealism

It may surprise some to learn that the conservative movement is based largely on right-brained strengths—like intuition, vision, and creativity. In my consulting experience, my conservative clients have generally been more visionary, more willing to explore their gut, and more willing to leave Comfortopia than my liberal clients. Consider how the conservative movement has captured the imagination of the American republic. Today, about one in five Americans describe themselves as liberal, while one in three prefer the conservative label. After World War II, many business leaders proudly wore their liberal colors, but today, in big business, being called a liberal is worse than being called irrational.

How did this shift occur? Ironically, at the same time that the anti-establishment movement was building in the '60s from the liberal left, a parallel movement was building from the conservative right.[2] This movement also had its roots in intuitive idealism—not the pragmatic, nuts and bolts, left-brained politics mastered by the men who built and controlled the political machines that ran states and cities.

Barry Goldwater put conservative idealism on the map with his failed presidential campaign in 1964, in which he championed a host of conservative ideas: Promotion of a free market economy and states rights, distrust of big government, hatred of foreign enemies, suspicion of any movement associated with civil rights, feminism, the environment, etc. As a young boy, I remember watching him accept the presidential nomination at the San Francisco Cow Palace in the summer of 1964. He said defiantly: "Extremism in the defense of liberty is no vice."

President Lyndon Johnson, the Democratic candidate, trounced Goldwater, but Goldwater's ideas lived on and became the basis of Ronald Reagan's political platform. Not coincidentally, Reagan's chosen profession of acting relies heavily on intuition and creativity. Although he died recently, the platform that he inherited from Barry Goldwater and fine-tuned into a red, white and blue gospel, has long since held the center of Republican thinking. Although these ideas are superficially bounded by left-brain structure and traditional values, when you look at them twice, they are very right-brain—intuitive, flexible, creative, spontaneous, self-organizing, and remarkably resistant to structure. For example, the conservative dogma that free markets always optimize distribution of wealth depends on capitalists creating innovative patterns of production and distribution. The free market is a continuous cycle of destruction and construction. And, sometimes, it appears to be completely chaotic. The more unfettered by structure, taxes, regulations, laws, union contracts, and even traditions, the easier it is for the free market to **intuitively** correct itself and create more wealth.

The New Personality Won't Fit in Old Bottles

The ascendancy of the right-brain culture emerges in the workplace in pressures from employees demanding creative work and quick success. Young people don't want to do the same thing every day and get good at it. The idea of doing what you did for three years (learn how to write a decent report or proposal) appalls them. They want innovation daily. Furthermore, they can't hold the idea of working 20 years for the mere opportunity to become an executive. They don't trust the structure. They don't believe in its integrity. It is not only young people who are impatient. When I first started hiring and developing people, I was surprised over and over by mature people who wanted to make extraordinary salaries in a few short years. And they didn't want the money for succeeding; they wanted it for the act of trying. They measured themselves by how they acted as employees (their performance), not by their results.

This stance made it difficult for me to convince them that their success rested on patiently building a strong foundation with the plain old bricks and mortar of the consulting business. I blamed the employees, the culture, and even myself. But now, through the process of creating Unrational Leadership™, I see this trend as the natural emergence of the intuitive, creative, non-linear side of our personality. As it rises to the surface, much of it will appear at first to be negative: self-centered, undisciplined, and irrational. Our challenge as leaders is not to force this energy into old bottles—this is a hopeless and futile task. Instead we need to tap these new forces and transform them into growth and results. **We start by understanding personality.**

The Four Functions

Dr. Carl Jung was a lifelong student of personality. (For more information on Jung's life and thinking, see Chapter Ten.) He spent his life exploring the paradox of how an individual personality grows within a common structure. In 1929, he published his breakthrough book, *Psychological Types*, in which he outlined a universal personality structure based on the four functions: sensation, thinking, intuition and feeling.[3] All humans have these four functions in differing degrees, and a slew of personality tests have been developed to determine how each individual expresses his or her personality within this structure of the four functions. Over 20 million people have taken the most famous test, the Myers-Briggs Personality Type Indicator (MBTI)—evidence of the profound desire to know more about personality and the long-term impact of Jung's thinking.

Jung described **sensation** and **intuition** as the perceptive functions—the two processes our personalities use for collecting data. The **sensation function** includes the five senses—touch, taste, smell, sight, and hearing. The **intuitive function** is the sixth sense—that ability we all have to see around corners. For example, our **intuition** warns us if a stranger who walks into our office is *trouble*.[4] The perceptive functions are irrational because we can't easily train or improve them.

The **thinking** and **feeling** functions are the judging functions—the decision-making processes for our personalities. Jung saw these functions as rational because we can exert conscious control over them. The **thinking function** applies logical, numerical, analytical factors to a decision. The **feeling function** (not to be confused with emotion) applies moral factors to a decision. For example, a person with a strong **feeling function** will make friends because she feels *right* when she is around a certain person. This person agrees with her—in every sense of the word. If a person enters her life who is a perfect match in terms of likes and dislikes and even emotions but does not feel right, she will have nothing to do with her. A dominant **thinker**, on the other hand, will choose friends based on the very things that the feeling person tosses aside: intellectual curiosity, commonality of interests, and the ability to excite the mind with a good debate.

Unlike the irrational functions, we can educate the rational ones. We can teach people how to sharpen their **thinking** by learning the arts of logic and science, and we can teach them how to strengthen

The Four Functions

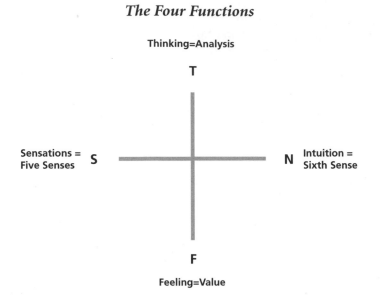

Thinking=Analysis

T

Sensations =
Five Senses   S

N   Intuition =
Sixth Sense

F

Feeling=Value

their **feeling function** by drilling them in secular and religious morality. Consider how our culture has been shaped by the choices that have been made in educating the rational functions. For centuries, the Church monopolized the education process and it focused its efforts on shaping the feeling function. The Church severely restricted intellectual exploration that questioned its moralistic view of the universe. However, as I pointed out in the beginning of this chapter, the personality tends towards equilibrium and the feeling function gave way to the thinking function. The process started in the Renaissance, when the pressure of thousands of bright and questioning minds loosened the Church's hold on the thinking function. In the last 500 years, the West has shifted its priorities towards educating the thinking function, leaving the feeling function to be shaped at-will by the family, the school system or the media. This shift has precipitated the widespread belief that our culture is experiencing a wholesale moral decline. Many authors and celebrities have hitched their wagon to this belief and have turned it into a movement: The Moral Majority.

This conflict between the feeling and thinking functions also plays out on the global stage. Middle Eastern countries like Saudi Arabia, Iran, and Pakistan don't leave the education of the feeling function to chance. The feeling function takes precedence over the thinking function. Their schools concentrate on inculcating Islamic values and place less emphasis on math, engineering, and the sciences. As a result, the development of technology in the Middle East (excluding Israel) lags far behind North American and Asian countries. In the meantime, the West, which is dominated by the thinking function, views the Middle East as a scary place filled with backward and irrational fundamentalists. Conversely, Muslim fundamentalists see the West as a degenerate land of Satan governed by immoral and intellectually bankrupt materialists. As I write this book, we are solving this conflict with military force and political power. I often wonder what solutions would arise if we looked at the conflict from the perspective of personality.

The Four Couplings are the Four Original Personality Types

Many people begin their education on personality by taking a MBTI. There are 16 different MBTI personality types, and even if you have taken a MBTI and learned your type, you have probably found it difficult to identify which one of the 16 types applies to the individuals around you. There is a simpler, more general method to identify personality types. It is based on combining Jung's perceiving and judging functions to arrive at the combinations of Sensate-Feeler (SF), Sensate-Thinker (ST), iNtuitive-Feeler (NF), and iNtuitive-Thinker (NT). These combinations are known as **couplings**. Isn't it fascinating how nature seems to prefer the number four? It has given us four directions, four seasons, four limbs and four different kinds of personality. Each of these four couplings has a distinct mode of collecting data (perceiving) and making decisions (judging). They're called couplings, because they couple the rational and irrational functions together. The figure below shows how the functions combine to form the couplings.

Although most of the popular works on personality types focus on the MBTI, a few scholars have returned to Carl Jung's original thinking on couplings.[5] I have had the good fortune to work with one of these scholars, John Giannini, a licensed Jungian analyst. He has encouraged my company to develop a much deeper appreciation of the couplings and how they operate as the fundamental building blocks of the personality. In his book about Jung's couplings, *The Compass of the Soul*, Giannini writes: "People all over the world distinctively live both practically and theoretically in one or more of the perceptive/judging combinations: ST, SF, NF, and NT."

The Four Couplings

Thinking

"ST" Sensing/Thinking   T   "NT" iNtuitive/Thinking

Sensing S   N Intuition

"SF" Sensing/Feeling   F   "NF" iNtuitive/Feeling

Feeling

What's Your Dominant Coupling?

Nature wires us with a unique configuration of the couplings, but one coupling is always dominant. It shapes your conscious personality. If you have taken a MBTI, the middle two letters give you a clue about your dominant coupling. For example, if the MBTI indicated that you have an ESTJ personality type, then start the search for your dominant coupling with the description of the Sensate-Thinker, the ST. The same logic applies to the other 15 MBTI personality designations. Start with the middle letters. Whether or not you have taken a MBTI, read the following four descriptions and see if you can identify your dominant coupling. I have given each coupling a name that reflects my focus on helping organizations succeed. These names are not fixed in concrete. Each culture finds its own names for the couplings. For example, in medieval times the couplings were named king (SF), warrior (ST), lover (NF), and magician (NT). Also, each description contains a negative behavior that captures the darker side of the coupling. Hopefully, this shadowy thread won't deter you from finding a name and description that resonates with your personality.

The Wise Leader Coupling—the Sensate-Feeler, the parent of the personality, the law maker and law giver, the upholder of all that is decent, the King and the Queen, the one who showers blessings and punishments, the warmonger and the tyrant, the township supervisor, the dealmaker, the partner in charge, the chairman of the board, the one who sets the climate, the person who asks: *What is right and what is wrong?*

The Committed Manager Coupling—the Sensate-Thinker, the doer of the personality, the chief operations officer, the detail guy, the one who makes decisions based on facts, the warrior, the conqueror, the defender of tradition, the city manager, the one person willing to sacrifice herself for the organization, the killer cop, the process guy, the one who knows how to make the numbers, the person who asks: *What do you want me to do?*

The Creative Facilitator Coupling—the iNtuitive-Feeler, the healer of the personality, the great empathizer, the lover, the one who knows how to build relationships, the artist, the comic, the painter, the idealistic teacher, the romantic novelist, the chaplain, the addict, the therapist, the marketing vice president who feels what customers will want in five years, the person who asks: *How can we make it beautiful?*

The Organizational Visionary Coupling—the iNtuitive-Thinker, the intellectual of the personality, the philosopher, the inventor, the scientist, the mad professor, the chief information officer, the magician, the high priest, the one who knows the secrets, the designer of the hydrogen bomb, the symphony conductor, the head of the National Security Council, the supervisor who taught you how to succeed, the person who asks: *Do you have a vision?*

Personality Tests Give Only a Clue

Identifying your dominant coupling through reading this chapter or taking a personality test like the MBTI will only give you the first clues to solve the mystery of your personality. It takes years for some people to learn and accept their dominant type. For example, three personality tests had told me that my dominant coupling was the Creative Facilitator, but in my journey to Unrational Leadership™, I began to see that I preferred to use my thinking function when I made decisions. Over and over again, I have made the intellectual choice versus the choice that agreed with my moral values. I think I tested to a Creative Facilitator because I wanted to see myself as a creative, sensitive moralist—a do-gooder. My sponsor, Pauline Napier, helped me think more deeply about my dominant coupling when she asked me: "Why do you think you have a strong feeling function? Every time you have a problem you try to think your way through it."

There is another factor that can complicate this search for the truth about your personality. Some parents will not tolerate the emergence of a dominant coupling different from their own. For example, a family with a strong Creative Facilitator personality might force a child with a dominant Committed Manager coupling into a Creative Facilitator straitjacket, stunting the child's growth and laying serious obstacles for future resolution. Perhaps, you have heard a 30-something friend say: "I feel like I have finally grown up!" This statement indicates that he or she has finally located the sweet spot in his or her personality—that is, the dominant coupling. Until this occurs, the person will feel alienated from family and self. Some people spend their whole lives not knowing who they really are. They choose careers, mates, religions, and political preferences based on a false understanding of self. If you wanted to be a poet, but your parents forced you into accounting, you have an idea of what I am talking about.

Our Left-Brain Culture

The couplings embody the left/right-brain split presented at the start of this chapter. The sensate couplings (Wise Leader and Committed Manager) reflect the functionality of the left side of the brain and the intuitive couplings (Creative Facilitator and Organizational Visionary) reflect what happens on the right side.

Although the right-brain personality is emerging, our culture is still dominated by the left-brain couplings. Our education system is largely a left-brain exercise[6]. As children progress through school, the right-brain activities such as art, singing, dance, creative writing, recess, and acting are considered electives and put on the back burner in favor of math, science, history and grammar, the playgrounds of the Wise Leader and Committed Manager. The prominence of left-brain education results in massive Western World discrimination against the intuitive couplings. For example, studies have shown that most children are highly creative before entering our school system and when they become adults, high creativity remains in only a small fraction of our population. This left-brain dominance is easy to see in the distribution of couplings in the United States in the table below. These figures are derived from the book *What Type Am I*, by Renee Baron.

The Committed Manager (ST)	The Organizational Visionary (NT)
• Will sacrifice everything for the Wise Leader • Directs the troops • Establishes process details • Ensures accomplishment of goals • Maintains organizational culture	• Gives honest feedback to leaders • Finds meaning in the organization's work • Creates the next breakthrough • Initiates younger leaders into board room • Inspires organizational vision
47% Male / 28% Female	*22% Male / 11% Female*
The Wise Leader (SF)	**The Creative Facilitator (NF)**
• Make the rules • Blesses the troops • Dispenses judgments—good and bad • Generates organizational culture • Decides organizational strategy	• Rescues bad projects or bad leaders • Troubleshoots conflicts • Inspires organizational creativity • Implements cultural changes • Facilitates informal communications
17% Male / 44% Female	*14% Male / 17% Female*
Total Left-Brained 68%	***Total Right-Brained 32%***

What the Unrational Leader Should Know About the Distribution of Couplings

1. Given the dominance of the left-brained couplings, it is easier for most organizations to follow a direction than it is to create new direction. Change is difficult for most organizations because it runs against the dominant personality in the culture.

2. Although the male Committed Manager may drive the organization, at home the female Wise Leader might rule the roost. Have you ever noticed how a tough manager turns into a boy scout on the weekends—loaded to the gills with Honey-Dos?

3. As the intuitive personalities become more commonplace in organizations, there will be more and more conflicts over vision, culture, communication, diversity, creativity, etc.[7] Intuitive types will need clearer vision, more systematic communication, and more meaning in their work in order to energize their whole personality.

4. As the right-brain rises, the Creative Facilitator will become increasingly important for helping organizations change, as they can have the most influence on the informal communication networks. Effective leaders will move Creative Facilitators out of the Human Resources departments into executive suites.

5. Men need to work on growing their Wise Leader coupling and women need to develop their Organizational Visionary coupling. Programs to develop these couplings will improve decision-making and increase intellectual energy within your organization.

I Almost Forgot the Inferior Coupling!

In addition to your dominant coupling, you have three other couplings. Two of these are known as **auxiliary couplings**. Think of

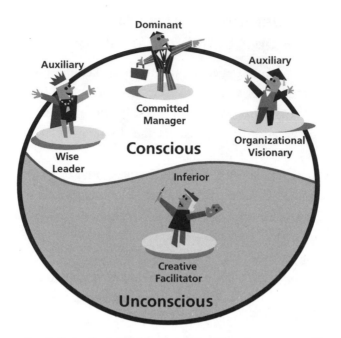

them as the left and right hand of the dominant coupling. The fourth coupling is known as the inferior coupling, because it resides in your unconscious and is the most difficult to develop. It shapes your unconscious personality and yields the most riches if you work to develop it. From a cultural perspective, the Creative Facilitator is our inferior coupling. **No wonder it is creating so much conflict as it emerges into consciousness!** The graphic shows the inferior coupling of the Committed Manager buried in the unconscious.

As you matured into a successful adult, you had to develop your auxiliary couplings. If you neglected them for the exclusive development of your dominant coupling, you faced difficulties outside your narrow area of competency. Your auxiliary couplings are located next to your dominant coupling. For example, as an Organizational Visionary, my auxiliary couplings are the Committed Manager and the Creative Facilitator. I was basically an intellectual dreamer until I went to college and found work after I graduated. These activities forced me to learn about managing process, following rules, and getting things done—the province of the Committed Manager. In my early 30's, I became a consultant and learned how to facilitate organizational change—a practice which forced me to develop my Creative Facilitator. And finally, as I built my company and my family, my inferior coupling, the Wise Leader, found its rightful place in my personality.

The word "inferior" can be misleading. If your inferior coupling is the Committed Manager, it doesn't mean that you can't become a great manager. The point is that you will have to work harder to bring some aspects of your personality into consciousness. For example, while serving as president of my company, I sometimes find myself in situations that make me feel clumsy, anxious, and overwhelmed with emotion. These situations almost always involve moral conflicts, the province of the Wise Leader. When decision-making is based on data or a battle between ideas or even creativity, my decisions come easily. But, when two or more "rights" collide, I have to use my Wise Leader coupling, if I want to make the right decision. If I just relied on my strongest coupling for moral decisions, I would tend to make snap intellectual decisions. Consequently, I have become increasingly patient with myself and now can face these difficult decisions without panic. The frustrating truth for the unrational leader is that he has to ignore the common wisdom of playing to his strengths and wrestle heroically with his weakness.

Raising the Wise Leader

I remember when my Wise Leader coupling was sorely tested during my service as president of a local youth football association. The mission of our association was to develop character—not win football games or develop future NFL quarterbacks. Our association fielded three tackle teams, from ages 8 to 13. At the end of one season, the coach of the freshman team, truly blessed with football genes, announced his desire to take over the junior varsity program as his son was too old to play for the freshman team and was moving up to junior varsity. He had gathered a group of passionate parents to support his campaign. Only one small detail stood in the way of the freshman coach. It was the junior varsity coach, who had only missed the playoffs by a touchdown. He wanted to remain head coach so he could coach *his* son. The coaches presented their cases to the board of directors. The freshman coach thought that his winning record and coaching ability made him a shoe-in for the job. The junior varsity coach thought that he had demonstrated his commitment to our mission of character development and had fielded a competitive team.

If you want to experience the irrational side of rational adults, get involved in youth sports. Groups of parents formed around each coach and pleaded for their candidate. Threats were made to quit and take players to another program. Many parents simply wanted me to fire the junior varsity coach because he had not won as many games as the freshman coach. Grown men actually told me in all seriousness: "If he doesn't coach this team, my Johnnie may lose his opportunity of a lifetime to be a champion."

This situation raised my Wise Leader coupling into consciousness. Where others saw black and white, wins and losses, I saw the collision of rights. Winning is a good thing in football, but so is developing character. My Organizational Visionary coupling responded by trying to create the grand vision that would make everyone happy. I reminded the parents that the real objective was our children's character development and pointed out how important it was to show the kids how to work through differences. Unfortunately, my silver tongue fled and I had to contend with the tossing and turning of the Wise Leader coupling. I was going to have to make a moral decision and some people were not going to be happy.

My training in Unrational Leadership™ supported me. I knew my emotions could easily overwhelm me, so I kept my cool. I listened patiently to every side. I responded to emails and phone calls. I asked my unconscious for data—through prayer and dreams. I tolerated my anxiety and refused to make a commitment until I had gathered the facts. I spoke to my fellow board members and tried to find a definition of a fair outcome. The moral situation, which seemed so clear to some parents looked like mud to me until the right decision became clear. I gathered the emotional strength and reason required to convince my board to retain the junior varsity coach.[8]

The Unrational Leader at Work

During the last holiday season, I walked out of a packed Michigan theater after seeing *The Return of the King*, and my daughter asked me why so many people in Detroit wanted to see a movie when they knew how it was going to end.

"People hunger for heroism in times of uncertainty," I told her. "Michigan wants a leader to take us back to the good old days, but as you will learn someday—you really can't go home again."

And so in this Middle Earth called Michigan our rational leaders talk about saving manufacturing. Can you think of a more heroic rescue? Since 1999, Michigan has lost one out of five of its manufacturing jobs—more than 200,000 manufacturing jobs lost since 2000. The rest of the nation is supposedly in recovery, but Michigan's unemployment numbers have increased for three consecutive years, including December 2003. Standard and Poor's bond rating agency cut our debt rating from AAA to AA—citing our weak manufacturing sector as the primary cause. But this sad story is more than numbers—when I drive to work along Eight Mile, made famous by the rap singer, Eminem, I see empty buildings and a forest of "For Lease" signs—grave markers for all the dead automotive businesses that will never return. As you can imagine, our leaders have a host of rational solutions for this challenge:

- President George W. Bush promised to name a Head of Manufacturing in the Commerce Department.
- Bush also proposed a $250 million jobs training program for laid off workers. (Note: This amounts to about $1250.00 for each one of 200,000 displaced.)
- Democratic politicians have proposed universal health care; laws to monitor pharmacy benefit managers; and changes in the tax code that will reward manufacturers for increasing US production.
- Politicians from both sides have talked about leveling the playing field with China. Unconsciously, China can be seen as Middle Earth's Land of Mordor, the home of the evil Sauron and his hordes of orcs.
- Our Governor Jennifer Granholm introduced a Seven Point Plan to help Michigan attract and keep jobs by establishing a One Stop Shop for business to secure permits and support for expansion.

As a small business owner who depends on a healthy Michigan economy, I read the papers and listen to the speeches and I wonder if our politicians (Wise Leaders) have lost contact with the appalling drift of things to come. This truth hit me hard last year when I conducted a focus group with some manufacturing managers on how their Michigan community could be more "factory" friendly. One of the participants said: "Look, I am a professional manager and I run this business for a foreign owner. Right now, this very day, my bosses are planning to move this factory to Asia, and there is nothing this community can do about it. Nothing. I am not worried about me. I will move to the next plant. But this community and its leaders? They don't get it. The real question they need to ask is: What is the New Economy?" I thought to myself: "That is the right question!" Let's see how an unrational leader might begin to answer this.

Michigan's political, business, community and labor leaders need to take personal responsibility for the situation. It is hard to believe that the boom and bust manufacturing cycle is finished—that we won't get called back, that a hot seller won't reopen a plant, or that our unions won't think of ways to force companies to stay in Michigan. But the truth is hard—the King must die. It is not the fault of any one party and finger-pointing will lead us nowhere. It is not China's fault or India's fault that they have so many people willing to work long and hard hours for a fraction of wages that our citizens earn. It is not the union's fault that they have negotiated lucrative contracts with the automotive companies. Let's not blame the government for implementing regulations that attempt to keep factories safe and our land, water and air clean. The current situation is built from a mess of unintended consequences that emerged from rational decisions over the last hundred years. In short, we got ourselves into this mix. We have to get ourselves out.

We need to think about creating energy—not efficiency. Efficiency is the province of the Committed Manager—the engineer, the plant manager, the production scheduler. In Michigan, from a collective perspective this personality coupling is worn out and needs to abdicate the throne to the intuitive couplings. Recently, I asked a group of seminar participants to identify what percentage of Michigan's economy depends on manufacturing. The lowest response was 30 percent and the rest were north of 50 percent. Currently, manufacturing comprises 17 percent of Michigan's economy. While we focus on this small slice of our economy, other opportunities flutter away. We should identify the opportunities that are bringing the most energy to this state and support them.

We need to confront and partner with our unconscious. In this case, our unconscious consists of the intuitive personality couplings that we have not fully developed. For example, education for the **future** is typically the province of the Organizational Visionary coupling. Think of the college professor giving a lecture, the master training the apprentice, or the mentor helping the protégé see into the future and you will have images of this coupling in action. Here is an example of how our state neglects this side of its collective personality. Although our Governor has called education "the fifth road on our map to a powerhouse economy," our legislature cut adult education funds 75 percent in a recent budget. In Michigan, adult education is a critical tool for helping our people adjust to economic changes. Why would our leaders give it short shrift? Because our leaders feel much more comfortable proposing initiatives that will please our collective left-brained personality. Have you ever noticed that training is always the first line item that gets cut in rough times? We don't see it as mission critical because we can't measure immediate results and that is what our Committed Managers demand. Adults are our most important resource for the future and we must learn how to tolerate the anxiety of waiting for the harvest.

We need to become much more creative in our search for economic opportunities. China and India have an infinite supply of people who will work for pennies on the dollar. The captains of manufacturing will continue to shift work to China, India and Mexico and other nations with large pools of cheap labor. The Darwinian nature of capitalism forces them to do this and no amount of tax shaving, retraining and incentives will stop this shift. Instead of competing for manufacturing, we need to compete for the talent. China will graduate 400,000 engineers this year (compared to our 125,000). If we strived to make Michigan friendlier to immigrants and actually recruited the best and the brightest to live in our communities, we could rely on this influx of talent to fuel the New Economy. Currently, young people are leaving our state—over 40,000 between the ages of 20 and 40 since 2000. We need fresh talent and most employers will tell you that immigrants tend to have a deep passion for the American dream.

We need to envision a future without so much manufacturing. Our leaders are fashioning a rescue based on this assumption: If the government hands out money, then manufacturing will want to stay in Michigan. This thinking ignores the dramatic shift in our collective personality. People are not programmable machines. What if people don't want to work in factories, or build factories, or maintain factories, or even live next to factories anymore? In *The Rise of the Creative Class*, Richard Florida, the Pittsburgh professor who popularized the Cool City concept, asked young people if they would rather become hairdressers or tool and die experts. Needless to say, the tool and die path offered substantially more money. The overwhelming majority chose the beauty salon. What is happening here? Our young people have a much stronger connection to their right brain. Talk to managers who work with young people and they will tell you: "They don't like rules, they don't want to work like I did, they want maximum flexibility to do what they want, but once you figure out how to turn their energy towards the organization, you won't find a better employee." What's Michigan's New Economy? Is it making clean water? Is it building a biotech powerhouse? Is it creating a string of Cool Cities or the world's tourist stop for understanding the rise and fall of manufacturing? I'm not sure, but I know one thing: ***The journey leads to the Right-Brain.***

One of the most poignant scenes in *The Return of the King* occurs when the fellowship sails away from Middle Earth. As a young reader of the trilogy, it was hard for me to endure the departure of my Middle Earth heroes. But I have come to realize that if they didn't leave, nothing would change. Manufacturing is leaving our state and many other states in the country, especially in the Midwest. Let's take advantage of the opportunity and create something new and wonderful.

Notes

1. Needless to say, reality television is only the most recent cultural development that depicts the folly of working for success, but I think it is the most persuasive, because it so uniquely rewards people for performing as themselves.

2. As a self-confessed political junkie, it is fascinating to see the Democrats focus on left-brained solutions: programs for health, jobs, trade, diversity, etc. Seventy years ago, even fifty years ago, the culture yearned for these types of solutions, but now, the emerging right-brained personality wants vision, ideology and security.

3. Jung also included the attitudes of introversion and extroversion in his thesis. They are beyond the scope of this book.

4. Recently, a man walked by me in the hallway of my office building. The hair stood on the back of my neck, but I ignored my gut and didn't follow him. Two hours later, I learned he had charged over $3,000 from two credit cards that he had stolen from my desk.

5. In his work on psychological types, Jung discussed the attitudes of extroversion and introversion, as well as the four functions. Isabel Briggs-Myers and Katharine Briggs took Jung's theory and with his encouragement developed an assessment tool. In that tool, they added the 'J' and 'P' designation which indicates which function you extrovert with. For example: The ESTJ is an extroverted, sensor-thinker, who extroverts with his judging function, i.e. the thinking function.

6. My experience with my children's education challenged me to modify my opinion of our education system. It may be changing to reflect the rise of the intuitive personality. My children started learning about team building, conflict management, systems thinking in the early grades and were encouraged to continue developing their artistic abilities throughout their educational careers. For example, in my daughter's high school, over 200 kids participate in seven

different choirs. In my high school days, this level of participation was unheard of.

7. Twelve years ago, I did personality testing with a local engineering company. Forty of forty-two managers were left-brain dominant. Last year, I repeated the test with a crop of new leaders in the same company. Over 50 percent of the new leaders were right-brain dominant. My staff is seeing a similar shift in personality test results in government and private sectors.

8. In the off-season, five coaches and eleven players went to a competing program. Unrational Leadership™ does not guarantee a Walt Disney ending, but it does bring about decisions that you can proudly share with your sons and daughters.

Important Concepts for the Unrational Leader

- The unrational leader is a student of personality.
- The right-brain personality is on the rise.
- The couplings are the four original personality types.
- We all have a dominant coupling that shapes our conscious personality.
- We all have an inferior coupling that shapes our unconscious personality.

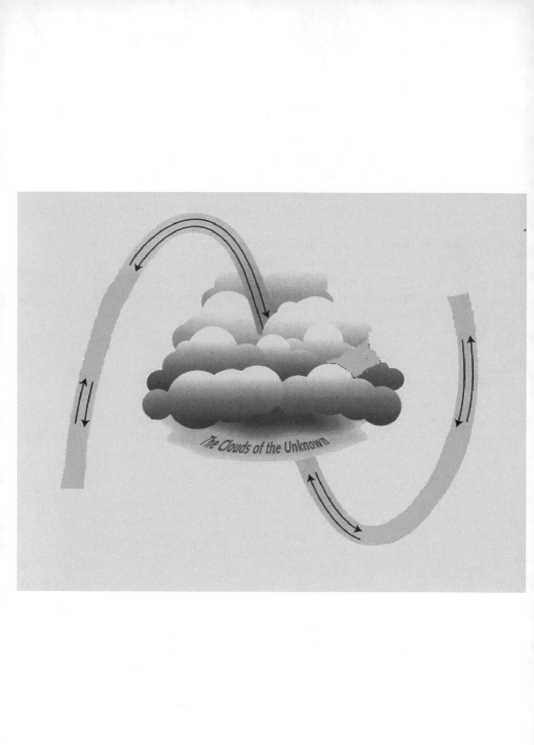

The Clouds of the Unknown

8 A Journey Through the Clouds of the Unknown

Y ou are now armed with an understanding of personality structure and the four couplings. You know that every individual's personality contains the four couplings. One coupling is dominant, two are auxiliary, and the fourth one is inferior. This most undeveloped coupling will soon play a starring role. In this chapter we will metaphorically land on IOPD Island and I will give you another layer of detail on how you can use personality to move mountains in your organization. I will present and describe:

- The major obstacle that stands in front of solving complex problems or delivering innovative programs.
- The Individual and Organizational Path to Discovery™ (IOPD). This model is based on the personality couplings. You can use it to understand why initiatives fail and how to leverage the personality couplings within your self and your organization to achieve your objectives.

- The psychological element in your personality known as the shadow and its impact on your dominant coupling.
- A case study in using the IOPD to resolve a real organizational conflict.

The Major Obstacle to Change is the Unknown

IOPD Island is almost always shrouded in clouds. These clouds represent the unknowns that we face whenever we implement a challenging plan. We call them the **Clouds of the Unknown**. Imagine driving to work on a foggy morning and straining to follow the taillights in front of you. You have an idea of what's ahead of you but you are not sure. Maybe the morning paper had a story about an automobile accident and images of a foggy pile up move through your mind. You keep driving, praying for a hot and early sun. You keep driving, because you think you have to get where you planned to go. Ah, it was very easy to make the plan (that's one reason why we like doing them so much), but driving through the unknown and arriving at your destination demands courage in the face of changing circumstances. Here is one of my favorite stories about courageously moving through the Clouds of the Unknown.

It was the spring of 1864 and President Lincoln had just given the reins of the Army of the Potomac to General Ulysses S. Grant. Grant's plan, in his own words, was "to hammer away at enemy armies, railroads and supplies until by mere attrition, if in no other way, there should be nothing left of them." On May 4, 1864, Grant lead his army of 120,000 into the woods of northern Virginia, in the opening campaign of his grand strategy to defeat Robert E. Lee. In this Battle of the Wilderness, Grant lost almost 18,000 men—nearly 10 percent of his force, while Lee's Army of Northern Virginia lost only 7,500 men. Ambulances filled with wounded men streamed north to the capital, and Grant missed opportunities in the battle to split Lee's forces and to smash him. Frustrated by the ferocity of the Confederate defenses in this first confrontation with the legendary

Lee, Grant faced a choice: Retreat to the north and lick his wounds like his predecessors (Burnside, McClellan, and Hooker) or sustain the attack. His veteran generals were used to backing down to Lee after the first taste of battle. Would Grant also retreat?

On the night of May 7, Grant rode east at the head of his army and approached a lonely junction in the Wilderness. A left turn would send the Army back across the Rappahannock, a route that would lead back to Washington. A right turn lead in an eastern circle to Richmond, via the Spotsylvania Court House. Grant pointed right and through the night, his Army passed and saluted him with cheers. According to Grant, the cheering " . . . was so lusty that the enemy must have taken it for a night attack."

The Standard Hurricane Problem Resolution Technique

In the modern organization, there is almost a genetic tendency to go around a problem. I call this tendency: The Standard Hurricane Problem Resolution Technique. *See Figures A and B.* As long as the pilot flies around the problem, he survives in the short run, but he doesn't solve the problem. The solution is to take the path through the hurricane. This path is not a straight line! It is filled with cutbacks and false starts—in other words it looks irrational. But, as I have said over and over, this irrational non-linear path is essential to success.

I remember the first time I led a group through the Clouds of the Unknown. I was a young consultant, assigned to help Ford Motor Company stamping plants prepare plans for launching new vehicles. During that time, Ford was introducing participative management throughout its system. Inspired by the quality improvement philosophies of William Edwards Deming, Ford leaders wanted to involve as many people as possible in vehicle launches to facilitate teamwork and early identification and resolution of problems.

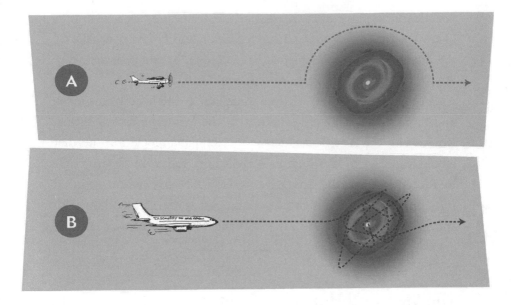

Joe, the Manufacturing Manager, asked me to spend a Saturday working with his team to plan a program for the Ford Econoline. I arrived in the plant's conference room at 7:30 AM. Forty guys sat up and down a massive brown table, sipping coffee from Styrofoam cups and smoking cigarettes. Joe occupied the front seat. He pushed a chair my way and grunted a good morning through a cigar. He introduced me to the group, told them that I was going to get them organized to do the launch and he left the room.

The door was still closing when his burly assistant stood up without looking at me and started telling the guys, one by one, what they had to do to make the launch successful. Then he recited a long and well-known laundry list of complaints about the guys from Dearborn and how the "suits" needed to get out of the way so the good guys at the plant could do their job. A few guys asked questions and even fewer took notes. The rest seemed to nod off into their coffee and the clouds of smoke that billowed in the room. I watched silently, waiting for the right moment to stand and deliver, but I couldn't see an opening. The burly assistant was running too fast around the hurricane and I couldn't catch him.

I didn't know whether Joe would come back. I have seen so many leaders announce changes and leave! So, I have to admit, I was surprised when he returned within the hour. For a few minutes, he watched his assistant go around the hurricane. Then, he glanced at me. I could see the steam moving into his forehead. He pointed his finger at me and thrust his chin like an umpire into the group.

"I brought this guy here to help you plan this launch. Now, you may think he is an asshole from headquarters, and maybe he is. But remember one thing—today he's my asshole and you better goddamned well work with him. Do you understand me?" His assistant sat down without a word and Joe concluded by turning to me and saying: "Charlie, it's your show."

Slowly, I stood up and faced those tired, gnarled men, with thick, nicotine-stained fingers and suspicious eyes. I wished for a joke, but as always, none came to mind, so I donned my invisible Creative Facilitator costume and quickly went to work. I asked them to take out a piece of paper and write down the top five issues they foresaw with the upcoming launch. After five to ten minutes of silent activity, I asked them, one by one, to give me their top issue, and I recorded it on flip charts. As each person spoke, I encouraged the group to watch for new ideas entering their minds—like sparks from a campfire. I went up and down the table, polling each person and more and more ideas surfaced. As the meeting progressed, grudging respect replaced suspicion and I began to lead them in a spirited brainstorming session. Joe watched with a wry smile, making an occasional comment that provided a broader perspective. By the end of the meeting, the guys were saying things like: "We should start every project with this exercise." As I was leaving the plant for a three-hour drive home, Joe took me aside, thanked me, and added: "Charlie, I hope you didn't take the asshole stuff seriously. I needed to talk to them in their language. Now, we can move forward as a team."

The Individual and Organizational
Path to Discovery™

As a facilitator, I helped Joe get his team through the Clouds of the Unknown. The Clouds of the Unknown sit in the middle of the four couplings, as you can see in the picture of the Individual and Organizational Path to Discovery™ (IOPD). As the Committed Manager moves into the Clouds of the Unknown, he and his leaders have to adjust their plans to meet contingencies, and deal with changes in direction, people, funding and technology. Joe's assistant was the Committed Manager. Joe was the Wise Leader. He had to deal with his assistant's unwillingness to change. I was the Creative Facilitator and Joe gave me the backing to help the group through the clouds. Plans don't know how to change themselves, and the energy to move

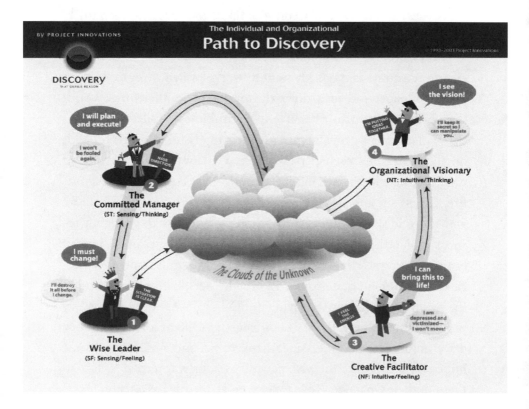

The Individual and Organizational
Path to Discovery

BY PROJECT INNOVATIONS

© 1993–2001 Project Innovations

DISCOVERY
THAT DEFILES REASON

I see the vision!

I will plan and execute!

I won't be fooled again.

I HAVE DIRECTION

I'M PUTTING IDEAS TOGETHER.

I'll keep it secret so I can manipulate you.

The
Organizational Visionary
(NT: Intuitive/Thinking)

The
Committed Manager
(ST: Sensing/Thinking)

I must change!

I'll destroy it all before I change.

THE SITUATION IS CLEAR.

The Clouds of the Unknown

I can bring this to life!

I FEEL THE ENERGY.

I am depressed and victimized— I won't move!

The
Wise Leader
(SF: Sensing/Feeling)

The
Creative Facilitator
(NF: Intuitive/Feeling)

through the uncertainty comes from the coupling of the Creative Facilitator, which shouts: "I can bring this to life!"

As the picture of the IOPD shows, the **energy for change** flows through all the couplings, back and forth through the Clouds. The basic steps for managing this flow are as follows:

1. The **Wise Leader** identifies the need to change.
2. The **Committed Managers** prepare plans and go to work.
3. An individual or organization moves through the Clouds of the Unknown and the **Creative Facilitator** helps bring the plans to life.
4. The **Organizational Visionary** derives the ultimate meaning and instills it throughout the organization.
5. True change has occurred and the cycle continues.

The Energy Must Flow through each Coupling!

The more difficult your challenge, the more important it is to tap the energy of each coupling. If it's a personal challenge, you need to put yourself in the position of each coupling and think from that perspective. If you ignore one of the couplings, you're headed for the Sea of the Dark Side. Lots of people want to pick my brain about launching a consulting business. **Not one** has ever brought a plan for me to review—they have brought visions and insights and callings, but never a plan. Not surprisingly, most of these would-be consultants seemed to operate from the coupling of the Creative Facilitator. Their mission in life is to help people by creating change, but they need to tap their Committed Manager coupling in order to start and run a successful consulting practice. I worked on my business plan for nine months before I started Project Innovations—even though I knew that the business would start in one room with one employee.

My dominant coupling is the Organizational Visionary, and it gives me tons of energy for writing and thinking, but to write this book, I had to engage all of my couplings in the project:

- I had to define a moral purpose for writing the book (**Wise Leader**).
- I had to develop a plan and monitor it (**Committed Manager**).
- I needed to inject my writing with creativity and passion (**Creative Facilitator**).
- I needed a vision of what the completed book would mean to my company (**Organizational Visionary**).

The same logic applies to undertaking a major project within a company. Let's imagine that you are a Committed Manager in charge of implementing a software application that will integrate your billing, timekeeping and project management functions. As you can imagine, this application will require lots of process change. For the project to succeed, energy must flow from each coupling into the organization. Here's how your company can do it:

1. The President (**Wise Leader**) must tell the organization what she wants to accomplish and why she decided to do it. The purpose must be more than improving efficiency or increasing profits. The personality does not live by bread alone! The purpose must address values like: Increasing your ability to serve your customers; extending the life of the business; or making your company the top dog.

2. As project manager (**Committed Manager**) you must lead the development of a plan and manage the implementation of the application. You should make sure that everyone affected by the plan understands it. If you do the plan in an ivory tower and throw it out the window to the organization, the project will fail. You have to assume from the beginning that you can't do the project by yourself.

3. The Human Resources Manager (**Creative Facilitator**) must champion the establishment of a strong partnership between the application users and the project team. She (or someone in her organization) should facilitate a partnering

session in which the team sets mutual goals and identifies a conflict-resolution process. The process should begin with a list of most likely conflicts and how they will be prevented and/or settled. In this way, the Human Resources Manager acts as the Creative Facilitator and helps you get through the Clouds of the Unknown.

4. The Leadership Team (**Organizational Visionary**) should have a clear understanding of the strategic implications of the application—what it means to the company's future marketing, engagement, data and financial management capabilities. A competent technologist can help with scenario planning. Amend the strategic plan to reflect the new understanding.

The Critical Path:
Committed Manager > Clouds > Creative Facilitator

In this chapter, I am especially focusing on the flow from the Committed Manager to the Creative Facilitator because it is such a perilous crossing to our left-brain leaders—and so necessary as the intuitive personality emerges! Joe had to get his logical, rule-bound, hierarchal team to think creatively, to break some rules, to color outside the lines. The rational manager tries to solve these challenges with communication, direction, or teamwork, and these efforts often help with simple challenges but not with problems that defy reason. These traditional solutions don't address the deeper challenge that the Committed Manager must face. He has to tap the Creative Facilitator, his inferior coupling. It is difficult for us to call on this dumb step-cousin. (Recall how difficult it was for the King to listen to the Young Knight, or how difficult it was for me to guide my football organization to the right decision on the junior varsity coach.)

To some Committed Managers, the prospect of tapping their Creative Facilitator is about as inviting as crawling into a manhole. The

Creative Facilitator resides in the unconscious of the Committed Manager and it frightens the hard-edged, action-oriented leader. It's soft. It's touchy feely and sensitive. It's the girlie man. He can't measure it and it doesn't seem to respect the clock. When he experiences it, he feels clumsy and slow. He avoids it at all costs. Isn't it ironic? The very things that the Committed Manager needs to achieve his objectives—flexibility, creativity, sensitivity—repel him the most.[1] The more he rebuffs the Creative Facilitator, the more fog accumulates in his consciousness. To the observer, it looks as if he is stubbornly walking into a steel door over and over, but inside he is fighting with every psychic muscle to stay with his dominant coupling, even if it stands in the way of the solution.

I'll bet you have met Pete. He is a classic Committed Manager and he's stuck in Comfortopia. I have watched him start many projects, run into trouble and refuse to ask for help. He would rather drive in circles before asking the lady on the sidewalk for directions. Only when he faces disaster will he call Human Resources and say: "Could we have lunch tomorrow? I am having a problem with my team and I don't know what to do about it." The Human Resources Director may or may not have a dominant coupling of the Creative Facilitator, but his or her office fills this role in the modern organization. In making the call, Pete begins tapping his unconscious and the Clouds of the Unknown begin to lift. I spend most of my time working with the Petes of this world. Sometimes they ask me for advice on moving through the Clouds. Here is what I say:

1. In the long run, you will accomplish more important work (versus busy work) if you adopt a creative hobby, like dancing, singing, poetry, drawing, playing a musical instrument or woodworking. These activities tap the Creative Facilitator coupling within your personality. Remember, the more difficult the hobby, the more you will have to struggle with your unconscious, and the more positive impact it will have on your personality.

2. Involve the people most directly impacted by your project. This is obvious advice, but frequently ignored by Committed Managers on the go, who say they don't really have the time when the truth is they don't want to confront the personality on the other side of the Clouds. If you are installing an assembly line, no matter how much time it takes away from your reporting, planning, and organizing functions, get down on the line and find out what your staff wants.

3. Try to be more aware when the Creative Facilitator emerges from your unconscious and produces frustration, confusion, and clumsiness. This will often happen when you are overloaded with too many changes and complaints. Believe it or not, your Creative Facilitator is helping you by raising these feelings. It is giving you a heroic opportunity to grow. It is saying: "Stop the world and get off!" Don't retreat so quickly. Stay in the Clouds. Look at yourself as a human being. Try to forget about competence for one hour!

4. Get your leaders to define a compelling moral purpose for the project. The strongest action by the Committed Manager starts from a moral foundation. Change without a moral foundation loses its energy when it runs into the

Clouds of the Unknown. You must have moral rationale for taking on an important challenge. Efficiency is not sufficient. With confidence that you are doing the **right** thing you can efficiently organize and plan the work.

5. Look for the Creative Facilitator in your dreams. When you dream about four people, you may be dreaming about your four couplings. Is one of the four a criminal or a sick person or a fool? If so, your unconscious may be trying to get you to recognize your inferior coupling. Here's a hot dream tip: Write a letter to the inferior coupling in your dreams and ask him what he wants from you! (See Chapter Nine for more information on dream interpretation.)

The Committed Manager as Cloud Walker

The Committed Manager can't solve the most difficult problems of our time without partnering with the unconscious. Only the tiniest fraction of our personality is identical with consciousness, with what we know as our thinking self. We spend many years teaching this fraction to add and subtract numbers, to classify things in hierar-

chies, to measure success in square feet and return on investment. But what happens next? If this fraction of consciousness loses contact with its roots, the basement with the dark closet, then personality growth slows and eventually halts.

The Committed Manager must learn to become a Cloud Walker. He or she can't escape a relationship with the Creative Facilitator. Sooner or later, the jilted coupling turns on the conscious part of the personality, resulting in addictions, depression, illness, smoldering rage, rigidity to change—and worst of all, the loss of verve.

It does seem contrary to reason to walk through the Clouds of the Unknown with a poet. But this is how life's greatest successes are achieved. For example, a few years ago, I recall reading a story about Robert Lutz. He was a successful automotive executive at Chrysler who moved on to General Motors. After reviewing GM's design process, he said that he wanted to quit designing cars with spread sheets. He wanted creativity. He wanted genius. He wanted a hunch that could be turned into a winner.

It amazes me how many Committed Managers say: "If I can measure it, I can manage it," when the most important contributions to their businesses come from the unconscious and are immeasurable. Think for a minute how much time is wasted collecting data on events and processes that have absolutely no bearing on the success of the organization. GM can measure every minute of the design process and every opinion from a potential customer, but if the inspiration of the designer does not exist or if it is killed, then the company will die.

Addressing the Flavor of the Month Syndrome with Wise Leader Energy

Have you ever heard someone say about a new project: "This is just the new flavor of the month?" Perhaps you have said these words in response to yet another email heralding a new morale-boosting initiative. When you say "Flavor of the Month," you may be recalling the last time that your leaders left you in the Clouds of the Unknown. The deeper you move into the Clouds, the more you will need support from your Wise Leader. If the Wise Leader abandons the change or shifts priorities, the Committed Managers retreat and say angrily: "I won't get fooled again." (See the IOPD Model on page 146.)

Once the Committed Manager moves into the Clouds, the Wise Leader must back him up. It doesn't matter if the CEO has a dominant Wise Leader coupling. The important thing is that he or she must not leave the Committed Manager alone to wander in the Clouds. Is there a better example of this relationship than the relationship that existed between President Lincoln and General Grant? Lincoln was absolutely committed to protecting Grant from Washington's backbiting and competitor warriors—especially after Grant's plan to end the war quickly went awry and he became known as the Butcher. Thousands and thousands of men died in places like the Wilderness and although Lincoln seemed to suffer each death, he refused to interfere with Grant, even when his own political future was on the line.

Leaders announce difficult changes, but when their managers are halfway through the foggy banks of implementation, they shift to the next big thing. When a Wise Leader (or someone in that role) asks me the most important thing he can **say** to his management team about a change, I say: "Tell your managers that you will fight for them. You may not always win, but you will always stand up and fight for them."[2] We think that we need fancy words to inspire our people, but what they want to hear is that you will defend them when they are in the Clouds.

When a leader asks me the most important thing he can **do** to support his management team during a change, I say: "Change yourself. If you want people to learn teamwork, learn it first. If you want them to become more innovative, stretch your own imagination." Of course, this advice reflects the first principle of Unrational Leadership™: Start all problem solving by taking personal responsibility.

Too many leaders want everyone but themselves to change. They point their fingers out into the organization and say: "You change." When it comes to their own personality, they are the last ones in line. What should you do if your leader abandons you in the middle of a project? I have helped many Committed Managers through this difficult trial. My advice is simple:

1. If this is **your** noble cause, keep going because the growth that you experience will far outweigh the suffering.
2. If this is your **leader's** noble cause, tell him that he must fight for you if **he** wants to succeed.
3. If this is **nobody's** noble cause, find a way to protect yourself and your staff and don't worry if you have to be cunning in order to do it.

Don't Get Trapped in the Shadow of Your Dominant Coupling

Unfortunately, dealing with our inferior coupling is not the only challenge in our heroic journey to get things done. In reviewing the picture of the IOPD, you may have noticed the phrases in the shadowy circles next to each coupling. These phrases (for example, the Wise Leader says: "I will destroy it all before I change,") represent the destructive shadow for each coupling. We must avoid getting trapped in our shadow, yet another part of our unconscious. In Chapter Ten, I address the shadow and how to deal with it. For now, I want you to become aware of how the shadow integrates with the IOPD.

Think of the shadow as the dim twin of your dominant coupling. It has its own personality and like any personality, it has both destructive and creative energies. People are surprised to hear that their shadow has creative energy. Prior to becoming a consultant, I had almost no energy for work after I left the office. The thought of becoming successful was buried deep inside of me. In fact, due in large part to my upbringing in suburban New York in the late '60s, I believed that the pursuit of material and career success was ignoble. When I left the Army for consulting, it released a creative fire from my shadow that still burns day and night 20 years later.

As for the destructive side of the shadow, Carl Jung wrote: "To become conscious of it (the shadow) involves recognizing dark aspects of the personality as present and real."[3] It is very difficult to **consciously** raise this dark twin into the light. More often than not, our shadow spreads over the light side of our personality on its own volition. We can't see it, even when it fires our personality with rage and blame.

"SF"
Wise Leader
(Sensing/Feeling)

When the **Wise Leader** operates out of the destructive shadow, he says: "I will destroy it all before I change." Tyrants (like Saddam Hussein or the King in *Rationality's Last Stand*) would rather lose their Kingdoms than **change** themselves. Have you ever had a boss who torpedoed his own ship?

"ST"
Committed Manager
(Sensing/Thinking)

When the **Committed Manager** operates out of the destructive shadow, he says: "I won't be fooled again." In our society, when the Committed Manager has been fooled too many times, he reacts by designing and implementing an avalanche of rules and laws to make sure he doesn't get betrayed. For example, if we talk on our cell phone **once** at work, a memo soon arrives warning us about taking cell phone calls.

"NF"
Creative Facilitator
(iNtuitive/Feeling)

When the **Creative Facilitator** operates out of the destructive shadow, he says: "I am depressed and victimized—I can't (and won't) move." For evidence of this shadow, buy a supermarket gossip magazine and observe the number of stories about celebrities who are battling addiction, weight problems or depression due to loss of their status. This coupling is the home of the creative individual, and when he loses the energy or self-confidence to create, he will often turn to addiction.

"NT"
Organizational Visionary
(iNtuitive/Thinking)

When the **Organizational Visionary** operates out of the destructive shadow, he says: "I'll keep it secret so I can manipulate you." Have you seen this behavior from your Information

Technology Group or your Legal Staff? These groups are largely staffed by Organizational Visionaries and when they get on the warpath, they almost seem to enjoy teasing you with your ignorance about the incredible complexity of their applications or their legal briefs.

One of the most dangerous shadows can be found in the person who **only** has your best interest at heart. The unconscious is not an Easter basket filled with sweet chocolates and colored grass. Some people teach that our deepest selves are fundamentally positive and that negative programming from our parents and our society has obscured this positive force from us. To become successful, all we have to do is reprogram our consciousness. This image of our inner self as an innocent babe is seductive, but I think the New Age disciples who buy it are in danger of becoming the Sorcerer's apprentice. Those who imagine that they don't have their own destructive shadow have the false confidence of the Apprentice. Because they are unaware of their own destructive side, they are casting spells that create floods—for themselves and everyone around them. These are the people who arrive in an organization and say: "I am only here to help you." They institute a series of brutal cutbacks without a single thought for the people they are supposed to help. Beware of the saint who is not aware of his dark side, for it will emerge in direct proportion to his good deeds.

It is impossible to eliminate the shadow or to avoid getting trapped by it. What you don't want to do is to let it destroy your ability to get things done. When you are trapped in the shadow, you can't move along the IOPD, and both you and your organization will have a very tough time growing. Here are five steps for dealing with your shadow:

1. Identify the most common elements of your shadow. At the beginning of the search, you had the opportunity to distribute the Unrational Leadership™ Effectiveness Survey to

peers and friends. The results from this survey might tell you something about your shadow. Hint: The more defensive you are about a result, the more likely you have surfaced your shadow.

2. Find a friend who can tell you the truth about yourself—who can tell you when you're not wearing any clothes. Warning: Don't chop off his head.

3. Whenever you start to consistently blame a "them" for your problems, you can be pretty sure that your shadow has trapped you.

4. Avoid all efforts to achieve perfection. This advice is meant especially for Committed Managers. Be purposely inefficient; be consciously chaotic and creatively rebellious.

5. Be a champion for the parts of the organization that you tend to shun. If you don't like HR, spend a day in their shoes. If you think your sales people are overpaid hucksters, spend a day on the road with them. Wherever your personality tends to dump, you can find the shadow. Go live in it and let it energize you.

The Unrational Leader at Work

Nothing drives a leader crazier than personality conflict. It gums up the works, wastes time, slows decisions, and decreases efficiency. Yet, conflict is endemic in the modern organization. According to the Dana Mediation Institute, the cost of conflict is immense:

- 30% of typical manager's time is spent on conflict;
- 50% of employee departures are related to unresolved conflict;
- 65% of performance problems are tied to strained relationships;
- 20% of Fortune 500 executives' time is spent on litigation, and
- in 1994, there were 18 million litigation cases in the US that cost an estimated $300 billion.

The IOPD gives leaders a tool for diagnosing and solving conflicts before a key employee resigns or the conflict escalates into a court battle. The following story illustrates how we applied the IOPD to help a Director of Operations and a Human Resources Director heal a wounded organization. Clashes between management and labor (including supervision) had led to a series of grievances, which then led to a search for an objective third party.

"They are all afraid of John. They said that he shakes from anger when he gets upset," said Dave, the Director of Operations.

"We talked to John about his over-the-top behavior, but he insists that a few sub-par performers are making trouble for everyone. He claims that they won't follow the rules, and he says that his supervisor, Mike, is one of the worst offenders," said Susan, the Director of Human Resources.

John had worked as a department manager for 20 years in Dave's division. Dave and Susan both characterized John as a highly intelligent, efficient performer, dedicated to achieving perfection, who had trouble getting along with some people. When we talked to John, we found an extremely bright man who liked to solve conflict with the rules—not his personality.

Mike, his protagonist, had worked for John in one capacity or another for 20 years. Currently, he worked for John as a supervisor. Mike saw his role as the classic middleman. He balanced management requirements from John with the needs of his staff. For example, a divisional rule stipulated that the men should keep their shirts on at all times while working outside—even on the hottest days. John insisted on enforcing the rule. Mike thought the rule needed to accommodate the needs of the men. He asked: "How can I supervise if I can't make decisions?"

As we interviewed the rest of the management and supervisory team, many of the threads tied back to John and Mike. We administered MBTIs to the team and learned that John had a dominant Organizational Visionary coupling and that Mike had a dominant Wise Leader coupling. A quick glance at *Figure B* shows how they sat on opposite sides of the Clouds of the Unknown. It was no wonder that John and Mike's conflict was at the root of the team's problem. Here is how we used the IOPD to diagnose the conflict:

1. John's inferior coupling was the Wise Leader. When he had to function as the Wise Leader to make moral decisions, he could not be as flexible as he was in his dominant coupling. When our inferior coupling is stressed, it leads us to all or nothing decision-making. For example, when John enforced the rules (like removing one's shirt), he tended to make black and white decisions because his personality did not give him the energy for seeing the grays and patiently assembling them into a picture that everyone could appreciate. (Note: He had no trouble with making decisions based on data or logic.)

"ST"
Committed Manager
(Sensing/Thinking)

John

"NT"
Organizational Visionary
(iNtuitive/Thinking)

Mike

"SF"
Wise Leader
(Sensing/Feeling)

"NF"
Creative Facilitator
(iNtuitive/Feeling)

Figure B

2. Mike's dominant coupling was the Wise Leader. He enjoyed bending the rules and still getting the job done. He saw fairness as a day-to-day discipline and constantly evaluated the rules for their applicability to a given situation. Yet, on the other hand, Mike had little time for John's vision of efficiency. It led him straight into his inferior coupling. To him, these were philosophies and high-minded processes that often got in the way of the real action on the ground. Though he knew it was wrong, he couldn't stop himself from complaining to his men about John's insistence on delivering exceptional performance.

3. John and Mike found themselves in conflict that showed the tension between the practicality of the Wise Leader and the idealism of the Organizational Visionary. Mike would approach John and say, "I'm trying to get my group to go to a job on time, so as an incentive, I'll buy them coffee if they're in ten minutes early." John would respond: "That's ridiculous. If they are a minute late, we'll dock their pay."

Each man saw his own dark and unattractive unconscious in the other man and neither of them wanted to walk through the Clouds and confront it until we introduced them to the power of the IOPD. We told them that they were stuck and that they needed to learn how to flow from one coupling to another in order to release the energy they needed to get through the Clouds. We also told them that if they could learn how to accept each other, they could make great strides in growing their own personalities. We led John and Mike (and the rest of the team) through a series of exercises:

- We asked them to adopt powerful images to represent their dominant couplings. We asked Mike to adopt the image of the King (a powerful, masculine expression for the Wise Leader). The King's role is to make decisions for the good of the people. We knew Mike would connect with this image.

When he had operated bulldozers, he would sit up high in what everyone called "his throne."

- We asked John to adopt the image of the Magician. Not surprisingly, the team readily acknowledged John's exceptional intelligence. They admired his ability to prepare budgets. They actually said that it seemed like he had a "crystal ball."
- We asked them to record their dreams and to look at the shadowy figures that emerged in the dreams. We asked them to examine themselves: Were they trapped in the shadow of their dominant coupling?
- We facilitated a team-visioning session that focused on vision and values. In this process, we tapped the positive energies of the Organizational Visionary and the Wise Leader.

In the end, Mike made a shift that changed the team's culture. He took personal responsibility for his unconscious—applying the first principle of Unrational Leadership™. Mike became aware that he operated out of his Wise Leader shadow—"I will destroy it all before I change." As a Wise Leader, the other supervisors and staff unconsciously took their lead from him. He had long ago relinquished his power to John and stuffed his positive Wise Leader in the closet. The shadow drove him to keep the troops angry by resisting John, while he proclaimed that he didn't need to change because John was the problem.

After we empowered Mike to take his rightful place as the symbolic King and taught him to become aware of John's inferior coupling (the Wise Leader), Mike took up the scepter and led his peers and people to a much deeper understanding of John. They began to see that John wasn't out to get Mike or them and John began to see that he needed to take it slow and get lots of feedback when he had to perform Wise Leader functions.

Although none of the other members of the group changed as significantly as Mike, the team slowly developed a new awareness of their different strengths and stress triggers. They became more cohesive in their work. For example, John and Mike resolved a recent employee productivity situation using their complementary preferences. John wrote a memo stating protocol and guidelines as referenced in the employee manual and then asked Mike to give it the Wise Leader touch. This teamwork resulted in a crafted message to the employee that set boundaries and acknowledged the employee's value. John slowly began to accept the style of others and Mike is no longer afraid to voice concerns and opinions. The team now holds a monthly communications session to sort out what is working and what is not. The bottom line: They walked through the Clouds of the Unknown, absolved their grievances, and began to grow as a team.

Notes

1. This book does not address the dynamic of the inferior coupling between all the couplings, but it is easy to extend the logic: The Creative Facilitator is repelled by its inferior coupling, the Committed Manager; the Wise Leader is repelled by the Organizational Visionary; and the Organizational Visionary is repelled by the Wise Leader.
2. This commitment is especially important in a downsizing situation. As a manager, you can never promise to save jobs, but you can and should promise to fight for every single one.
3. Quote taken from Carl Jung's *Aion.*

Important Concepts for the Unrational Leader

- The major obstacle to change is the unknown IN OUR PERSONALITY!

- In the IOPD, energy for change flows from the couplings through the unknown (or clouds).

- The path from the Committed Manager to the Creative Facilitator is the critical path for accomplishing great things.

- The Flavor of the Month syndrome is caused by the retreat of the Wise Leader.

- Don't get trapped in the shadow of your dominant coupling.

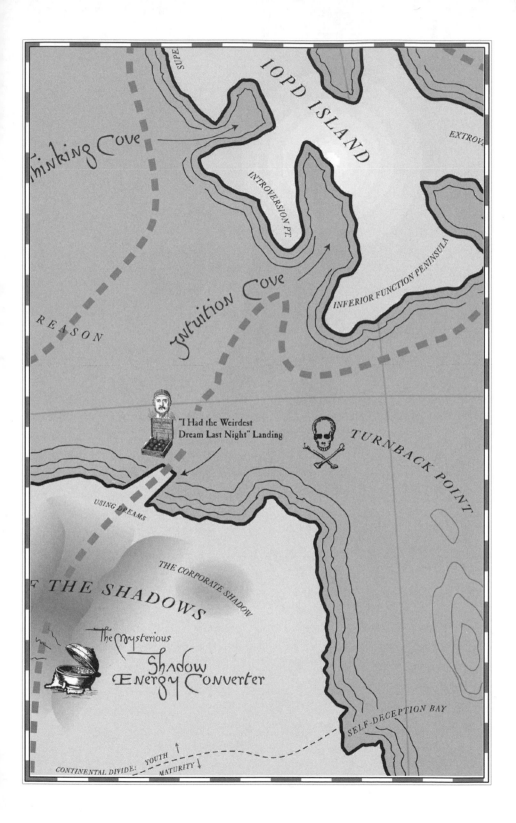

9 I Had the Weirdest Dream Last Night!

Y ou made the short passage from IOPD Island and you are preparing to go ashore at the I Had the Weirdest Dream Last Night Landing. This chapter is about dreaming, and you might as well face the truth. Your leadership team will give you crazy looks when you tell them that you are working with your dreams. Things will get worse if you announce your plans to make dream sharing a regular agenda topic in your monthly strategic planning meetings. Here is a simple response that works from the shop floor to the corner office. Tell the naysayers that when they dream, a friend from their unconscious is calling, a friend that may have very valuable information. Would any responsible leader think of ignoring calls from a friend for months, years, or even a lifetime? When they remember a dream, they answer the call; when they write it down, they show respect, and when they interpret a dream, they establish a dialogue with their friend, the unconscious. This dialogue is one of your best Unrational Leadership™ processes. With dreams you can see around corners and use what you see to make better decisions. If you dare to work with dreams in your organization, you can achieve the following benefits:

- Reduce conflict and stress within the leadership team through more meaningful communication.
- Expand the creativity of your team by exercising their ability to think symbolically and strategically as they struggle to understand their dreams and what they mean to the organization.
- Increase the leadership capacity of your team through the personality growth that naturally occurs through dream recording and interpretation.
- Give the next generation the courage to creatively challenge you and your leadership team.
- Produce unique data for long-range planning by giving your team glimpses of the future.

Working with Your Dreams is a Quadrant Two Activity

When you arrive on Unrational Island, look to the left and you will see a large sign that reads: *Quadrant Two Activity Straight Ahead!* At first puzzling, the sign's meaning quickly becomes clear. In *The 7 Habits for Highly Effective People,* Stephen Covey introduces a matrix for improving personal efficiency and effectiveness. A basic summary of this matrix, which has helped me improve my time management, follows:

- Quadrant One activities are both urgent and important and must be done.
- Quadrant Two activities are non-urgent, yet important activities. They are optional but vital to quality of life and organizational performance.

- Quadrant Three activities are urgent non-important activities that don't really contribute to your mission (despite your illusions to the contrary).
- Quadrant Four activities are non-urgent, non-important activities—like taking cigarette breaks.

According to Covey, scheduling and accomplishing Quadrant Two tasks *is the heart of effective personal management. It deals with things that are not urgent, but are important. It deals with things like building relationships, writing a personal mission statement, long-range planning, exercising, preventive maintenance, preparation—all those things we know we need to do, but somehow seldom get around to doing, because they aren't urgent.*

Recording and interpreting your dreams is a classic Quadrant Two Activity and should be a routine task on your schedule, as normal as any other important non-urgent activity—changing the oil in your vehicle, maintaining your insurance portfolio, or preparing and implementing a Five-Year Growth Plan. On average a person recalls two to three dreams a week. If you and your team pay attention to these dreams, they can give extraordinary benefits and competitive advantages. And most importantly, it is one Quadrant Two activity that won't affect the bottom line.

Where are You Driving Your Organization?

This true story is an example of how dreams can warn you of impending danger. Jeff Butler (not his real name), my number one client on January 1, 2000, was the CEO and founder of TPL Inc. After making a killing in Canadian gold mining stocks, Jeff started TPL in 1987 to leverage the convergence of the computer and the telephone, a phenomenon that he saw before almost anyone else. Under Jeff's special brand of leadership, TPL had grown over 30 percent annually since 1992—strapped to the rocket of the telecommunications explosion and fueled by TPL's innovative optical switching products.

In 1998, Jeff hired me to help him take TPL from a $300 million company of 3,000 to an international company with revenue on the upside of $2 billion. I will never forget the first time I visited TPL. Located in the Deep South, the TPL headquarters (envisioned and designed by Jeff) was a Temple to Technology in the cotton fields—stupendous, shiny steel-and-glass buildings teeming with adults smiling like scouts in blue shirts with sunburst logos. I walked into Jeff's office. It was a large and inviting space in the center of the gleaming temple. From my research on TPL, I knew that Jeff was in his 50's, but he had the slim tiger energy of a 35-year-old Master of the Universe. He paced around his desk, holding three conversations simultaneously, eating bologna sandwiches.

When Jeff saw me, he smiled gleefully. My first thought was: "I am supposed to be selling him—not the other way around." As a battle-hardened consultant, I believed that I was beyond getting wowed by anyone, but Jeff's charisma blew me away. For the entire hour he did not sit. He spread his vision of the converged future, where everyone in the world could ride waves of light to wealth and happiness through his switches. He walked me to the TPL war room and proudly showed me a colorful, hand-drawn chart of the company's meteoric rise: "Charlie, the starship has lifted off and our XM-300 is the product of choice for any company entering the telecommunications space. The door to this opportunity is staring **us** in the face. Are **you** going to help us open it?"

No consultant could have refused Jeff's offer. I responded passionately, affirmatively, and true to the spirit of our first meeting, Jeff opened the doors of TPL to me. Within weeks, I became a partner in evaluating the executive team, designing the succession management program, and scaling the organizational structure for rapid growth. I also became Jeff's trusted advisor—a member of his kitchen cabinet. I shared the principles and tools of Unrational Leadership™ with him. Although the ideas puzzled him, he left Comfortopia and participated in some dialogues with the Magic Rock (see Chapter Two). The company continued to grow wildly. At the 1999 Leader-

ship Team Conference, Jeff told the assembled executives that I had
been one of the most positive factors in the company's success.

Before I went to sleep on the evening of January 1, 2000, I asked
my unconscious to show me a *vision for the first year of the new century*. My unconscious answered with the following dream:

> I'm helping a guy tie up a boat. Then, Jeff picks me up in a
> 4X4. Everyone in the town knows him because he is so reck-
> less. He takes his 4X4 to a cliff. It looks like the Grand Canyon
> down there! I am afraid he expects the thing to fly. I am afraid
> he expects me to fly with him. I think I might just follow him.
> If you have worked for Jeff, you know the power of his
> charisma. No, thank God, he and I get out of the vehicle and
> he pushes it over the cliff. It falls and bounces four levels. He
> climbs down to the truck. I am amazed that he thinks it will
> still work. Then from the other side of the canyon, he creates
> a bridge of planks upon which to drive the truck over the
> abyss. I get it! He tries to do these things for the challenge of
> getting over the danger.

The dream made me nervous. Although you could make a case that
it celebrated Jeff's daredevil leadership, it also implied that he was
taking the company over a cliff. When I shared it with him, he
looked at me as if I were crazy. He quickly changed the subject. He
didn't want to talk about it. He was not an executive who could be
forced into a conversation—even by his favorite consultant. Worried, I took the dream to his executive team and they dismissed it
with a laugh. To them, working with dreams was a frivolous Quadrant Four activity.

A couple weeks after I had my dream, Jeff bought another company, paying more than 30 times the gross revenue. TPL could not
digest the acquisition and the new executive team that Jeff brought
in couldn't deliver. TPL missed its growth targets. At the same
time, the telecommunications industry, Jeff's customer base, drove

off their cliff and two years after I had my dream, TPL declared Chapter 11.

A Dream can be as Valuable as a Quarterly Report

A rational leader may dismiss that dream as a fluke, but I have listened to countless dreams from leaders of all stripes and found over and over that a dream, in one stroke, can provide more valuable information about a situation than a wheelbarrow of quarterly reports. You might remember the story of an executive who listened to an interpretation of his dream and saved his country. His name was Pharaoh and he had a series of perplexing dreams. He looked around for an interpreter and heard about a Jewish prisoner renowned for interpreting dreams. His name was Joseph. When the Pharaoh told Joseph that he had dreamt about seven lean cows eating seven fat cows, and that seven lean ears of grain had swallowed up the seven plump ears, Joseph saw the images as symbols for seven fruitful years followed by seven years of famine. He advised the Pharaoh to save one fifth of the agricultural production during the seven good years. Pharaoh followed the advice, saved the Kingdom and appointed Joseph to high office. In teaching leaders how to work with their dreams, I have observed:

- A group of community leaders conducting a dream circle to break a deadlock in tough negotiations over a contentious regional issue.
- A corporate leadership team incubating and sharing their dreams about the company's ten-year vision.
- A group of consultants using their dreams to brainstorm ideas for developing more business.
- A team of regional leaders listening to their dreams for clues on how to revitalize a declining economy.

- An executive team using a monthly dream circle to energize the next generation of leaders.

Changing Lives Through Dreams

Dreams can do more than help your organization. They can give you the courage and energy to make important life decisions. Have you lost your energy for your current position, but can't put your finger on the cause? Here is a story of a corporate engineering manager who changed his life because of a dream. When Bob called me, I was surprised. I had not talked to him for a year, and he had rarely talked to me during the Unrational Leadership™ program that I presented at his company. He started the program with a lot of skepticism, and like most rationalists, he epitomized the phrase: "I'm from Missouri." Before his call, I was sure that he had never left Comfortopia.

> Charlie, I called to tell you about my dreams. Remember you told us to write them down? I thought you were crazy! Well, I kept having the same three dreams, and I remembered the interpretation tips that you gave us in your class. All the dreams involved college. In the first one, I couldn't get out of the dorm. The halls went on forever in each direction. In the second dream, I got out of the dorm, but I couldn't find my class. No one would tell me the schedule. In the third dream I found the class, but discovered I had to take a surprise test. When I started thinking about these dreams, it hit me. In college, I always knew what I was looking for. I wanted to become an engineer to serve the public.
>
> What did you do with your insight? I asked.
>
> I realized that in my work as a consulting engineer that I had lost my direction. The consulting work was like the hallway. It looked like it was going on forever and ever. And, to tell you the truth, it seemed like I could never get out of the office. And when I went home, I couldn't pay attention to my

kids because my mind was always on work. Then I realized that I was failing the most important test in life—taking care of my family. All these thoughts weighed on me for a week and I talked them over with my wife.

Bob, did you make a career change? I said, hesitantly.

Yes. I left the company and now, I am a manager for the State.

Wow!

Yeah, I love it! I spend more time with my family; my stress level is down, and I'm enjoying my work again. And you know something, Charlie? The college dreams have not returned since I figured them out. Thanks for your teaching. I know I was a little skeptical, but they sure changed my life.

Transforming an Ambivalent Superstar

When I sat down for my first coaching session with Ralph, it didn't take me long to learn that he was ambivalent about his role at ABC Engineers. Although one of the company's rising stars, he was exploring other opportunities—including starting his own business. ABC Engineers hired me to coach some of their aspiring leaders and Ralph was a poster child for the process. He was ripe for saving. I listened to his tale of ambivalence and told him to write down his dreams. "They will give you clues about your future," I said. The assignment didn't overly please him, but he said that he would try.

During the second coaching session, Ralph admitted that he had suffered a recurring dream from childhood. In the dream, a terrorist entered his house and forced his family into the basement, where he began to torture them. Ralph fought the terrorist. It got to the point where his wife turned on the light and watched Ralph wrestle with the sheets. I told him to talk to the terrorist before he went to sleep and ask him what he really wanted. "If he wanted to kill you, why would he keep coming back? Why wouldn't he do it once and be done with it?" I asked.

On the third coaching session, Ralph walked into my office with a big smile. "I talked to the terrorist before I went to sleep," he said. "And when the dream came, I shook hands with him. My wife saw me do it and she woke me up and said: "You made friends with him, didn't you?" The terrorist was a symbol for his unconscious fear of success. As I continued to work with Ralph, his ambivalence wilted and he unleashed his energy for the company. You could send Ralph to a hundred leadership development programs, but how many could teach him the lesson that he learned from wrestling with his dreams? This is the power of tapping the unconscious through Unrational Leadership™, and I have seen it work on superstars from 25 to 60.

Recharging a Tired Veteran

As a leader, one of your most difficult challenges is energizing the middle of your organization to confront and assimilate strategic changes. Many rational leaders use incentives, threats, rule changes, and reeducation to drive change. As I described in Chapter Eight, the middle manager that plunges into the Clouds of the Unknown clinging to his leader's mission, has probably been abandoned more than once in the fog. The unrational leader knows that he needs to tap the unconscious of the middle manager. The acceptance of change has to come from within, and he can set the stage for this acceptance through dream work. Why? Because when a middle manager fights through his fear of his own unconscious and lifts a difficult dream and puts it on the table to assimilate, he conquers a piece of his fear. His confidence increases; his ability to adjust process expands; and his decision-making becomes crisp. **He lets go of his fear of being abandoned.** Want some data? Here is an excerpt from an email that I received from a middle manager (an ex-Marine Corps Captain) two years after concluding an Unrational Leadership™ program in his company.

I must tell you Charlie, with all the adversity here, I am able to cope and maintain my focus due to your program. Those teachings gave me a new perspective on everything I deal with or look at in this company. I kept up the dream journaling for two years. I see symbols everywhere. I see things in people and their search for personality. I know this sounds like a testimonial, but my level of anxiety has been the lowest it has been in years and I think it's because of your company's teachings.

Dreams Have Gotten a Bad Rap

Even though you may be a powerful leader, maybe even the CEO, your experimentation with dreams will be more successful if you understand the source of the resistance from your staff. By the way, not all the responses will be negative. Don't be surprised when your Chief Operating Officer says: "I have always wanted to learn a little more about my dreams." Without knowing it, he may favor the Ancient Greek perspective on dreams. The Ancient Greeks, those paragons of philosophy, science, art and war, turned dream interpretation into a religious, healing and practical art. In Ancient Greece, over 200 temples were dedicated to Asclepius, the most popular healing divinity of the Hellenistic world. Imagine visiting your local dream temple (you can think of it as a franchise) and presenting a leadership challenge to a dream consultant. Maybe you have a problem with one of your executives or you're thinking about buying a company or your daughter wants to marry a guy that you don't like or your doctor just told you that you have high blood pressure. You talk over the situation with the consultant and together you ask Asclepius to bring some answers in a dream. You sleep in the temple and when you wake up, your dream consultant helps you interpret your dream, using the *Oneirocritica*, the largest and most complete book of dream lore from the ancient world.

On the other hand, you may get resistance to dreams from people with strong religious beliefs. I remember advising a technology team in a large health care provider to document their dreams to help them with some project conflicts. The good news in this story is that the project manager recorded a dream about a family fight, a dream that led him to the hypothesis that his team was avoiding a major conflict. He had one-on-ones with the team members, flushed out the problem, and dramatically improved his project performance. The bad news is that the quality control specialist, a sweet woman near the end of her career, approached me a few days later and whispered: "I don't know if I can write down my dreams, Charlie. My faith has taught me that some dreams come from the devil."

When I heard her say this, a patronizing urge welled up within me, but as I have researched the history of dreams, I learned that religious prejudice against dreams runs deep and shouldn't be taken lightly. In the Book of Jeremiah, the Israelites were sternly warned about trusting the dreams of false prophets. In some versions of the Bible, the books of Leviticus and Deuteronomy warn the Chosen People not to observe their dreams. St. Jerome, best known for translating the Bible into Latin in the fourth century, a version which became the authoritative Catholic Bible until the modern times, had a series of troubling dreams that led him to believe that dreams were dangerous. In his translation of the Bible, he inserted negative language about dreams and propelled the Church to a long-standing distrust of dreams.

In the Middle Ages, religious leaders taught that the devil could tempt followers in dreams. These were the sexual demons, the incubi and succubae, which seduced virtuous men and women in their sleep. For example, in the sixteenth century, Benedict Peterius, a Jesuit priest, wrote: "The devil is most always implicated in dreams, filling the minds of men with poisonous superstition and not only uselessly deluding them but perniciously deceiving them." And, even the modern Catholic Encyclopedia states: *As a matter of fact dreams are now—we speak of civilized peoples—seldom heeded; only very ignorant and superstitious persons ponder over the "dictionaries of dreams" and the "keys to the interpretation of dreams" once so much in favour.*

The majority of the nay-saying will come from your rationalists, who will tell you in the same irrational breath that: 1) they never dream and 2) that their dreams come from eating bad pizza. I am serious about this. Many years ago at an executive teambuilding off-site for an East Coast based telecommunications company, the president told his team that the strange dream he had the previous night was caused by bad pizza. Not surprisingly, this silly argument from an executive who was known for his ability to pay attention to the bottom line was well received. An informal follow-up survey of our clients revealed that 62 percent believed that **bad pizza** is the number one cause of dreams.

I think that these rationalists have spent too much time on the Colossus of Rationality, where they probably learned and forgot the Activation-Synthesis Model, a dream theory developed by two Harvard researchers, Robert McCarly and J. Allan Hobson. The Activation-Synthesis Model, one of the many theories that attempt to disprove that dreams have any psychological value, states that dreams are basically rubbish. McCarly and Hobson hypothesized that during sleep our brains are flooded with electrical activity. Our minds try to impose order on the signals by creating the weird disconnected images that we experience in dreams. Sounds like a Bad Pizza Theory, doesn't it?

Even Sigmund Freud, who pioneered the development of dream therapy to heal mental illness, contributed to the negative stereotype about dreams. He saw the source of dreams, the unconscious, as a dangerous repository of primitive instincts. Thus, dreaming was a clandestine process for satisfying deep and hidden urges—many of them sexual. For example, let's say I love my female boss and am unwilling to experience my sexual tendencies directly. I might dream that a good friend is throwing her out of the window of a large office building while I am standing aside in horror. In this way, I get rid of the problem without dealing with it consciously.

Without knowing it, most people adhere to Freud's theories that the unconscious is singularly dangerous. It makes them very leery about recording their dreams, let alone sharing them. You can test this by suggesting to a group that they record and share their dreams. Invariably, at least half the group will shake their heads and a few will announce to a round of knowing snickers: "There's no way I'm going to share a dream with anyone in this room!"

Your best theoretical counterattack to the rationalists is Carl Jung, an early follower of Freud. Jung believed that dreams were communications from the unconscious, filled with symbolic messages about the past, present and most mysteriously, the future. Jung had a bitter breakup with Freud, generated in part because Freud insisted on interpreting Jung's own dreams from a sexual angle. Jung believed that sexuality was only one of many sources of dream symbols. Jung reviewed over 30,000 dreams in his work as a psychoanalyst, and he turned Freud's theories inside out by asking: "What do dreams *reveal* about our unconscious?"

To him, paying attention to your dreams was definitely a Quadrant Two activity.[1] He theorized that dreams serve two functions. First, they compensate for imbalances. For example, an introvert might dream about speaking to large crowds. Second, working with your dreams helps you develop your personality—a process that Jung called "individuation".

Jung believed that people resist dreams for a simple reason: Consciousness tends to resist anything that emerges from the unconscious. So, as you move deeper into Unrational Island, expect to meet some resistance to dreams. Again and again you will confront those awful twins, Fear and Ignorance, that characterize the post 9/11 business climate. But, at the risk of repeating myself, I guarantee that the number of people who will greet your initiative with open arms will surprise you. The urge to understand dreams is one of the strongest forces pushing us towards individual and collective growth. Today, our schools don't teach us about dreams, even though they arise naturally, even though they offer objective information about the state of our personality, even though they can give us important clues about the future. One day with your help, my grandchildren might attend a high school class entitled "Dreaming 101".

The Biggest Pay-Off comes from Recording Your Dreams

Years ago as a project management consultant, I sold project management software and associated consulting services to help clients build complex schedules. While training people how to use the software, I always told them: "You bought this software for the reports, but the bang for your buck is in preparing your plan. At least 80 percent of the value you receive from this software will be determined by the plan that goes into it." The same principle applies to working with your dreams. Everyone wants to know what dreams mean, but your pay off comes from the pre-work, i.e. recording each and every one of your dreams. Think about plodding, nose to grindstone like a hedgehog. When you recall a dream, write it down, whether or not you understand it.

In the long run, you will only "get" a small portion of your dreams, but the real benefit from the discipline is that it inoculates you against an attack from your unconscious. Have you ever seen an executive go into a rage, a manager make a series of uncharacteristically poor decisions, a leader decide to have a crippling affair with someone in the organization, a president pursue an acquisition even though every bit of rational information went against the deal? We call these "leadership mistakes," but we should call them "unconscious attacks". Imagine if you could protect yourself against these mistakes (attacks). Furthermore, consider the fact that all the expensive training, quality initiatives, wise consultants, and airport reading you can buy will offer you no protection whatsoever when your unconscious overwhelms you.

When you record a dream, you inject a small piece of your unconscious into your conscious personality, just as polio vaccine injects a small piece of virus into you to stimulate the creation of antibodies that protect you from the full-blown disease. I remember getting my first polio vaccine. I stood in a long line of nervous kids and parents. I remember my Dad telling about what happened when polio came into a community. He said that everything shut down—swimming pools, schools, and restaurants, even movie theaters.

Think about the unconscious. It can be like a virus. We can't see it, measure it or weigh it, but it rules the world all the same. It's on the television every night and it scares the hell out of us. We feel it every day at the office—in the suppressed anger of our vice president's face, in the slumping resentment at the loading dock. But, when we consciously vaccinate ourselves with irrationality, we can stand against it whether it emerges in the boardroom, on the plant floor or in the living room.

"But Charlie, I Never Dream!"

"Sally, that is a bunch of baloney," I said to the veteran Deputy of Public Services for a large midwestern city, during a session on dreams. "According to Mark Blagrove, Vice President of the Association of the Study of Dreams, the average person recalls 2.4 dreams per week. Almost everyone dreams. Nightly. To remember your dreams you must tell your unconscious that your receiver is turned on." She frowned and shook her head. "You will dream if you practice the following procedure that I developed through years of recording my dreams. I guarantee it. Half of the people with your disbelieving condition dream the same night; most dream within a week; but a few stubborn ones take a little longer. Sharpen your pencil and take notes."

1. Before falling asleep, place a journal with a pen on your nightstand.

2. Relax, close your eyes and repeat the following three times: *"I will dream. I will wake up. I will write down my dream.*

3. Take three deep breaths and click your heels three times. Yes, Sally you will dream and this heel clicking is completely irrational and absolutely critical to dream production.

4. Do this without fail for seven days and a dream will visit you.

5. Don't wait to write it down. The average dream disappears from memory in less than 30 seconds.

6. Treasure this first dream after you record it. Use it to write an epic poem. Draw a picture of it. The unrational leader's first dream contains a special secret about his journey, that when revealed, will help him unlock the treasure. Don't expect a feature movie. My first dream on Unrational Island was a short scene. My childhood best friend (who I hadn't seen in decades) arrived as I was remodeling a house and told me: "It will take five years to finish." It took me a couple of years to understand that my unconscious was saying: "Relax, Charlie . . . it will take you five years to remodel your personality."

7. Don't worry if you don't dream every night. Sometimes, you might wait a month for a dream.

After the session, I visited Sally's office intermittently. Every time I popped my head in her office, I got the same response about dreaming—a firm negative shake of the head. I always asked: "Did you click your heels?" And, she would scowl in return. A year after I first met her, she walked into an Unrational Leadership™ workshop and gave me a sly smile. I was a little tired of hearing her tell me that she didn't dream, so I just said hi. Then, during my presentation on dreams, she surprised the class and me by announcing: "It took a while but I had a dream last night for the first time in my memory. It felt great. And, yes—I did click my heels!"

Dreams Speak in Symbols, Not Signs

People ask: "Okay—I recorded a dream. What comes next?" Well, my first piece of advice is don't keep your dream journal in the open where your partner can read it. It takes a little evil to be good, and some people don't have the strength to keep their own secrets. Once upon a time, a client flew from Texas to Michigan to as he put it: "Sit at the feet of the guru." I introduced him to Unrational Leadership™ and cast a spell upon him when I recited the epic story of my voyage to Unrational Island. I told him that the fastest way to experience the unconscious was through dreaming and he said: "Write me an invoice, Charlie. I am a buyer." When he left my office, I thought I saw tears of admiration in his eyes. The next day, he called me before I finished my first cup of coffee and said angrily: "Your dream procedure worked all right. I dreamt about having an affair with another woman. If my wife found out that I cheated on her, she would kill me!" He quickly ended the call, and I haven't heard from him since. At least I was a guru for one day.

This story brings me to an important aspect of dream work: **Dreams speak in symbols, not signs**. A sign tells us to turn or stop or that New York City is 600 miles east. Symbols are things that represent something else and they resonate emotionally with the perceiver. For example, the dove is a symbol of peace, or the heart is a symbol of love, or the bear is a symbol for Russia. If you treat your dreams as signs, you won't move far into Unrational Island because most dreams are weird. They don't have recognizable signs. Rationalists, especially highly educated ones like my former Texas protégé, always start their journey by converting their dreams into signs (so powerful are the Sirens of the Colossus of Rationality).

Joseph would be a footnote in the Bible if he had not seen the seven plump ears and seven fat cows as symbols for seven years of bountiful crops. As I am sure you know, the ability to think symbolically is an important leadership skill. A leader adept with symbols knows why she has to say hello to the cleaner when she meets him on the elevator;

Charlie's Dreams Mostly by the Numbers	
Number of dreams recorded since December 12, 1996:	445
Name of person in first recorded dream:	Chuck
Number of dreams in which Chuck appeared after 12/12/96:	0
Number of dreams that involved Grandpa Charlie's farm:	16
Number of dreams in which my father appeared:	8
Year that my father died:	1974
Number of dreams in which my mother appeared:	6
Number of dreams in which Pauline Napier appeared:	1
Number of hours spent in dream analysis with Pauline:	100
Number of dreams in which my children appeared:	62
Number of dreams in which a plant grew from my hand:	1
Number of plants that have grown from my hand:	0
Number of dreams in which I heard music:	5
Number of estimated hours per year that I listen to music:	730
Number of dreams that featured male conflicts:	48
Preferred conflict management style (as tested):	Avoidance
Number of dreams that featured female conflicts:	0
Percent of dreams that involved some work theme:	26
Number of dreams in which a devil or monster appeared:	11
Number of dreams in which an angel rescued me:	0
Number of dreams in which God appeared:	3
Number of dreams that involved dead bodies:	31
Number of dreams in which I had sexual intercourse:	1
Number of estimated thoughts regarding sex since 12/12/96:	43,810
Number of times I killed someone in a dream:	8
Number of dreams that featured a gorilla:	1
Number of repetitive dreams (exact same):	0
Percent of times that I received a dream when I asked for it:	100
Number of dreams in which I was late for a test:	0
Number of dollars that I lost by dismissing a dream:	$2,000,000

why she has to send personal get-well cards to the spouses of her top executives; and why she has to find simple yet meaningful words to communicate the company's vision. People connect emotionally and energetically with symbols; **they run over signs.**

You can quickly improve your symbolic thinking by organizing and classifying the symbols that appear in your dreams. As you can see from my dream table, working with dreams doesn't have to be completely serious. Your unconscious personality has a sense of humor.

Do's and Don'ts of Dream Interpretation

When you introduce dreaming to your group, you need a strategy for dealing with nightmares. You will have nightmares, especially in the beginning of the process when you first open the locks on your unconscious and release the trapped energy. Your subordinates will have them too, and as a result, some will opt out of the process. Don't ever force someone to deal with his or her dreams. After an Unrational Leadership™ workshop on dreams, a strapping, athletic executive approached me, pulled me into the corner, and told me that he didn't want to have anything to do with dreams because whenever he dreamt he had nightmares about crashing a plane. His face was set to defend himself, but I told him that he didn't have to record his dreams. "The rule in this workshop is radical freedom," I said. "Stay with us for the rest of the journey and see what happens and by the way, see if you can figure out how to land that plane."

The secret to working with nightmares rests in the center of the Unrational Leadership™ process. The dream material provides the irrational data, and then the rational mind takes over and makes sense of the fright. Of course, the repetitive nightmare is the worst. During the first year of recording my dreams, I had several horrible dreams about concentration camps, in which Nazis chased me through camps of blood and torture. Once, I escaped by diving in a latrine. (You can imagine how I felt awaking from that one.) When I tried to interpret these dreams, to find the message from my unconscious, I couldn't get past the belief that I was actually visiting concentration camps. In other words, like my Texas friend, I was looking at signs, not symbols.

One evening, while reviewing my dream journal, a fit of determination seized me. I decided, no matter what, that I had to interpret the concentration camp dream. I listened to my inner voice and it told me to use the 5WH problem solving process, a very **rational** technique I had learned many years ago as a rookie-manufacturing consultant. 5WH stands for Who, What, When, Where, Why and How. The process requires you to take your problem and methodically probe it with the six questions.

I started the game. The questions of who, what, and when didn't help me at all. The Nazis (who) were chasing me (what) in World War II (when). Then I asked myself: "Where are the camps?" and a voice shot from my unconscious like lightening through the Clouds of the Unknown: **"The camps are in your own head, Charlie."**

Until the voice spoke, I had an unconscious belief that the camps were really in Europe. The rational 5WH process raised the belief to the surface and it trigged a series of revelations. I asked myself: "When do you make the camps?" My dream journal showed that I had the dreams when I was really stressed at work—after a series of long flights or high-pressure presentations. Through the dream, my unconscious was telling me over and over: "Sometimes, you are a Nazi to yourself. You must stop or you will kill yourself with relentless Nazi efficiency." I realized that I had become a slave to my work. It had turned into a monster that chased, chained, and in some ways, tortured me.

I decided to change my work-alcoholic ways and my big chance came when my daughter asked me to coach her softball team. At that time, I was a frequent-flyer poster child, gold on three airlines simultaneously. I had a million excuses lined up, but I looked into my future and saw this epitaph: "He never said no to a client." I couldn't face this ending, so I agreed to coach her team. You probably want to hear that the decision didn't cost me any business. Sorry, I did lose some billable hours and even a client. But, I gained something that I can't ever measure or replace—three incredible years with my daughter on the softball field. There are three happy endings to this story: My daughter and I won a league championship, I have never had another dream about Nazis, and the strapping executive called me six months after he completed the Unrational Leadership™ program and shouted: **"Charlie, I landed the plane!"**

Don't delude yourself about dream interpretation. An authority no less than Carl Jung wrote: "So difficult is it to understand a dream that for a long time I have made it a rule when someone tells me a dream and asks for my opinion, to say first of all to myself: 'I have no idea what this dream means.' After that I can begin to examine the dream."[2] And, based on my experience with dreams—interpreting my own for several years and listening to many, many dreams from clients and friends—I agree with Jung. You may be the CFO, the Director of Public Communications, or the Chief Engineer, but when you stand in front of a dream, more often than not, you will begin without a clue. I always start the process with the feeling: "I had the weirdest dream last night." Walk towards the dream, and **you will know when you have reached the right understanding.** Not by confirming it with a book or by visiting a therapist or by sleeping in a dream temple. No, you will feel a right interpretation deep in your gut. Your inner voice will speak to you as it did when I asked myself: "Where is the concentration camp?"

Do adopt or create your own process for understanding your dreams. I developed a five-step process based on Pauline Napier's guidance and my own experience.[3] With many profound insights and stimulating questions, Pauline guided me through the rough places on Unrational Island. Although I don't recommend professional help for most people, a professional can be an invaluable aid in understanding dreams. Jungian analysts like Pauline are trained in dream interpretation and are especially helpful in identifying the universal stories and symbols embedded in them.

1. Look for the story in the dream. Most dreams have a story inside of them—a heroic quest, a journey, a war, a breakup, a crime, a romance, etc. Ask yourself what roles you and the other characters play in the story.
2. Look for the reoccurring symbols and try to connect them with your personality. For example, I dream about houses, and I think the house is a symbol of my personality. Some of my clients have had a similar experience with trees.
3. Identify your associations with the story and the symbols. If I dream about Grandpa Charlie's house, I have different memories and emotions than I do when I dream about my boyhood home.
4. Ask yourself: "What is the unconscious trying to tell me about my life?"
5. Finally, the most profound question a leader can ask about a dream is: "What are the ethical implications of this dream?" The practice of using irrational material to make tough ethical decisions is the hallmark of an unrational leader.

Although I use the *Dictionary of Symbols and Imagery* by Ad de Vries for hints and clues about my symbols, don't rely on books or web sites to tell you what symbols mean. They can help, but in the long run you will get much more value from your own work. The house that symbolizes my personality might be a different symbol for you. Maybe it is a symbol for your country of origin or your family. It depends on the personal associations that arise whenever you see the symbol in your dreams.

Do ask for a dream when you need leadership advice. Once upon a time, I had a wonderful long-term engagement with a client. As the assignment wound down, I couldn't say good-bye, so I looked to my dreams for advice. The night before a critical leadership meeting, I dreamt that I was in Biblical Galilee with one of the client executives. We witnessed a minor miracle by the 13th Apostle, and the client executive commented: "We don't think much of that apostle."

I asked my unconscious for the ethical implication of the dream and it responded clearly: "Your client needs a different miracle worker." The toughest ethical decisions occur when a set of morally correct actions collide. (See Chapter Thirteen for a discussion on ethical decision-making.) As a consultant, I believed that I could still add value to the client (one morally correct action). Also, I was earning significant billable income for my own company (another morally correct action). I swallowed hard when I heard my unconscious voice because the **right understanding was emerging from my gut.** Later that morning, I walked into the leadership meeting and told them my dream about the miracle worker. As I watched their faces respond to my dream, my inner voice confirmed my first intuition. Indeed, they needed another miracle worker. The path to a difficult ethical decision became clear, and I announced that I needed to end the assignment. I half hoped to hear, "Please stay", but they were relieved. We both needed to move on.

Introduction to Dream Circles

After you discipline yourself to pay attention to your dreams, the next step is to bring the practice into your organization by organizing a dream circle. Are you ready for this challenge? It looks very difficult, but once you climb the first mountain, the rest of the hike is a walk in the park. A dream circle is a group of people who meet to share and understand their dreams. The circle has ancient roots. In the traditional Hawaiian culture, the entire family would discuss important dreams in the morning. Dream sharing is a key educational tool for the Senoi, a Malaysian tribe well known for tending dreams. The Hopis keep good dreams secret while bad dreams are discussed in groups to purge dreamers' negative thoughts.

I have organized many dream circles for employees and clients. Yes, there are always a few people who don't want to share their dreams. Let them sit in the circle and watch you grow. In my company, we share our dreams monthly to kick off our business development meeting. After each dream, we ask: "How can this dream help us sell more business?" The process has delivered major benefits: Our team has become one mind with one mission in pursuit of a single goal—becoming America's resource for Unrational Leadership™. Key accomplishments on the path to achieving our goal include:

- Creating and rolling out Unrational Leadership™ marketing collateral, including our new web site (www.projectinnovations .com);
- shooting an innovative video on Unrational Leadership™;
- certifying several consultants in administering the Myers-Briggs Personality Test;
- developing several unique training programs based on the Unrational Leadership™ process, including: Innovations in Rainmaking and Innovations in Regional Collaboration;
- selling Unrational Leadership™ programs and processes to business and governmental clients;
- and, most importantly, expanding the personalities and professional capabilities of each team member.

The Unrational Leader at Work: Conducting a Dream Circle

1. Start the process by inviting 5 to 15 people.
2. Tell the people you want them to ask for dreams about an organizational challenge, a growth initiative, leadership development, etc. It doesn't matter if their dreams have any relationship to the topic—what matters is patiently recording the dreams.
3. Conduct the dream circle in a circle of open chairs or around a circular table.
4. Start the dream circle by explaining the rules:

a. What is said in a dream circle must stay in the dream circle.

b. Repeat the aforementioned rule to make sure people get it. They can't discuss the dreams with their therapists, their spouses, their mistresses, etc.

c. No one has to share a dream.

d. No one has to comment on another person's dream.

e. All comments should begin with: "If I had that dream—"

5. As the host, break the ice by sharing a dream. Let's say the dream is as short as: "I was rebuilding my house and my best friend from my childhood stopped by and said that it would take five years to finish the job." Here is how the commentary might go:

a. Debbie: "**If I had that dream,** I would think about the house that my husband and I remodeled when we first got married. It seemed to take forever."

b. Chuck: "**If I had that dream,** I would be sad. My best friend died when I was 14 and I have never gotten over it."

c. Bill: "**If I had that dream,** I would see the best friend as a part of my personality that I have neglected for too long. I have been looking for the energy to rebuild my life. Maybe this friend can give it to me."

6. Stop any comments that smack of an interpretation. The circle gets its power through collective ownership of the symbols and stories, not in figuring out someone else's dream.

7. When all dreams have been shared, close the circle by asking each person to comment on the challenge you posed in the invitation. For example, what has this circle taught you about strengthening our core leadership competencies, what has this circle taught you about intra company collaboration?

Notes

1. For some of Jung's best writing on dreams, see his introduction to *Man and His Symbols*.
2. Taken from Carl Jung's *Psychological Reflections*.
3. When I first worked with Pauline, I was dumber than a doorknob when it came to my dreams. Whenever she asked me what my dreams meant, I replied: "I don't know. You tell me." Finally, in exasperation she lit a fire in me by saying: "Think Charlie think!"

Important Concepts for the Unrational Leader

- Working with your dreams may seem weird, but it's just another Quadrant Two Activity.
- Pay attention to dreams and you may save your company!
- Dreaming is a natural self-development process that has gotten a bad rap.
- The biggest payoff comes from recording your dreams.
- Dreams speak in symbols, not signs.

The Mysterious Shadow Energy Converter

On March 25, after the curtain had fallen on the *Frederick Taylor's Mysterious Shadow Energy Converter*, after an audience that was filled with dignitaries accorded the cast a generous reception, Carl Jung took the stage himself at the Psyche in the Round theatre. Suddenly, admiration took wings and landed in the clouds, and opened all hearts for the Great Doctor. Slightly stooped, but brimming with pride, Jung drunk in the prolonged and thunderous applause, until Frederick Taylor bounded on the stage with an energy that defied all reason. The audience went wild and Heaven smiled on the men.

10 Frederick Taylor's Mysterious Shadow Energy Converter[1]

A Play in Three Acts

CAST:

Dr. Carl Gustav Jung—famous Swiss Doctor, notorious for womanizing

Elizabeth—in lifetime, a maid to Queen Victoria, assigned by the Management to serve Jung

Sophia—Jung's beautiful, adoring and ambitious assistant

Frederick Taylor—famous American industrial engineer, notorious for swearing

Tracy—Detroit-area show girl, hockey coach and devoted mother of two

Tracy's Mom—long-term employee of Discount Retail Corporation, mother

Friend #1 of Tracy's Mother—long-term employee of Discount Retail Corporation

Friend #2 of Tracy's Mother—long-term employee of Discount Retail Corporation

Friend #3 of Tracy's Mother—long-term employee of Discount Retail Corporation

Dr. Carl G. Jung, (1875—1961) was born in Switzerland, the only son of a Protestant Minister. His eight uncles and his maternal grandfather were all in the clergy. He began his apprenticeship in psychiatry in 1900 at the Burgholzi Mental Hospital. He married Emma Rauschenbach in 1903. They had five children. In 1905, he became a senior doctor at Burgholzi and a lecturer in the medical faculty of the University of Zurich. His first visit to Sigmund Freud occurred in 1906. Elected president of the International Psychoanalytic Association in 1909, he split with Freud in 1913 and founded the Analytical Psychology Club in 1916. He was blacklisted in Germany in 1940 for protecting Jewish psychiatrists. He founded C.G. Jung Institute in 1948. He wrote and published numerous scholarly works. On June 6, 1961, the last evening of his life, he opened one of the best red wines in his cellar. An hour after he died, a great storm broke across Lake Zurich.

Frederick Taylor was born 1856 into the upper class of Germantown, Pennsylvania. At the age of twelve he began battling nightmares and insomnia. To his mother's dismay, he passed on Harvard and served a four-year apprenticeship at a machine shop. He married Lou Spooner in 1884 and was the loving father of three adopted children. He was the first US Tennis Doubles Champion, an avid baseball player and the inventor of Scientific Management—a process of standardizing, organizing, classifying and accounting aimed at eliminating waste and improving efficiency in business. He claimed that his system would create Utopian cooperation between management and labor. Vilified by workers as the father of the time study, he was summoned to Congress in 1911, as the result of labor unrest associated with his system. In testimony, he said: "Mark my words we never take a human instrument that is badly suited for its work anymore than we would take a bad machine. We take a proper human animal just as we would take a proper horse to study." One of the most influential thinkers of modern times, he died in 1915.

Act 1, Scene 1:
The Shadow in the Modern Corporation

A group of distinguished intellectuals gather around a massive oak conference table in the Old World library in the university section of Heaven. It is early in the 21st century. Stacks of leathery books rise to the ceiling. Dressed in professorial black with wire-rim spectacles, the intellectuals politely sip tea from a sterling silver service maintained by Elizabeth, a portly English maid. Dr. Carl Jung, famous Swiss psychiatrist and seminar leader, stands at the head of the table. In Heaven as on earth, Jung's students sit as rapt disciples with one exception—Frederick Taylor, a stately man dressed in tennis shorts seated in the rear of the room, fidgeting with a tennis racket. In front of Jung, there are several thick tomes and a watch. At his left, sits his beautiful assistant, Sophia. In Jung's Heaven, he has been given his simplest dream: to be the teacher. We meet Jung as he is closing the first session of a seminar on the Shadow in the Modern Corporation.

Carl Jung: In closing today's seminar, the shadow is a matter of no small importance in the modern corporation for it contains the instinctual, uncivilized, animalistic qualities, that the corporation wishes to hide from itself and from others.

Frederick Taylor's Mysterious Shadow Energy Converter ———— 197

The shadow consists of all of those things that the corporation doesn't know about itself. These things may be repulsive or creative. Of course, consciousness seeks to rise into the light but it also brings the shadow, which most often appears as destructive. When the shadow appears, we are severely and unconsciously tempted to project it on to the "other" so that it can hold our evil.

Thus, the shadow is the unholy twin of the ego. They are opposites, chained to each other for life. Though the shadow is the thing that no sane or moral person wishes to be, Herculean labors to destroy or escape it are completely useless and in fact, most dangerous to the self or, as in this case, the corporation.

Neither the corporation nor the individual can become conscious of the shadow without looking into the mirror of the self. Only this mirror, like Narcissus's pool, stands to warn and protect us from the shadow.

In the corporation, the chief leader bears the burden of contending with this shadow. If he fails, then darkness descends on the organization and everyone is cast into the pit. The great contest with the shadow must begin with recognition of the darker parts of the personality—no small task for the CEO who is surrounded by people who are afraid to tell the emperor that he is not wearing a stitch of clothing.

As you might know, in my lifetime I had little interest in corporations, but they are clearly taking over the world and . . .

Elizabeth (*moves from the shadows to Jung's left side and whispers*): Professor, the time limit—

Carl Jung (*glances at his watch*): Thank you, Elizabeth, but I am almost finished with my remarks, yes?

Alas, it is all too easy for corporate executives to fall into their shadows. Here is one all-too-familiar example of a fallen executive. (*Jung grabs a document from the pile in front of him, quickly finds the page that he wants and begins to read. Sophia, Jung's beautiful assistant, hides a frown.)*

In the year 2000, the Discount Retail Corporation (DRC) had spent almost a century stimulating and capitalizing on America's rush from the darkness of the cities to the light of the suburbs.

During that year of the New Millennium, the Board of Directors hired a chief executive, who proceeded to drive a healthy company into bankruptcy within 18 months. During this period, the chief executive collected over $20 million in compensation. He made many poor decisions, including the hiring of a subaltern, who earned more than $10 million. When these two men finished milking this aged cow, billions of dollars had been squandered, thousands of jobs had been lost and hundreds of supporting companies had been forced out of business.

Needless to say, both men were handed million-dollar parachutes while the people that slaved in their dirty stores struggled to find bread and milk.

Sophia, please remind me to write a thank you note to Heidi for her wonderful research on the DRC situation.

Sophia (*with a jealous grimace at the mention of Heidi*): Yes, Dr. Jung.

Carl Jung: Is there a remedy to these crimes? Politicians with their campaign war chests stocked by corporations like DRC will say: "Most CEOs are good. There are a few bad apples and we must strengthen our laws and redouble our enforcement efforts to remove them from the barrel."

And, the little hens at the business schools will cluck: "The fault really lies with the Board of Directors. If the shareholders held them accountable, we could largely eliminate the kind of irresponsible and immoral behavior displayed by the DRC robbers."

My friends, these efforts, although well-intentioned, ignore the conspiracy of the shadow. In the vastness of the modern corporation, it lodges itself in every possible nook and cranny. The most insidious effect of this is the corporation's ability, with its muscles of rationality, to transform the most irrational decisions into logical and unassailable mountains of reason. So, as you Americans say, everything is whitewashed!

How else can we explain the Board of Directors granting over $20 million in retention loans to the DRC executives who drove the company over a cliff? (*Jung's voice begins to rise.*)

No, my friends, these kinds of decisions have nothing to do with reason. They result from a lack of consciousness about the shadow and its influence on decision-making. Unfortunately, after nearly a century, the world of the living is no more prepared for my theories than it was the day I died.

Elizabeth (*moving from a dark corner with an insistent cough that is a little louder than the first*): Herr Professor, you have run out of time.

Carl Jung: Ya, I hear you. I am not finished.

Elizabeth: Herr Professor, you will never finish. And I have warned you before about being prompt. Look at your watch! It is now the time to let our guests leave.

Carl Jung (*irritated*): Your unpredictable interruptions are untimely and ill appreciated!

Elizabeth: I am going to count to three. One . . .

Carl Jung: Elizabeth, that is enough for now. (*Elizabeth retreats in the shadows of the conference room, and Jung frowns.*) Please excuse my irritation. But, as you can see, in my Heaven I am also permitted to wrestle with my life-long fear of my mother figures. (*Jung pauses for a sip of tea.*)

Prior to World War II, I wrote about the psychic invasion of Germany by the "blonde beast." My foreknowledge rose from the dreams of my German patients. In this New Age, men dream of the terrorist, who wanders outside the law and creates mayhem. Osama Bin Laden was the most notorious terrorist of the late 20th century and, ironically, Bin Laden was sired by one of the most successful executives of the 20th century—a self-made titan in the construction industry. Even superficial research into Bin Laden's life reveals many parallels with the modern executive: He established bases in host countries with little regard for native custom; his team was all male and bound in guilt by secret oath; and his organization excelled in transfer of money and information across national borders. What is the difference between Bin Laden and the Modern Executive?

Frederick Taylor (*stands waving his tennis racket at Jung*): Dr. Jung, isn't it a little hypocritical for you of all people to be condemning people for making money? Isn't it true that you depended on the rich to promote your books? Isn't it true that your hourly treatment rate was 50 francs in 1930? Hell, if we take inflation into account that is more than $600 Y2K dollars. And, how many DRC clerks could've afforded that fee? Hah! (*Taylor clutches his tennis racket and strides forcefully to the front of the room.*) Throw me some more of the soft bullshit, Jung. I can knock it over the net with ease.

Sophia (*rising*): Sir, your outburst is not only rude but also characteristic of the terrorist himself. Please sit down and allow Dr. Jung to finish his lecture. Our time with him is brief; we must take advantage of it!

Frederick Taylor (*moves to the door*): Bah! In this God-forsaken place there is too much time.

Act 1, Scene 2:
The Scientific Manager Visits Dr. Jung

> **(Carl Jung's office in Heaven):** Jung smokes a pipe. His office is lined, floor to ceiling with bookshelves and filled with statuary. A magnificent Tibetan mandala hangs on a wall. Underneath rests the Shroud of Turin—covered, and to Jung's left is a life-size statue of the Venus de Milo. Over the office door, a plaque reads: "Bidden or not, God is here." We hear a loud and insistent knock on the door.

Carl Jung: Please enter.

Frederick Taylor (*hurries in wearing tennis shorts and glances at his watch*): Dr. Jung, it seems even here my time is limited! I have been asked to join a Scientific Management Committee dedicated to making Heaven more efficient.

Carl Jung: Mr. Taylor! Welcome to my office. Even in paradise your services are valued. And, I must admit, there is much sloppiness in this place. I can barely tolerate the impudence of Elizabeth. Will your committee fix her for me? (**Jung smiles.**) May I offer you a glass of wine?

Frederick Taylor (*looking around the room. His gaze rests on the statue of Venus*): Thank you no. Dr. Jung, I abstained from alcohol my whole life. Why would I entertain the habit now? If you please, I will stand. Studies have shown that standing makes for shorter meetings.

Carl Jung (*following Taylor's gaze to the sloping breasts*): I presume you are no longer angry with me, eh?

Frederick Taylor: You are referring to my outburst? On Earth, I was known as a fierce—and, I am afraid, wearisome—debater.

Carl Jung: What brings you here, Mr. Taylor?

Frederick Taylor: I am here on a personal matter, Dr. Jung, but before I reveal it, I want to tell you what I did after your lecture. I visited some DRC stores. The stores are disorganized and dirty. The help is unfriendly and sickly. Surely, they would benefit from prunes. I made my children eat prunes at precisely 7AM. Their bowel habits were magnificent!

Carl Jung (*sotto voice*): Echh, bowels again. Last night I ate supper with my old colleague Dr. Freud and he talked on and on about the toilet. Perhaps he didn't notice I was eating chocolate mousse.

Frederick Taylor: But, I also went to a Sprawlmart. Are you familiar with that company, Dr. Jung?

Carl Jung: I am afraid not, Mr. Taylor.

Frederick Taylor: Dr. Jung, the Sprawlmart Corporation is a wondrous organization, and it is the monster that killed DRC—not your executive shadow. Sprawlmart stores are bright, filled with stock and manned by a million friendly people. Look in any town at the difference between the two stores. Both sell the same goods at the same damn prices and are staffed by the same class of undereducated and shiftless people. But one is filled with shoppers and the other is nearly empty. Dr. Jung, do you want to know why Sprawlmart is so successful? Because they practice Scientific Management, **the only proven methodology for combining efficient production and happy workers**. Why, they even measure the width of the smile on the cashiers' faces.

Carl Jung: Mr. Taylor, your ideas and your life unleashed a profound change in the 20th century civilization. You damned the old God to a carnival sideshow and gave the West a new God—Efficiency! How long do you think Sprawlmart will stay on top? Your precious Efficiency will suffer the same fate as Jesus.

Frederick Taylor: The hell with debating, Jung. I came here to ask you about a dream. I understand that you developed a theory of dream interpretation based on Freud's work. I have not been able to locate Dr. Freud.

Carl Jung (*sardonically*): Have you looked in the Oedipal Section? I believe you will find him there with his mother.

Frederick Taylor: That is the second time you have mocked Freud. Dr. Jung, have you truly resolved your feelings for him?

Carl Jung: What a bold question. You Americans are aggressive and extroverted in every conceivable way. Now tell me this dream of yours.

Frederick Taylor: I began to have this dream when I was 12 and it has recurred throughout my life and death. As a child, I was so terrified of the dream that I built an apparatus of wooden pegs to awaken me when I turned on my back. But no machines could stop this nightmare.

Carl Jung: I am not surprised. The unconscious is much more powerful than any machine. Tell me more.

Frederick Taylor: In the dream, I am caught in a vast mechanical colossus—a dark labyrinth of angles and passageways. I spent my life inside of massive works, but this machine is a true monster. It is essential that I determine how to make the machine move. I never solve the riddle. So, I tossed and turned night after night trying to make the damn thing go. Evidently, God condemned me to the task for eternity.

Carl Jung: And, if you fail?

Frederick Taylor (*with emotion*): I am not sure of the exact punishment, but I believe the machine would have swallowed me if I refused to work on it.

Carl Jung: How do you feel about this dream now, Mr. Taylor?

Frederick Taylor: The machine still haunts me and sometimes I feel that its long arms are reaching into the center of my very soul and choking it. What do you think, Dr. Jung?

Carl Jung: Mr. Taylor, what I think matters very little; what you think and feel about this dream is everything.

Frederick Taylor: What! What nonsense! You are probably upset with me for my outburst in your symposium. Is that why you won't tell me what it means? Okay, I'm sorry, damned sorry. But in my lifetime, I was so misunderstood. Enemies hounded me at every turn—most of them liberal politicians or union leaders who refused to give a fair day's work for a fair day's wage. They didn't understand the true nature of my vision. When my research team documented and measured work, we were not trying to turn people into machines. My greatest desire was to lift the workingman out of poverty through the elimination of waste. If only the politicians would have kept their hands away from my work, the Japanese and Chinese would not have stolen our core industries. (*pauses and smiles*) Now, the Chinese, they know how to practice Scientific Management. They have no unions to interfere with efficiency. Why, the workers think nothing of laboring 14 hours a day, six or seven days a week. And, Dr. Jung, they even sing at work.

Carl Jung (*handing a business card to Taylor*): Mr. Taylor, only you can solve the puzzle of your dream. Like so many great men, your work transformed the world, but it left one part of your soul untouched. The time is most ripe for self-reflection. Strike out upon the frontiers of your unconscious and wrestle with this dream. Take this card, go to the Temple of Aphrodite, and then return to me.

Frederick Taylor: Dr. Jung, aren't you going to help me? What is this? (*holding up the business card*) A temple? I have no intention of visiting a Greek temple. This is ridiculous. Good day!

Act 1, Scene 3:
The Temple of Aphrodite

The scene opens at an ancient Greek Temple easily identified by an experienced Hellenic traveler as a temple to Aphrodite, the Goddess of Love, Beauty, and Fertility. Bright butterflies and birds flutter, dive and soar. The scent of roses fills the air. Taylor, in tennis shorts, rushes through a labyrinth of hedges next to the temple. Tracy Adams, an attractive blonde with a shimmering toga falling over her right shoulder, suddenly appears at Taylor's side and startles him.

Tracy Adams (*in a kittenish voice*): Hel-lo sweetheart! Did I surprise you? I thought you might be lost.

Frederick Taylor: Young lady, I should say that I am not lost! I was told that the most efficient path in this maze contained 5,209 paces. I am simply validating this estimate, while of course measuring the time it takes to perform this labor.

Tracy Adams (*pressing against his arm and whispering in his ear*): Honey, why don't you take a break and visit my club. (*She gestures at the temple.*) It's only for true gentlemen, like you. Tall and handsome, well groomed and kind, generous with their wallets and sweetie pie, they know how to treat a lady.

Frederick Taylor: Madame, I am founder of the science of management. Although I value your good manners, I cannot afford to waste another second—

Tracy Adams (*laughs heartily*): Baby doll, you're wound tighter than Aunt Pat's ass! What's your name? Could it be Mr. Stud?

Frederick Taylor (*absentmindedly removes Jung's card from his pocket*): My name is Frederick Taylor.

Tracy Adams: Well, Mr. Taylor, it's a pleasure. If you're lucky, I'll even dance for you.

Act 2, Scene 1:
Your Mother Works at DRC?

> Inside the Temple of Aphrodite, Frederick Taylor, dressed in soft, white robes, reclines on a velvet divan in the shade of swaying palm trees. Tracy Adams, wearing her toga, dances seductively to the music that floats on the warm breeze. Taylor is clearly enthralled. When the music stops, Taylor begins to clap. Tracy Adams smiles lovingly, bows and falls onto the couch next to Taylor. He pulls her into his arms.

Frederick Taylor: I have something for you, my dear. Ever since you started dancing for me, I feel different inside. I can't put my finger on the change, but something is finally moving within me. I quit that ridiculous committee on making Heaven more efficient.

Tracy Adams: Efficiency, smishency. Who cares? I only know that nice people deserve nice things, and Frederick, you are very nice.

Frederick Taylor: You don't know this about me, but when I was alive I was quite theatrical. I wrote you a poem, Tracy. (**He stands in front of her proudly and begins reciting from memory.**)

Where the Goddess Lives

Look near the tip of Tracy's tongue
Where the heavenly fountains play wet notes
On her swaying saxophone hips,
And you will find Her laughing!

Or, follow the sacred trail between her breasts,
To the flat plains on her stomach
Where my eyes worship white skin
And She sits too, celebrating Love.

Even if you search the darker places,
Under her sweet feet or scrumptious arms,

You will hear the Goddess coolly chanting
To the spring beat in her eyes.

Where the Goddess lives . . . is a temple . . . for my passion.

Tracy Adams: Frederick that is so lovely! No one has ever written me a poem before. It is so sexy! You know, if I still worked at the Heavenly Tops, I would kiss you and break the rule. They always told us: Never kiss the customer on the lips. But, I wouldn't care. Not in your case.

Frederick Taylor: Tracy, I would have been most honored to receive your kiss. By the way, have you ever heard of Carl Jung? He is a teacher in the University of Heaven.

Tracy Adams: Never heard of a Dr. Jung but I served shots to a lot of guys named Young. The idea of a university in Heaven is pretty decent. I wonder if my Mom heard of Jung? She actually went to college for a couple of years before DRC.

Frederick Taylor (*with sudden interest*): Your mother works at DRC?

Tracy Adams: She's worked in that rat hole as long as I can remember. She hated me working at a gentleman's club, but told me it was a lot smarter than getting screwed by DRC. What about this Young dude?

Frederick Taylor: I asked him to interpret a recurring dream and he handed me a piece of paper with the words: "Go to Aphrodite."

Tracy Adams (*getting up to resume her dance*): I think I'd like to meet this guy.

Act 2, Scene 2:
We Have Targets on Our Backs

Monday night at a restaurant in a Detroit suburb, four middle-aged women sit around a booth eating dinner and talking about DRC. Their voices seem to float over a Denny's sign. It is a monthly ritual for these good friends. Dressed neatly in discount rack clothing, they have the gentle, worn and slightly suspicious faces of women who have spent their lives in department stores dealing with obnoxious customers and overbearing bosses. Their souls are exhausted, and you can see it when you look into their eyes. But, they hide their eyes from most people because they have become accustomed to making themselves invisible. Cumulatively, they have 145 years of service with DRC and they know that they are an endangered species—full-time retail workers with benefits. In the middle of the stage, from a suspended perch, sit Tracy and Frederick. They listen to the women. Tracy strains to hear her mother's voice.

Tracy's Mom: As usual, we got our Meanies yesterday. Just like clockwork. At 12:30 they streamed in from the churches, all riled up by the preachers about their sins and, of course, who do you think they take it out on—us, the DRC girls who can always absorb one more nasty comment.

Tracy Adams (*smiling at Fred*): That's my mom! She always talked about the Sunday Meanies. She said they were Christians with attitudes.

Frederick Taylor: Let's get closer. I want to see their faces.

Tracy Adams: Cool it, Fred. We can't get closer. Can't you feel the barrier? I think it has something to do with you, because I generally don't have any problem getting next to my mom.

Frederick Taylor: That is ridiculous. I have never done anything to hurt a woman. When I was at the peak of my fame, I sacrificed everything for my wife.

Tracy Adams: Fred, shut up with your 'I am such a good boy' routine. I am trying to hear my mom.

Tracy's Mom: . . . and I would give anything to be called by the Grand Jury that is going after those two crooks. They need to be washed, hung out and dried. But good! (*Pause*) I had the strangest dream last night. There were Chinese terrorists in the city. They destroyed it and then flooded it. Only three of us survived. We helped each other run and hide, but they kept chasing us. Then, it was the weirdest thing—they guaranteed that we would die and I woke up.

Friend #1: Wow, that's weird.

Friend #2: Do you think that it has to anything to do with 9/11?

Frederick Taylor: She is talking about terrorists, isn't she?

Tracy Adams: Yeah. My mom always has the wildest dreams.

Tracy's Mom: I don't know. Who really knows? I probably had too much pizza last night at Tom's sisters. Hey girls, let's help out the prosecutors and prepare our own indictment of our fearless DRC leaders.

Friend #3: We could start by listing all the stupid and evil things that DRC has done to us throughout the years.

Friend #2: We don't have all night! I have to open the store tomorrow.

Friend#1: I'll start. Last year I was invited to meet the CEO. Remember those meetings he was having with us workers? Where he was supposed to answer our questions about his New Economic Program? Well, before I went, my manager told me that if I asked a single question she would fire me on the spot as soon as I returned.

Friend #2: Yesterday, in front of the customers, my manager started yelling at me: "WHERE THE HELL'S THE HELP?"

Tracy's Mom: I'll never forget the time they asked me to a shareholder's meeting. What an honor. First, they told me to buy some new shoes and a decent dress. I had to pay for this honor myself, needless to say. Then, when I got to their fancy-schmancy hotel, they had me park the shareholder's cars six blocks away in the rain. They told me if they heard me answering any questions from a shareholder that I would be fired the next day.

Friend #3: They like to tell me that three part-timers could replace me tomorrow.

Friend #2: We have targets on our backs, girls. We have five weeks vacation and make $15.36 an hour. They hate us.

Tracy's Mom: They froze our pension in 1995. But when I call the toll-free number to find out about mine, the lady tells me that she can't give me any information because I am 47. She says I have to wait until I am 55 before they will talk.

Friend #1: Fat chance of any of us lasting that long on this ship.

Friend #2: I don't know about you girls, but I am going down with the ship. It's like the Titanic.

Friend #3: I know what you mean. It's like that scene in the movie where the old man and woman lay in bed and hold hands as the ship is going down. I have no energy for swimming.

Tracy's Mom: Let's not get morbid, girls. We are preparing an indictment, you know.

Friend #2: Okay, how about the CEO's live broadcasts where he was pounding on the podium and telling us that everything was fine and dandy and that we were turning the corner and that we should invest our money in the stock. Do you think the Grand Jury would want those tapes?

Tracy's Mom: I have a video of my boss pounding his fist on the service desk yelling that I am screwing him because I am taking a vacation.

Friend #1 (bitterly): I'll bet that SOB never bought a single share.

Friend #2: But, he walked away with $9 million, didn't he?

Friend #3: They ought to get him for the Shopper Always Program. Do you know our store manager made us clap whenever the Shopper Siren sounded? And, it didn't matter where we were in the store. We had to clap and shout: "We Love Shoppers! We Love Shoppers!" The customers thought we were idiots. And, if the manager saw we weren't clapping, we could be written up.

Frederick Taylor: Tracy, the Shopper Always Program is a good thing. I used to tell my clients that I would only work with them if there had absolutely rigid and inflexible standards. Workers must obey them, whether they are right or wrong.

Tracy Adams: That's a pile, Fred. Can't you hear them? How can they serve customers if they feel humiliated?

Tracy's Mom: They make us stand in front of the cash registers every morning and do the DRC cheer in front of the customers.

Friend #1 (more bitterly): You know what I would like to do to him? If I had the chance, I would make him experience the *Eight Foot Customer Rule* that he forced on us. Whenever we are within eight feet of a customer, we are supposed to ask them if they need help. In our store, if another employee sees you within eight feet of a customer and you don't say anything, then he is supposed to rat on you at the staff meeting. When he does, you get a toilet plunger painted gold. You have to carry it around the whole day until you can find an employee breaking the *Eight Foot Customer Rule* and rat on him.

Frederick Taylor (*sounding righteous*): I used spies all the time in my consulting work. Is there a worker alive who doesn't spend every minute thinking about how to work as slowly as possible?

Tracy Adams: Fred, I used to serve shots to a lot of customers like you—hockey players, baseball players, football players, politicians, doctors, lawyers and cops. I think I even danced for a senator, but I was so drunk I don't really remember. All of you had one thing in common.

Frederick Taylor: What!

Tracy Adams: You all thought your shit didn't stink.

Tracy's Mom (suddenly): I don't think I can stand getting yelled at one more time.

Frederick Taylor: I was well-known for yelling and swearing at my workers. It makes them work harder. I have measured this result personally.

Tracy Adams: I think that was my mom. She sounds so tired.

Tracy's Mom: Girls, I don't know what to do. Last week, my doctor told me I had to have a biopsy to check for breast cancer. He said I need it right away. When I told my boss, she asked me why I couldn't get it done after the holidays. Then, she told me that she didn't know if they would have a job for me when I came back. I know it's weird. After all they have done to me, I don't want them to fire me.

All the Friends: Why didn't you tell us before?

Tracy's Mom: I should be glad to get fired. For all these years, I have gotten home on Christmas Eve after my family has eaten dinner, dead tired. And, then the day after Christmas, I'm up at 5 am to get ready for all the jerks that want to return their gifts. I should be glad . . . but I can't feel it because I keep thinking of Tracy and how much I miss her at Christmas. *(**She breaks down and the girls huddle around her.**)*

Tracy Adams: Oh, Mom, I miss you, too!

Frederick Taylor: I invented the rest break, did you know that, Tracy? A good rest increases worker happiness and productivity.

Tracy Adams: Look, Fred. Has anyone ever told you that you talk about yourself too much? I don't know exactly what you had to do with the wonderful DRC System that Mom got stuck in, but I think you had lot more to do with it than I will ever imagine. Here's the deal. If you want to see me again, you better find a way to stop these asshole executives from making Hell on Earth.

Act 2, Scene 3:
Transformation Comes From the Weak

Carl Jung is in his office smoking a pipe. His door is open. Fredrick Taylor approaches slowly and knocks at the door. Fredrick is not loud and insistent. Rather, he pauses and enters the office thoughtfully.

Frederick Taylor: Dr. Jung, may I take a few minutes of your time?

Carl Jung: Mr. Taylor, I was hoping you would visit me again. In fairy tales it is always the poor, weak or handicapped ones that bring about the transformation so desperately needed by the world.

Frederick Taylor: Jung, I take that as a compliment. I have heard that you like jokes, so I will surprise you with one. Abe and Saul, who had always loved baseball, were sitting on the park bench talking. You do know baseball? It was one of my favorite sports.

Carl Jung: Who has not heard of America's favorite pastime?

Frederick Taylor: Saul said, "Abe, do you think they play baseball in Heaven?" Abe replied, "I don't know, but I'll tell you what, if you die first, come back and let me know. If I die first, I'll come back and let you know." Saul replied, "You got a deal."

About a week later, Abe died from a heart attack. Some days after the funeral, Saul went alone to sit on the park bench and feed the pigeons. He heard a voice, "Saul . . . Saul." He looked, saw no one and said, "Abe, is that you?"

Abe said, "Yes, and guess what? There's good news and bad news about baseball in Heaven." Saul said, "Oh, yeah? Let's hear it." Abe said, "The good news first. There is baseball in Heaven." Saul said, "That's great, Abe. How could there be any bad news about that?" Abe replied, **"You're pitching next Friday."**

Dr. Jung (laughing): A wonderful joke, Mr. Taylor! Your heart is light, yes?

Act 3, Scene 1:
The Mysterious Shadow Energy Converter

An eternity has passed since the first session. Another group of serious, distinguished-looking intellectuals has gathered in the Old World library. Carl Jung and Sophia sit next to each other near the head of the table. Tracy Adams, who is now a regular, sits next to Sophia, while Elizabeth, the portly English maid, serves tea and cakes. At the head of the table, we see Frederick Taylor, looking relaxed and confident in tennis shorts.

Carl Jung: Now, we will hear Mr. Taylor speak on the executive shadow. As some of you may know, Mr. Taylor's ideas spawned the corporate revolution of the 20th century. If you were a businessman in the 20th century, almost every management technique that you applied can be traced back to Mr. Taylor.

The modern executive presents a most difficult case. He is cursed with the disease of competence, and trained to shun every weakness, inferiority and irrationality. Thus, he avoids the roots of his salvation and spares no effort in pruning the slightest irrational growth in fear of encouraging parts of his personality that might lead to failure. If he can be taught to bring a little of his darker self into the light and hold it, he might gain the strength to make a courageous decision. Now, let us hear what Mr. Taylor has to say about this matter.

Frederick Taylor: Thank you, Dr. Jung. You are most gracious. It took me too long to learn one of the basic rules of Heaven: You must do what you want to do until you find what you're meant to do. When I walked on earth, I wanted to create a Utopia in the American factory. In my death, I discovered that I was meant to learn about my shadow.

Dr. Jung started my quest when he compared the modern executive to Osama Bin Laden. It upset me and made me quarrelsome. I just couldn't imagine executives flying planes into buildings or setting off bombs in marketplaces. And, that conviction remained solid until I was led by Dr. Jung to the Temple of Aphrodite, and then by Miss Tracy Adams to the shadows of DRC. (*Tracy beams*)

Perhaps some of you remember this insignificant retailer? It has long since disappeared. In the final years, a young CEO drove it into the grave, a feat for which he was amply rewarded. This is a matter of corporate record.

As a consultant, I created the processes that helped executives tyrannize their organizations. In my work on Scientific Management, I believed that the modern organization must put the system ahead of the individual worker or leader. But, I didn't factor in the idea of a person's shadow, let alone the power of the personality. Man does not live by systems alone!

Dr. Jung, you have called the shadow our "unknown face." The more we avoid it, the more it inserts itself in our decisions. **Leaders who don't pay the shadow its due are ruled by it.** The shadow is like the roots of an oak tree. You may not see the roots, but if you destroy them, the tree will have no way to gain nourishment and it will topple. In the same way, any attempt to destroy the shadow destroys the leader. But running away from it only makes things worse. In my life, a shadow tried to speak to me through a dream. But I was too stubborn to listen to it. We must learn how to deal with our shadows or suffer a lifeless life. Here are some principles that I've created to help executives deal with their shadow.

1: The Shadow is mightier than any spreadsheet.
2: The most dangerous Executive is always Innocent.
3: Vengeance is the Shadow's most loyal friend.
4: An Executive without a Fool is like a Manager without an Objective.
5: The first step in solving any irrational problem involves the Shadow.
6: The mirror is the best tool against the Shadow.

And, my favorite but most difficult given my past:

#7: Any efforts to achieve absolute efficiency are doomed.

Thank you.

(Amidst sincere applause befitting the great man, Taylor begins to unroll a drawing on the tabletop. He gestures for Dr. Jung to help.)

Get up everybody and gather round. I want to show you some good old-fashioned American ingenuity. *(Taylor grabs Jung's shoulder.)* Carl, this is it! Do you know what it is? *(Jung shakes his head.)* It's a prototype drawing of a Shadow Energy Converter. With the proper engineering, it will process 100 supervisory, 77 managerial and five executive shadows per eight-hour shift. And of course, the operators will receive two 15-minute rest breaks and 45 minutes for lunch. (*Taylor smiles proudly*).

Carl Jung: Mr. Taylor, your mysterious drawing is further proof that we are chained for eternity to our pleasures. Bravo! As Shakespeare said, "So smile the **heavens** upon this holy act. . . . "

Act 3, Scene 2:
Find Something that Works

The Temple of Aphrodite

(Outside the Temple): Jung approaches Taylor, as he is about to enter. *(Sweet music, the rustling of palms, a warm breeze, a rose scent)*

Carl Jung: I knew I would find you here.

Frederick Taylor: Why don't you come in and relax?

Carl Jung: I only send my clients here. I do not indulge. I only wanted to ask you if you resolved your dream. It is of professional interest to me.

Frederick Taylor: Resolved? One must find something that works, eh Dr. Jung? I concluded that the machine was a symbol for my mother.

Carl Jung: Your mother! How insightful, Mr. Taylor. My own mother terrified me as a boy. She was the real power in my family.

Frederick Taylor: After a few visits to the Temple, the dream stopped. Your prescription was quite irrational but effective.

Carl Jung: Yes, through your relationship with Tracy, you raised a piece of the shadow to the light and looked at it with a stern moral eye. You found enough courage to change. It is a most difficult moral task—holding a shadow without becoming overcome by it. Let me ask you, Mr. Taylor, do you think your American executives can confront the shadow of the Terrorist?

Frederick Taylor: They must! If they cannot, despite all their power, education and advantage, then who will? They are the new gods.

THE END

Note

1. Author's Note: This play is based on the real-life experiences of a group of women who worked for a national retail corporation. He is indebted to them for their courage.

Shadow Energy Converter
THE UNDISCOVERED SHADOW
CONTINENTAL DIVIDE: YOUTH MATURITY
UNRATIONAL ISLAN
MANDALA BEACH
THE VALUES CHANGING MOUNTAINS
SECOND HALF OF LIFE PASSAGE
THE SWAMPS OF MATURITY
MORALS
THE ETHICAL DECISION DEVICE
TION BAY
NEW VALUES BEACH
S

11 The Swamps of Maturity

This chapter is about aging. How does the aging process affect your leadership? Should you change your leadership style for the up-and-coming generation? Or, does one leadership style work for all ages? Can you effectively lead people who are older than your parents? Will they follow you if you wear a stud in your ear? What strategies can you implement to take advantage of the fact that time doesn't stop for the brightest of executives? But getting morbid isn't the way to move towards the Treasure of Unrational Leadership™. As the novelist Graham Greene wrote: "Let's leave death to the professionals." In this chapter, we look at how the stages of life impact leadership, and how a leader can use that knowledge to energize and engage employees of all ages.

The work occurs in the Swamps of Maturity. As you can see on the Map to Unrational Leadership™, these swamps are north of the treasure. The ideal path skirts the swamps and goes directly from the Second Half of Life Passage to the Ethical Decision Device. But one stray step off the path and you are lost. I was in my mid-forties when I entered the Swamps of Maturity. I had seen clients, friends and employees walk into them. I thought I would cleverly navigate around them. As I look back, I smile at my innocence. One moment, I was hiking a certain path and the next moment I found myself in the swamps less traveled.

Filled with wet, spongy land and percolated with rivers of regret and secret longing, the Swamps consumed me for longer than I want to admit. When I reached the middle, the sun seemed to desert me and ghosts from my past rose from the bubbling bog to tease me like the Raquel Welch poster on my best friend's bedroom door. I took so many steps in the dark, it's a wonder I escaped at all.

Where is Your Sun Today?

The aging process has a tremendous impact on leadership. The un-rational leader knows that youth and age must be served different courses. He knows that the strength that took him to the top must be sacrificed sooner or later for the good of the organization. The Sirens from the Colossus of Rationality warn us to treat everyone the same, regardless of age, but it is a prescription for a tired and de-feated company.

Carl Jung, who devoted his career to helping clients understand and resolve mid-life challenges, compared the passage of life to the journey of the sun. Born at dawn with a boundless horizon, you arch up through childhood to your peak at high noon. You then slowly descend into old age and the earth. Where is your sun today? Are you climbing toward your peak burning with energy and light? Or, are you past your zenith struggling to return your chariot to dawn?

We associate maturity with old age. It's a mistake. You can achieve maturity in any stage of life. If you look up "maturity" in the dic-tionary, the definition speaks to becoming "full-grown, ripe, fully-developed." We love the company of mature teenagers, and what is more frustrating than an immature grandparent? **The goal of the unrational leader is to create a mature personality.** How will you know when you are a mature leader? Carl Jung gives us a clue in this writing on the development of personality: "(Mature) personality, however, does not allow itself to be seized by the panic terror of those who are just waking to consciousness, for it has put all its terrors behind it. It is able to cope with the changing times, and has unknowingly and involuntarily become a *leader*."

The Four Stages of Life

Jung divided life into four stages. *See table.* The **first-stage** runs from birth to puberty, the **second-stage** from puberty until middle age—somewhere in the range of 35 to the early 40s. The sun climbs through the first two stages (or first half). The major psychological goal is *adaptation.* The child learns the rules from parents, school, and culture, and then begins to practice them at puberty. He or she grows into adulthood, pursues a career and social standing, leaves home physically or symbolically, finds a mate, and raises children. Adapting is no easy task—you know this if you have a family member who is lost to drugs, depression, or has a personality that rubs everyone the wrong way, making it difficult to hold a job or build long-term relationships.

The first two stages concentrate on mastering the outer world and ignoring those inner vicissitudes. It's about success, acting with resolution, feeling right about things and, most importantly, finding your strengths and shaping them into useful tools. **It is all about fitting in.** As teenagers in the '60s in New York, my friends and I mocked the "fit-ins"—the kids that followed the rules and earned the approval of teachers. Not surprisingly, by the time we finished college or left home, almost all of us were racing to "fit in" to the middle class. The second-stage ends around 40, when you look in the mirror and ask yourself: "Have I turned into my father (or mother)?"

The **third-stage** marks the beginning of the unrational leader's inner quest and the start of the second half of life. It begins with a call from the unconscious. This call obeys a law that Heraclitus, an ancient Greek philosopher, identified centuries ago: Any strength, taken to its extreme, turns into a weakness. Thus, the strong ego that we worked so hard to build in the first half of life must yield grace-

The Leader's Personality and Stages of Life				
Stage	Age	Challenges	Obstacles	Mark of Mature Leader
1	0 to 18	Growing into an independent adult	Bad parenting and/or bad luck	Smart enough to walk away from the shadow of his or her peers
2	18 to 40	The outer heroic journey— positive adaptation to community life	A personality that runs against the grain	Strong enough to face his or her shortcomings as a leader and to work on them
3	40 to 65	The inner heroic journey—developing the underdeveloped side of the personality—the inferior coupling	A culture that does not value the inner heroic journey (confronting and partnering the unconscious)	Wise enough to make ethical decisions when standing in the middle of a dilemma
4	65 to ?	Accepting the role of elder and shaping the culture for the next generation	Staying alive and being heard	Loving enough to give back her or his wisdom to the next generation

fully to the undeveloped inferior coupling (see Chapter Seven for more on the inferior coupling). This stage begins after 40 and continues until the onset of the **fourth-stage**, when we withdraw from the fires of everyday life, put on the elder's cloak and begin to prepare for death.

After the sun passes the midpoint, autonomous changes occur in our personality. Lost childhood traits emerge from our unconscious. Our inclinations weaken, some pleasurable activities lose their luster and others take their place. I began to experience these changes during my 44th year, when I felt a strong desire to return to my youth—to spend a weekend reading a novel or driving the highway on a hot summer night with rock 'n roll music blaring. We realize that money won't create happiness, even though it can create many opportunities for pleasure; we stop working weekends and worrying about success and failure. We discover the pleasure in watching our children express *their* talents—my daughter singing, my son pitching. We think more about death—when will it happen? Will my life be truly meaningful at the end? We put on 20 pounds and don't care what anyone thinks about it. We turn back to God.

At this time, men find themselves giving up their competitive warrior energies and moving toward more "feminine" activities. It is amazing to me to see many men in their late 40s take up gardening—raising flowers and caring for plants with the same (in some cases more) tenderness than they gave to their children. Women find themselves becoming more "masculine"—leading the charge in their communities—running school boards, starting businesses, leading their men to new frontiers.

I am not old enough to write with experience about the fourth-stage of life. As I have indicated throughout this book, elders like my Grandpa Charlie, Pauline Napier, and John Giannini have profoundly influenced me. They defy the law of conservation of energy. They repeatedly give more than they receive. Carl Jung believed that the role of the elder was to shape the culture for the next generation. Only the elders can stand above desires for things and status, and only the elders have the requisite experience of living. Elders shape the next generation effortlessly.

For many years, I have visited my Uncle Edgar and Aunt Rosa. Edgar Fleetham, 89 years old, eldest brother of my father, has lived in the same house his whole life in rural Michigan. My uncle loves politics and the conversation always takes a turn towards my perception of national politics. I think Roosevelt was the last Democrat to get my uncle's vote. Once I told him that the president and his administration were too angry. He snapped back: "Why, we can't afford a gentle president now!" Aunt Rosa, a woman who has distilled the essence of Christian love and tolerance into the bones of her personality, looked at her dear husband of 69 years and said: "Edgar, why can't the president be gentle? Can't a gentle man also be strong?" Then, the second miracle occurred. Edgar looked into Rosa's eyes and said: "Yes, dear. You are right." I absorbed two lessons that afternoon: Learning never has to end and neither does love.

Leadership in the Second-Stage of Life[1]

The dominant theme for the second-stage leader is doing for others so she can do for herself. She has to learn how to fit in, to join the crowd—that's where she finds her followers, that's where she builds her network. Young leaders climbing the ladder in an organization must think first about what the boss wants, what the customers want, even what the staff wants. In most cases, what the young leader wants comes at the end of the priority list. Why? The young leader must learn how to put the demands of the culture first. If the leader's character is strong, the decisions will be good (i.e. in accordance with the cultural demands). A young Mafia lieutenant, a young head of regional marketing at Pepsi, and a young Catholic priest all have one thing in common: They try to figure out what others expect of them so they can deliver it and get ahead. After they have satisfied others, they will do for themselves and receive the appropriate rewards of salary, bonus, office size, title, promotion and glory.

The Extremes: Getting Stuck and Getting Out

There is a place in the Swamps of Maturity known as the Extremes. The last time I flew over it, I saw second-stage leaders building fires and trying to transmit smoke signals. Why are second-stage leaders so prone to extremes? Young and hungry leaders focus their energy on developing their dominant coupling. Sometimes they take it too far. They over-adapt. They act as if they know everything and what they don't know doesn't really matter. Often, they unconsciously surround themselves with elders who can see their flaws—an autonomous response to the personality's need for balance. Sometimes these elders engage consulting firms like mine to deliver the bad news to their Master of the Universe.[2] Here is what over-adaptation might look like for each coupling:

- **Wise Leader**—Politicizing every decision and thus the entire organization.
- **Committed Manager**—Turning time management and project management into religions and forcing mass conversions at the point of a measurable objective.
- **Creative Facilitator**—Putting people before profits, before effectiveness (and sometimes, before survival).
- **Organizational Visionary**—Trying to build the perfect mousetrap with every project (it never gets done).

Once, I was brought into a company owned and managed by a 29-year-old who had cashed in on an IPO. He had the persona of a Greek warrior drunk with visions of glory—a sure sign that he had a hyperactive Committed Manager coupling. He peppered his language with military talk about long marches, sieges, pincer movements, and unconditional surrenders. He'd announce a cost-cutting initiative one day and the next day charter a plane for a press conference. He'd assure the staff their jobs were secure and then eliminate a department. His company was growing fast and needed more and more executive competence. Everyone around him, including the board of directors, feared he wasn't cut out to lead the organization into its next phase of growth. He was brilliant, quick on his feet and indefatigable, but he refused to listen. His company went under in short order. He escaped with the cash, but he didn't escape the Extremes. He was stuck in his hyperactive personality.

When the second-stage leader gets sick of extreme muck and mire and decides that he wants to get out of the Swamp, the strategy is simple: **Grow the auxiliary couplings.** In our cruise around IOPD Island in Chapter Seven, we learned about the auxiliary couplings, the left and right hands of our personality. We start our careers by finding and relying on our strength—our dominant coupling. Baseball offers a good analogy. A youth pitcher has to have a good fastball, but if he doesn't learn a change up and curve, he won't get past the high school level. As we expand our leadership range and take on more responsibility, we have to go to the underdeveloped sides of our personality and say: "I need your help!"

By the way, attempting to tackle the inferior coupling is too frustrating and arduous for a second-stage leader. For example, trying to force the Committed Manager through the Clouds to confront his Creative Facilitator would be like trying to make a high school football team more sensitive by taking them to see *The Way We Were*. It won't work and will make any movement more difficult because the personality will re-entrench itself in the dominant coupling.

With the strategy of growing the auxiliary couplings in mind, let's see how the unrational leader with a dominant **Committed Manager** coupling could apply the Five Principles of Unrational Leadership™ to help himself get out of the Swamp.

1. **Start all problem solving by taking personal responsibility:** Unrational leaders always assume personal responsibility— you got yourself in the Swamp, it's your job to get yourself out. It's not the fault of your mother or your predecessor. Draw a colorful picture (the colors bring out more emotions) of yourself stuck in the Swamp. Take the picture to a respected elder and ask for his or her advice on how to escape.

2. **Aim at increasing energy, not just efficiency:** You need to start conserving energy. Aren't you tired of those 16-hour

days? Aren't you sick of balancing your time? Aren't you fed up with squeezing your life into the end of the toothpaste tube? To cure the obsession with efficiency, put yourself in a role that is new and uncomfortable. If you dislike small talk, ask employees about their weekend; if the microwave is your only cooking utensil, prepare a gourmet meal. Be inefficient in something for the next 20 days, and you will learn to let go of some of your perfectionism. At the same time, you will feel a surge of energy and will actually perform better. Consciously adding digestible bits of discomfort to your life is a long-term Unrational Leadership™ strategy.

3. **Confront and partner with the unconscious:** The unrational leader walks into the fire of the unconscious and wrestles with it until she achieves a partnership. In your case, that fire can be found in your auxiliary couplings. There are two ways to work this principle. First, get yourself involved in activities that energize your auxiliary couplings—the Wise Leader and Organizational Visionary. Run a volunteer organization (Wise Leader); get involved in politics (Wise Leader); create a new product or service (Organizational Visionary); or show a younger person the ropes (Organizational Visionary). Another idea is to record your dreams and look for the auxiliary couplings. They will be same-sex characters. For example, look for cousins, long-lost friends or business partners. I can't tell exactly who they will be or what coupling they represent, but I can tell you if you look for them that you will find them. Write letters to them explaining your situation and ask for help.

4. **Creativity drives change:** Rest. This principle taps the Creative Facilitator, your inferior coupling, something that you can look forward to when you arrive at the third-stage of life.

5. **Look two generations behind and look two generations ahead:** Write an abbreviated autobiography and write por-

tions of it at work. This will be your launching pad for con-
necting the past to the future.

Energizing Second-Stage Employees

Third-stage leaders frequently wonder: "How do I motivate this
younger generation? They don't want to work like I did. Work is not
at the top of their agenda." The third-stage leaders are right about
one thing: The young generation is different. According to a 2004
Herman Trend Alert:

> Reflecting a trend we have seen in the current workforce, the
> teenagers chose family and fun over money in level of impor-
> tance to them. Nearly 65 percent voted for less money and
> more time for family and fun over more money with an invest-
> ment of more time. This data is consistent with other research
> where 48 percent of today's workers made the same choice.
> Money is no longer the primary motivator.

As I noted in Chapter Seven, the personality in our culture is shifting
from the left-brain couplings to the right-brain couplings. More and
more workers will value intangible experience (fun and family) over
material things (money). Needless to say, there is a pony in this barn.
If the next generation isn't so focused on money, it will relieve your
payroll expenses. Having supervised many next-generation employees, I have adopted the following motivation strategies with some
success. They are based on the principle that different generations
need different leadership approaches.

1. **Build your culture around the team:** The next generation is
   driven more by peers and less by hierarchy. At Project Innovations, teams form spontaneously to plan and deliver a
   project. Although at times these teaming efforts want for
   efficiency, they more than compensate by creating energy
   (motivation).

2. **Create radical freedom with a few simple rules:** The next generation doesn't like a lot of rules. They like informality. We don't take attendance at Project Innovations. We don't fill out forms. We work where we want, when we want and as long as we want. We follow three simple rules (and they're not written down): Create value for the client, create profit for the company, and create your personality.

3. **Tap their unconscious:** The process fascinates the next generation and really connects with their intuitive function. At Project Innovations, we practice Unrational Leadership™ at every turn and the next generation loves it.

4. **Help average employees become above average:** Let them make the choice to grow. If they can't, help them out of the company. The next generation wants more than a job. They want to find themselves *in their job*. Average performers, however well-intentioned, don't inspire other members of the team to grow professionally.

5. **Never under employ the next generation:** They like fast, fresh futures. I always give my people a little more than they can handle today and tomorrow.

Leadership in the Third-Stage of Life

The dominant theme for the third-stage leader is that he must **do for himself so he can do for others**. In contrast to the second-stage leader, who concentrates on listening and responding to the voice of culture, the third-stage leader turns in toward the self. Jung believed that the second half of life begins with an updraft from our unconscious. It is the call of the self. Lightning strikes the neglected side of our personality. The outgoing person who neglected silence, the disciplined woman who avoided spontaneity, and the creative man who has not planned for the future—all three are lightening strikes waiting to happen. Suddenly, like sparks from a campfire, neglected, unwelcome urges float into consciousness. The strong ego that we worked so hard to build in the first half of life must yield to the unconscious.

The third-stage leader must attend to this fire. The unconscious challenges him to assimilate the energy. Before a critical decision, the second-stage leader asks everyone: "What do you think?" The third-stage leader asks: "What do I really want to achieve here?" The second-stage leader paces before the battle; the third-stage leader takes a nap. The second-stage leader needs an epic poem; the third-stage leader appreciates the haiku. The second-stage leader runs the discussion; the third-stage leader facilitates the dialogue. For the second-stage leader, the beginning is always close at hand; the third-stage leader is calmly facing the conclusion.

How do I Know When I've Hit the Third-Stage?

1. I smile when I watch the young bucks charging at each other in a meeting.
2. I find it easier and easier to identify the risks in a strategic plan—without diminishing my commitment to the enterprise.
3. Long-buried memories suddenly emerge while sitting at my computer.
4. I prefer my advice (and my reports) in simple sentences.
5. I have formally surrendered my quest to change the world.
6. I get more satisfaction from helping others grow than I do from personal success.
7. More and more simple decisions are filled with competing goods.
8. I am in it for the long haul—even though the yardstick gets shorter and shorter.
9. I find myself pondering the meaning of life—and getting somewhere.
10. I have given up trying to control the people who work for me (and myself).

Watch Out for the Bottoms

In the center of the Swamps of Maturity there is a place known as the Bottoms. Below sea level, the Bottoms are filled with murky stagnant waters. Garlands of moss and slimy snakes hang from the branches of weird, twisted trees. The sun turns into a pale shadow. People get stuck in the Bottoms when they refuse to pay attention to their unconscious. Here is some testimony from a friend:

> Charlie, I fell into the Bottoms at the age of 46, just after my software development business started to disintegrate when NASDAQ crashed. I had thought I was invincible, but now I see that I had been running away from the setting sun. What was it like in the Bottoms? The worse things got, the more I REFUSED to change. I clung to my WAY. It felt like my soul was eating me up from the inside out. For reasons I couldn't explain in a hundred years, I bought another company. And for reasons I couldn't explain in two hundred years, I had an affair with a young sales gal. My soul didn't care about my bottom line. Life chewed me up and threw me down until I learned how to listen to my self. And you know, I was lucky. I managed to save the core of my business and more importantly, my family. I have some friends who are still stuck in that hole.

Not everyone who gets stuck in the Bottoms is depressed. Not everyone experiences a mid-life crisis.[3] Sometimes, they are just confused. Something is going on inside of them and they don't know exactly what it is. Lots of people wander into the Swamps at the peak of their careers, when their star shines brightly on the outside. Despite their success, they wonder privately if "this is all there is to life" and why "this perfect life isn't enough for them anymore." If they have spent their energy on external success, they suddenly find a need for self-reflection, quiet, and privacy. Conversely, if they have been inwardly focused, they discover urges to speak out passionately for a cause.

As chief operating officer, Peter carried his firm for 10 years. He had incredible talent for managing costs and squeezing out profits through good and lean times. His work habits were prodigious—first to arrive and last to leave. He had a dormant love for basketball. Out of the blue, not long after turning 40, questions of guilt began nagging at him. Was he a good father, a good husband? Would all this work pay off? Why was he killing himself to achieve? Despite these questions, he continued his exceptional performance.

Then, a good friend, whom he had not seen in several years, suffered a heart attack. Peter's visit to the hospital left him shaken. He only needed one night of brooding about death, his children's future and his college years before he said: "This is not a dress rehearsal. I'm going to change!" He joined a basketball league, volunteered to teach catechism at his church, quit working weekends and now leaves the office before 6 p.m. He also prays each day for health and another chance to do well. What has happened to the bottom line at his company? Its gross revenue has doubled in the last four years while simultaneously increasing its profits.

Coping with the Third-Stage of Life

The best strategy for coping with the third-stage of life (and the Bottoms) is to integrate your inferior coupling into your personality. The inferior coupling is the fourth coupling, the one that resides in your unconscious. Although it is the most difficult coupling to develop, integrating it into your personality is an essential challenge of the third-stage of life. Once your inferior coupling makes its claim, you will spend your third and fourth stages forging a relationship with it. In Chapter Eight, I showed how the Committed Manager must partner with his inferior coupling, the Creative Facilitator, in order to solve problems that defy reason and overcome the challenges that inevitably occur when plunging into the Clouds of the

Unknown. Now, from the perspective of the third-stage leader with a dominant coupling of the Committed Manager, here are some tips for integrating your inferior coupling into your leadership toolbox. As with my advice to second-stage Committed Managers, I will use the framework provided by the Five Principles of Unrational Leadership™.

1. **Start all problem solving by taking personal responsibility:** Answer these questions to stimulate the Wise Leader within you. The more the questions tire you, the more you need to answer them.

   - What is your definition of good and evil?
   - Reflecting on the most important decisions that you have made in the last year—how did the concepts of good and evil enter into your decisions?
   - Make a list of the most difficult challenges you are currently facing in your organization and identify the good and evil components of the challenges.
   - What are the five things you must do to increase the level of good and decrease the level of evil in your organization?

2. **Aim at increasing energy, not just efficiency:** This principle is targeted at stimulating your Committed Manager coupling. In the third-stage of life, you need to distance yourself from this dear strength without losing confidence or energy. I strongly recommend that you review your responsibilities, identify the ones associated with the Committed Manager coupling, and delegate a portion of them to subordinates. In other words—**let go**.

3. **Confront and partner with the unconscious:** This principle is associated with plunging into the Clouds of the Unknown. The third-stage unrational leader must walk towards her inferior coupling. While you walk, hold on to

this thought: Love is the ability to suffer with someone.[4] It might be instructive to compare Lincoln and Hitler. They both led their countries into great wars. Hitler could not stand the sight of blood, refused to personally suffer the consequences of his warmongering, and had no feeling for the people that he killed. Yet, he never failed to remind the people how much pain he personally endured for them. On the other hand, Lincoln willingly took on the suffering of his people. He had the capacity to grieve for lost life. Somehow, Lincoln inoculated himself from the worst ravages of the war and managed to remain human in the face of it.

4. **Creativity drives change:** As you know, this principle taps the Creative Facilitator, your inferior coupling. It will emerge when you least expect, and I don't want to offer any illusions that you can manage, control, or perfect your inferior coupling. You can't command your unconscious. The best thing you do is to learn patience and tolerance when it does emerge. What can you do to increase your patience? You need to expose yourself to as many Creative Facilitator activities as possible. Attend a poetry reading, take a drawing class, or learn how to facilitate a meeting. I can see your head shaking, but eventually you'll find the right activities.

5. **Look two generations behind and look two generations ahead:** This principle energizes the Organizational Visionary coupling. Help the next generation prepare for the future. Carl Jung believed that our unconscious erupts in the third-stage of life to give us the energy and wisdom to contribute to our culture. My Unrational Leadership™ workshops almost always include the pairing of experienced leaders with younger staff members. Here is a small sample of comments from these mentors/coaches:

   • "I realized how much I had to offer when I found myself, for the first time, explaining how things really work. I had been taking my 'wisdom' for granted!"

- "I loved helping her solve thorny problems, especially the ones that involved conflicts in her team . . . when she told me at the end of the program that I had made a difference in her life, I have to admit I felt some pride."

- "My coaching sessions became something to look forward to. Much more rewarding than most of my meetings! I noticed they gave me energy and sparked my creativity in other parts of my job—impacts I never expected."

- "Probably the most striking benefit was creating a vision of what my protégé could become in five or ten years if she stayed the course. I wish I had had a mentor when I was her age."

Transforming Third-Stage Employees into Elders

If you want to turn-on third-stage employees in your company, give them a chance to operate as elders. I once facilitated a strategic planning process for a small engineering company. Henry, an engineer in his 50s, a true elder in the company and mentor to the younger engineers, had an idea. He wanted the company to devote a small percentage of its profits to "crusades," projects in poor communities, maybe even in third-world countries, to build wells, sewage treatment facilities, small bridges, and the like.

Henry was a lone voice for a while, trying to convince the company leaders that they should spend *profits* helping others. "How would we manage this?" the leaders asked. Others said, "If our people want to take time off to do this work, and *of course* it is good work, we'll support them in one way or another." As Henry continued to speak passionately about wanting to make a difference, about the rewards of helping others, he started to win people over to his vision and the company adopted his crusades. The president told me a few months later: "I haven't seen Henry so excited in years. This crusade has really fired him up!"

Your employees don't become useless when they round 55! Silver hair gives wisdom not only to media personalities and aging athletes. A seldom-used definition of *elder* is "an older person with some authority or dignity in a tribe or community." The word "authority" implies "jurisdiction" or "judgment." A person needs considerable life experience to make judgments that may affect generations. Elders have collected enough wisdom to avoid rash decisions. Elders have learned that you can want *everything* but can only have *something*, and that sometimes you must walk away from the good as well as the evil. Here are three tips for transforming employees into respected elders:

- Invite them to give non-binding judgments on moral issues, by virtue of their age (not competence or accomplishments— these are the awards of youth). It's important to invite rather than direct; wisdom doesn't settle for command.
- Invite them to comment on your plans, especially the ones for grand and sweeping changes. Invariably, they will point out what can go wrong and remind you of past failures. Listen deeply before you sweep away their caution as mere resistance.
- Invite them to tell stories of what they have learned about life to the young people in your organization. I use this idea frequently in my Unrational Leadership™ programs. I invite the oldest people to sit in the front of the room and face their younger comrades. I ask them to talk about the most important thing they have learned about life in their work. The elders who have been through this experience invariable tell me that it is the first time anyone has ever honored them **simply** for their age. They hold on to the experience for years.

Letters to the Unrationalist:
Real Challenges in the Stages of Life

My company publishes a newsletter, "The Unrationalist." The newsletter features an advice column. Many of the questions concern the stages of life. Here is a sampling of letters and responses.

Dear Unrationalist,

I'm a 33-year-old engineer and was recently promoted to my first supervisory position. The young people (who used to be my friends) think they know more than I do. I thought the opposite was supposed to happen when you got promoted! And the older folks, who used to help me, treat me like I'm irrelevant. It is very frustrating and I am almost sorry that I took the promotion. What should I do?

Caught in the Middle

Dear Caught,

I could tell you to have a meeting with both groups, explain your expectations and forge a partnership with them. And it might just work! But, let's get unrational for a minute. Your kids (i.e. your ex-friends) want to fit in and they are wondering if you are old enough to help make that happen. Of course, they would never admit this. So, forget about performance and start judging them (in quiet and cunning ways) on their dress, communication style, presentations, etc. They'll come around in short order. As for your older team members, they have already figured out the game. They know that they belong. They want to make sure that a task is the right thing to do before they do it. Start your conversations with the question: "Do you think this is right?" Always remember, you have to lead from the stages of life—both yours and theirs.

Dear Unrationalist,

I am a 34 year-old wife and mother of two children. I love my family, but I have never found what I really want to do with my life. I have so many ideas and urges that sometimes I get confused. If I follow them, I know my husband and family will say I am crazy. But, the things that I do try seem to have no relation to my dreams and besides that they never work. Every room in my home is filled with junk from a different networking marketing scheme—from the soap under the sink to the cases of make-up in my closet! Should I go back to school or dive into full-time work? I don't want to screw up my family, but I am really frustrated. Help me before I turn into a witch in the kitchen.

Witch in the Kitchen (to be)

Dear Witch,

You are stumbling through the second-stage of life without being conscious of your journey. You are trying to escape the fundamental challenge of the second-stage: You must do for others so you can do for yourself. Make a list of the demands your family places on you and find out which of them energize you and which leave you exhausted. This will give you some idea of your strengths and weaknesses, and may even reveal your true calling. Focus on ways to use your strengths to satisfy your family's needs without exhausting yourself. As you figure out this puzzle, the clouds in front of your decision regarding school or full-time work will clear.

Dear Unrationalist,

I am a 45-year-old manager in a small engineering firm. I am one of the most loyal and dedicated employees. Everything was going well until a couple of years ago when I started blowing up at the slightest problem. Of course, this led to friction and I responded by watching my people. Literally. I walk around the office and spy on their conversations. So no one trusts me anymore. Recently, they sent me a coach to teach me Anger Management skills. He's a good guy and has helped me become aware of when I'm going to blow up, but the feeling is driving me crazy.

A Smoldering Volcano

Dear Smoldering,

Everything has been planned in your life, down to the finest detail, everything except for your untamed unconscious. Until two years ago, you imprisoned it in the darkness of your shadow. But now that the rascal has escaped and lit a Great Fire, there's no turning back. Just because you can't see your unconscious, doesn't mean it doesn't exist. Just because your friends don't talk about it, doesn't mean it doesn't exist. Smoldering, you can't play it safe. Here's what you must do: You must find a voice teacher and learn how to sing. Even if you believe you have no talent for singing, you must sing. Your voice will transform your fire into contentment.

Dear Unrationalist,

My dear husband retired two years ago from a high-level governmental position. Prior to his retirement, he was the most ordered of men. Now, he is a complete slob. He lives and sleeps in the same clothes. If he changes his underwear once a month I'd be surprised. I have tried to be a good role model by showering daily and keeping the house spick-and-span, but he won't change. He won't admit that he's dirty. Now, I'm ashamed to have my friends visit and I certainly don't want to have sex with him anymore. What should I do?

Invaded

Dear Invaded,

Welcome to the second half of life! Your dear husband no longer worships the god of reputation. He gave this god every ounce of his strength for 30 plus years and now he's worn out. His unconscious has become the new sheriff, and it is not pretty—or is it? Here's what you do: Start a dream journal and record your dreams. If you begin to assimilate your dream images, his unconscious will be comforted and bank its fires. Although you may not believe it, in these types of situations, if one of the partners takes on the challenges of the unconscious, the other will be helped. This approach will take about nine months. In the meantime, create a separate bedroom for yourself and tell him that it's sacred space. No males allowed.

The Unrational Leader at Work

Recently, a friend asked me to serve on a committee for the American Consulting Engineering Council (ACEC) to explore the concept of the trusted advisor. What is a trusted advisor? According to David II. Maister, Charles H. Green, and Robert M. Galford, in their book, *The Trusted Advisor,* a trusted advisor is "the person the client turns to when an issue first arises, often in times of great urgency: a crisis, a change, a triumph, or a defeat." I have been working with engineering consulting companies for many years and have served as a trusted advisor to many executives. The ACEC thought I might be able to contribute an external perspective to their explorations.

Becoming a trusted advisor is a Holy Grail quest for a consultant. When you find it, you open the door to extraordinary personal and professional rewards. This powerful connection allows both client and consultant to leap over the impersonal and sometimes degrading owner-vendor relationship. Obviously, it can accrue significant advantages to the trusted advisor when clients want help solving a problem, but this kind of relationship offers much more than profits. Operating as a trusted advisor has helped me build lasting and deep friendships with clients, to the degree that I vacation with clients and exchange holiday visits. Engineers, lawyers, doctors, therapists, architects, accountants and leaders of professional services firms want to know: How do you become a trusted advisor? How do you train your people to become trusted advisors? Or, even more fundamental—are trusted advisors born or are they made? Let's see how an unrational leader would answer these questions.

1. **Are trusted advisors born or are they made?**

   Some people are born with the talents that make it easier to become a trusted advisor. These talents include: the ability to listen, to think on your feet, to form intimate relationships, and to give good advice. How do you leverage these talents? The key to becoming a trusted advisor is growing a personality that can stand on its own two feet and have something useful to say about how the world works. Trusted advisors are not sycophants.

   The requisite personality growth occurs in two waves. In the second-stage of life, the trusted advisor-to-be must develop his strong coupling. This development brings professional competence—the foundation of the advisor. In the third-stage of the life, the professional can grow by developing his inferior coupling. For people with left-brain personalities, the challenge is moving through the Clouds of the Unknown and wrestling with the irrational elements of the human heart: vision, love, creativity, fun, and dependency. For the people with right-brain personalities (actually quite common in some professional service firms), the most common challenge is to tap the Wise Leader coupling, a process which adds a moral flavor to one's advice.

2. **How do you train people to become trusted advisors?**

   Becoming a trusted advisor has rational and irrational challenges, which is, of course, the bailiwick of Unrational Leadership™. From the perspective of the unrational leader, a successful training program would address five critical learning objectives:

- What are the core values in my profession? Do I share these core values? Do my clients share these values? How do these values influence my advice? Do my clients know what I stand for?
- In practical terms—cost, quality, time, and content— do I know how to identify what my client wants and to deliver the goods? I have observed a few trusted advisors who lacked professional core competence, but they usually attach themselves to one or two clients, and their longevity is tenuous. To make it short: You have to know what you are doing to become a trusted advisor.
- Do you have the courage to tell your client that she is headed over a cliff, that she is not wearing any clothes? This is the challenge of sitting in the fire, of walking through the Clouds of the Unknown. In the short run, aiding and abetting your client's fantasies can improve your bottom line. I have kept clients because I averted my eyes, and I have lost clients because I told them the truth. In the long run, you will stop growing if you can't find the courage to give your client the help she needs the most—information for growing her personality.
- Can you make friends with a client? Some people have tremendous problems mixing business with personal relationships. It seems so much safer to draw a thick line between the two worlds. Some people will trust you based on your performance, but it is friendship that leads them to trust you with their hopes and dreams. These "fantasies" are

the hard and objective data of any long-term relationship.

- Do you know how to become a mentor? In Homer's tale, *The Odyssey,* Mentor was Odysseus' wise and faithful counselor, entrusted to watch over the household during the Trojan War. Mentor tutored Odysseus' son, Telemachus, and his name became a pseudonym for trusted advisor and friend. Mentoring is one of the oldest career-development methods. A good mentor has three characteristics: experience, perspective and distance. The trusted advisor should understand the mentoring process and should be an active mentor in his own organization.

3. **How do I become a trusted advisor?**

Leave Comfortopia and start the quest for Unrational Leadership™.

Notes

1. The purpose of this book is to help organizational leaders, so the rest of this chapter will focus on second and third-stage leaders as they call the shots in most organizations.
2. Young bulls like the prestige of working with a consultant, and elders like the breathing room!
3. Not everyone who ignores their unconscious ends up in the Bottoms. Many people walk through the second half of life with the charms of Forest Gump. Most likely, their children won't be so lucky.
4. My sponsor Pauline deserves the credit for this powerful definition. See Chapter Five for more on Pauline.

Important Concepts for the Unrational Leader

- Your life's journey is like the rise and fall of the sun.
- Each of life's four stages has a different development challenge.
- Second-stage leaders do for others so they can do for themselves.
- Third-stage leaders do for themselves so they can do for others.
- Transform third-stage employees into elders to drive more value into your organization.

12 The Rain Always Follows the Sun[1]

TrueHeart's father died away from the shadows of Snow White's manor. TrueHeart carried him to the river of the Seventh Mountain, constructed a funeral pyre and prayed while the flames consumed the body.

Exhausted to his soul, TrueHeart decided to forget his quest to rouse the Princess. He started a new life. He walked across the land until he found a small farming village, whereupon he traded his weapons for a patch of land and a cottage. Soon, he found a wife—the mayor's daughter. They had children and for 15 years lived contentedly until the Black Plague swept through the land and took his family. In complete despair, he sold his plot and cottage for 300 crowns of gold and at age 40 returned to the Dark Forest to ask Brigid for advice.

"Brigid, I've decided to return to the Kingdom of my youth and awaken the Princess. What say you?"

"Do you remember our conversations about the stages of life?" Brigid asked.

"Vaguely," TrueHeart replied, for he remembered almost nothing.

"Watch out for the third-stage of life," Brigid said. "That is my advice to you."

"That is not enough for me!" TrueHeart said with unexpected sharpness. "Can't you tell me more?"

"My dear TrueHeart," said Brigid tiredly. "I would be happy to give you more, but I must charge you the usual fee."

"Fee?" replied TrueHeart, a little indignant at the apparent loss of his special relationship with Brigid. "I don't remember a fee. I must be getting old."

"My friend, the Black Plague has destroyed not only your family," Brigid said as way of explanation. "Its shadow has claimed us all. I now charge 100 crowns for advice."

"Yes, times have changed," said TrueHeart. "I will respect your fee because of what you have already given."

Handing Brigid a hundred crowns, TrueHeart waited eagerly for his advice. Taking a deep breath, Brigid announced: "The rain always follows the sun."

"You jest!" TrueHeart exclaimed. "I gave you a hundred crowns for that?"

"Well, my old friend, I am sure you will remember it," Brigid remarked.

Convinced that he needed more advice, TrueHeart handed her another 100 crowns.

Looking him square in the eyes, Brigid now said, "Your greatest strength will become your greatest weakness."

Frustrated, TrueHeart shook his head angrily. "Your advice has no muscle that can move these old bones! Is there any substance remaining in that ancient wit?"

Wanting to hear a real secret and forgetting how many years he had worked to earn the gold, TrueHeart thrust the last of his money into Brigid's hands. "Now give me something I can use."

Without hesitation, Brigid quickly announced: "Do for your-self so you can do for others."

Rolling his eyes, TrueHeart got up to depart. "What about Moira's sleeping spell on the Princess?" he said at the door. "How will it finally be broken?"

"Take this," said Brigid, rising and thrusting a smooth stone into his hand. "My mother gave it to me, and I dedicated it to you long ago. Save it for your most desperate prayer."

A sad smile touched TrueHeart's lips when he realized that all his hope might rest inside a rock, yet he thanked Brigid and started his heroic journey home. Seven days later, he emerged from the Dark Forest and entered a bustling camp of men. They welcomed him with meat and wine.

"Good stranger, make your camp with us," said one of the men. "We have discovered gold in yonder hills. You look too old to dig, but you could help build the village or mind a store. There is much wealth to gain."

Fortune's smile had turned on him, and he felt a strong urge to try his luck in the gold rush. Then, he remembered Brigid's advice that the rain always follows the sun—it meant that bad luck will often follow good fortune. TrueHeart reluctantly de-clined the miner's offer. After eating, he thanked the men for their hospitality and walked out of the camp. Within an hour, he heard the clap-clap of a horse and turned to see a man cov-ered in blood clinging to the animal's mane.

"Good sir, run for your life!" the man bellowed. "Brigands from the Dark Forest have attacked the camp and slaughtered all but me." TrueHeart ran away as quickly as he could, and only when he felt safe did he reflect on Brigid's advice. "What new traps lay ahead?" he wondered.

Many days hence, a bustling village appeared before him, alive with the sights and sounds of a fair. He quickly found himself in the village green and a wrestling tournament. The champion's prize was immense—300 crowns—and competitors had come from far and wide. Although he had not competed since his days at Snow White's manor, a burst of youthful en-ergy filled him and he entered the contest, hoping that he might win the prize.

Once in the ring, TrueHeart's youthful vigor returned, and he became the crowd favorite. All memories of the Black Plague and his lost fortune vanished in the warm afternoon. He won match after match as the crowd cheered along. At the end of the day, TrueHeart had earned a place in the next day's cham-pionship round. As he prepared for sleep underneath a tree, he became aware of how deeply his muscles ached. Then, Brigid's second warning came into his consciousness: "Your greatest strength will become your greatest weakness."

The next morning, claiming tired bones, he withdrew from the contest. However, he stayed to watch the outcome. Not sur-prisingly, the youngest and strongest wrestler won. TrueHeart thought: "I could've beaten him and won the gold. Damn that Brigid."

Soon, a procession of maidens flocked around the champion, crowned him with a laurel wreath and presented him with the

300 crowns. Then, they grabbed his hands and led him out of the village. Perplexed that no one joined the procession, True-Heart crept around the village and followed the sounds of the singing maidens and boasting champion.

At a grove of trees, safely hidden, TrueHeart watched as the maidens served the champion wine and more until the man was delirious with pleasure and exhaustion. Ashamed of watching, TrueHeart prepared to leave when the maidens suddenly tied the naked hero between two trees. Stunned, True-Heart realized the women were intent on slaying the champion. TrueHeart, remembering how he saved his father from Snow White, instinctively prepared to rescue the young man. However, he could not forget Brigid's second warning, "Your greatest strength will become your greatest weakness."

He felt old and thought of his dead wife and children. For the first time in his life, death frightened him more than the urge to be a hero. With adult fear, TrueHeart hurried quickly away from the scene. Before long, blood-curdling screams filled the air. TrueHeart ran faster.

After many nights of troubled and guilty sleep, TrueHeart reached the Kingdom's borders. The land was wild and overgrown. After all these years, the King and his people still slept. Walking on the outskirts of the castle, TrueHeart recalled the Kingdom's last days—the King's thirst for war, his own love for the Princess and his pledge to Moira to travel to the Dark Forest and learn Brigid's secrets of Unrational Leadership™. It all seemed like a fairy tale to him.

When he arrived at the castle gate, vines covered it from the base to the turret tops. Only the tattered banners of the Nine Habits remained, flanking the bleached skull of the Fool. He tried unsuccessfully to enter through the main door. Then he tried to scale the outer wall, but his body would not obey him.

Sitting to ponder his next move, he thought: "Am I cursed now? Have I lost my wits in this third-stage of life? Why am I

chasing this dream of the Princess? I should have stayed in my village." His despair grew until he took the stone that Brigid had given him and prayed that his troubles would release him. Suddenly, an old woman approached him.

"Brave and strong knight, as you can see, I am very old," she said. "I live in the woods nearby and my loyal husband has died. I am quite alone and helpless. Come to my cottage and chop wood so I can start my fire and cook a fine stew. I will share it with you."

TrueHeart was about to assent, when Brigid's third piece of advice came to him: "Do for yourself, so you can do for others."

"I am sorry, old woman, but I cannot chop wood for you today," TrueHeart replied. "I am too tired, and I need my rest."

"But, I will surely die," wailed the woman. "Please help me. You are a knight and have sworn to protect the weak and innocent."

"Today, I cannot," TrueHeart, insisted. "Perhaps, tomorrow I will have more energy."

"I beg you, good sir!" the old woman pleaded.

Squeezing the stone for strength, TrueHeart shook his head and refused again.

"May God curse your heartlessness!" the woman screamed.

TrueHeart was about to change his mind, when the old woman abruptly turned and stumbled away. Surprised at her quick departure, TrueHeart followed her from a distance, watching from behind a large tree as she entered her cottage. Soon enough, a large snake emerged.

TrueHeart wondered if it was the same snake that he had met in the woods when Moira attacked the Kingdom. He had no desire to test his theory. He slumped back to the castle only to discover that the door had been open all along. He entered the walls in the twilight and found himself in the main courtyard.

He struggled to adjust his youthful memories to the courtyard's present state. It was filled with a jungle of vines, scrambling rodents and crumbling buildings. He wandered through silent, narrow alleys to the massive oak door of the royal family's quarters. He pushed on it. It wouldn't move. He pushed again and again, but the crumbling chaos smothered his remaining energy.

TrueHeart stumbled to a nearby bench and fell asleep before any fears had time to catch him. The next morning, he awoke and saw a snaky, spidery mandala on the massive oak door. It both pleased and troubled him for he had not noticed it the previous night. He gazed at it as the sun rose to greet it. He wondered what it foretold for him. He traced the web in the mandala and the door opened.

"What magic is this?" he asked.

Note

1. This chapter was inspired by the fairy tale: *Solomon's Advice.*

13 The Ethical Decision Device

The biggest threat to our world is a leader who forms his moral convictions without suffering any doubt, a leader who looks at the Sea of the Dark Side and can't see himself in the sea monsters. This is the lesson of history and the curse of our future as technology gives leaders more and more destructive power. For example, consider Kim Il Jung, the president of North Korea. If he launches a nuclear attack on his neighbors, the warheads will contain the same moral certainty as the president who defends his nation against terrorists. We may accuse the North Korean of immorality, but from his perspective, his decision is completely moral. Ironically, the lack of doubt increases his confidence in his own morality. This is moral blindness and it occurs in leaders of organizations large and small. How can we help leaders really **see** both sides of a moral equation? It's not a trivial question. The world's destiny hangs on the psychic threads of the nine leaders who belong to the Nuclear Club.[1] If one of them loses his nerve, millions could die in the blink of an eye.

While researching this chapter, I unearthed a schematic for an Ethical Decision Device. At first, I had trouble understanding how the device might work, but as I uncovered more information, I began to grasp its nature. Designed by ancient unrational leaders and erected many centuries before the Age of Reason, the Ethical Decision Device produces the precise amounts of light required to see many sides of a moral dilemma. Unfortunately, I could read every book written on the topic of virtue and still lack the capacity to make moral and ethical decisions. You can't learn this most difficult skill of Unrational Leadership™ through reading. It is won by courageously standing in the middle of one's own fire, waiting for the unconscious to reveal a creative solution, and grabbing it like the last rope to heaven—such is the nature of the device.

Morals and Ethics are not the Same

If you look up "morals" and "ethics" in the dictionary, you will find that they are almost synonymous. But, if you examine the roots of the words, you will find an interesting distinction. "Morals" descends from the Latin word *moralis,* which translates—*of manners or customs.* On the other hand, "ethics" descends from the Greek *ethos,* which translates—*character, custom.* At this point in our research, the words align perfectly. But, if you go to the deepest root of *ethics,* you will find the Indo European *swedh* which translates as *essential quality, own character.* I think these differing roots help us see the difference between moral and ethical behavior. To be moral is to adhere to the customs of the day; whereas, to be ethical is to adhere to customs of the day *and to your own essential quality.*

In the beginning of this search, I defined Unrational Leadership™ as leadership that uses both rational and irrational methods to achieve a desired outcome. Following the customs of the day is the rational aspect of the moral decision-making process. Before a leader can be ethical, he has to be moral. Even though one can be moral and extremely destructive (as shown in the introductory example), moral leadership is the cornerstone of decision-making that optimizes the good for your culture. The unrational leader must know, and for the most part, must adhere to the presiding morals. Morality can be furthered through training and discipline. This education is the province of the Wise Leader coupling. Obviously, customs change across countries and cultures, but in the United States, I have seen and experienced a remarkably common set of idealistic morals in business, government, and non-profit organizations:

- Be honest in all dealings
- Make a promise, keep a promise
- Have the courage to act with integrity in all matters
- Treat everyone with mutual respect
- Always develop the next generation of leaders
- Put the organization ahead of yourself
- Energetically pursue the goals of the organization
- Walk your own talk
- The customer/taxpayer/client/employee is Number One
- Strive for excellence in everything you do

Our Moral Compass has Shifted

Are we losing our moral compass? True north is no longer headquartered in the left side of our brain. The needle is swinging from left to right in parallel with the rise of the intuitive personality. Not surprisingly, people ask: "Have we lost our bearings? Does anyone remember the meaning of right and wrong?" People want to know if they can trust their leaders. They wonder if politics is an immoral calling. The compass is swinging too fast, and many people long for the times when it was easy to see the difference between good and evil. There is plenty of data to fuel this uncertainty: From the recent flood of corporate bankruptcies and the pedophile scandals in the Catholic Church to the impeachment of President Bill Clinton, our most visible and important symbols of moral leadership have been shaken to their roots.

I can see you smiling over my analysis, for it always has been this way: Each generation looks back to the old days and sees higher "standards of moral behavior." But, I think this time it's different. I think we are witnessing a quantum leap, a revolution in the evolution of our society. What makes it so revolutionary? Two factors: 1) technology has largely freed us from worrying about daily survival and 2) the disintegration of rationality has led to a general reconsideration of our core values. For example, recent studies have shown that up to 25 percent of the American population has become disenchanted with a material-based value system—a staggering 500 percent increase from a similar study done in the 1960s.

This is a sea change, but you don't have to go to the library to experience it. As an aging baby boomer, I am astounded at the difference between the way I grew up and the way my kids are growing up. We seem to have one thing in common: a middle class upbringing. Beyond that, everything else appears different. When I try to tell my kids how it used to be, they shake their heads as if I am spinning fairy tales. They can't imagine the world without the Internet or without videotapes or without school lockdowns, or with entire blocks where every family was intact or a playground where kids played without parents watching anxiously for child snatchers. This afternoon, my son can get online and locate pornography that has images beyond the furthest frontiers of my adolescent fantasies. Or, he can watch the beheading of an American in Iraq.

The unrational leader can't bury his head in the sand and pretend that we can go back to the world of *Leave It to Beaver*. And, he can't strike a blasé pose and say that everything will work itself out in the end because things always do, don't they? There is no standing still anymore (unless you have been seduced by the Colossus of Rationality). Everything is changing and the unrational leader must develop a strategy for leading himself and his people through this revolution. The strategy begins with the first principle of Unrational

Leadership™. People want leaders who will take **personal responsibility** for their decisions. Recently, at an Unrational Leadership™ workshop, I asked a group of clients why they had joined their firm. One of the managers said that the old president had impressed him at the interview when he said: "We back up our work. We take on our mistakes. We admit them and we fix them." This moral approach inspired this manager to leave a promising position for an uncertain opportunity.

A Leader Must Act Decisively to Stop Immorality

It is said that Maat, the Egyptian Goddess of Justice, decided the afterlife fate of a soul by weighing the person's heart next to the feather of truth. If the heart was balanced with the lightness of the feather, the person was welcomed to join a banquet with deities and the deceased. If the heart was heavier than the feather, Ahemait, the Goddess of the Underworld, devoured the person. If an employee cheats on his timesheet, if a volunteer steals money from the ticket till, if a contracting officer extorts gifts from a vendor, the leader must confront the behavior. Needless to say, it is easier to talk about moral leadership than it is to practice it.

I will never forget my exit interview when I left the Army after five years. The executive officer asked me to explain my decision, and I gave him a stock answer about not seeing a long-term opportunity in the organization. I didn't want to tell him why I was really leaving. A year earlier, I had been promoted to lead a small logistics team on a weapon systems program. One of my guys ran a real estate business from the office. He had been doing it for years and had never been touched. Every day he sat at a desk across from mine and worked his network. He refused to do his real job and refused to travel. Despite warnings from my wiser friends to live with the situation, I shined up my idealistic sword and took him on. I followed the discipline process to a tee. But, the realtor threw me a curve. He went on sick leave and returned with a note from a psychiatrist alleging that I had created an overly stressful work environment. The bottom line: He returned to work and resumed selling houses, and I received a stern warning for failing to follow disciplinary process.

In the course of the exit interview, the executive officer asked me what I thought of the management in the organization. The question surprised me, as I was pretty far down the totem pole. I assumed that he had no idea of my conflict with the realtor. One of the morals of the Army was "don't move problems up the chain of command unless you are looking for trouble and work." I hemmed and hawed a response, not wanting to burn any bridges. He startled me by saying sadly in a "I hope you're listening" tone: "Too many managers in this organization have compromised themselves. They let their friends shirk their duty, they falsify their expense forms, and they lie about overtime. As you move forward in your career, remember that you can't lead an organization if you compromise its moral foundation."

Paradoxically, these words helped me feel better about my experience, as I realized that even though the realtor had beaten me, I had fought the right fight. The words also gave me a much deeper appreciation of the challenge of leadership. Sustaining a moral organization was no easy task, as I could hear in the executive officer's weary explanation and see in his resigned eyes.

Not too many years ago, a government organization hired me to train their maintenance department on gender diversity. One of the guys hated the program. He showed his disdain by reading work material during portions of the workshop and then, denounced the workshop as a huge waste of time. His boss called this behavior: "productive venting." But, it irritated me and it discouraged the men who actually wanted to learn something about diversity. In the third workshop, I called him out on his behavior in front of the group.

After the session, I sat in his boss's office writing a report, and the guy stormed into the office, enraged. (Only later did I learn that he was practiced at the art of explosion.) He towered and glowered over the desk, yelled at me at the top of his lungs and came within inches of hitting me. As an adult, I had imagined that my days of physical fright were over, but in that moment, my churning stomach and my shaking voice educated me quickly. I was truly afraid, and I didn't know how to respond. The secretary who sat outside the office thought the guy was going to kill me and she was on the phone with Security when he stomped away.

Angry, I filed a police report, contacted a lawyer, and warned my family about this man. I wrote an official letter of complaint to the chief of the organization, asking for some disciplinary action. I even walked away from the contract, determined to get a response to my complaint. His boss (my client), who was well aware of this man's character, told me with a sly smile that he wasn't afraid. Then, he stonewalled me and said that I had to convince **his boss** that I had a case. Then, I heard from that boss that nothing could be done. Why? I was only an outside vendor and I had no standing unless a government employee had experienced a similar outburst from this man.[2]

The Retreat of the Wise Leader Coupling is Creating a Moral Crisis

Recently, I read a story about a man who had been fired, after a long and successful run as the manager of a large city for lying on his job application about his education. On his application he claimed he had a college degree (which was a base requirement for the job). The lie had lain dormant for years, and when it surfaced the man dodged the issue until the media trapped him like a rat and forced a confession in front of the city's elected officials. A few months after his resignation, he granted an interview to a local newspaper (yes, the same one who helped crucify him) and said: "People can be disappointed in what I did, but nobody can judge me."

Nobody can judge him? Why? On the surface this man seems filled with arrogance, but if you look at his statement as a symbol (just as we look at dream images as symbols) a different meaning emerges. Nobody can judge him **because there is no one to judge**. In one sentence, this administrator underscored the symbolic consequence of the shift from the left-brain to the right-brain personality. The Wise Leader, the coupling of Solomon, Augustus, Queen Elizabeth I, Abraham Lincoln, and Harry Truman has retreated into the shadows and shaken our capacity to effectively judge self and others. The symbol of the wise judge is the missing ingredient in our modern morality, and the signs are easy to see. (See *the next page* for clues to weak moral leadership.)

Extremism is replacing wisdom in our culture. Religious fundamentalism is spreading like fire throughout Christian and Muslim societies, as people desperately search for absolute wisdom in the Wise Leader coupling in an increasing intuitive, relative world. Unfortunately, at the extremes, the Wise Leader turns into a tyrant, and the gods of the fundamentalists are scary indeed.

The father, one of the two pillars of the family and along with the mother, the primary psychological source of the Wise Leader for children, is disappearing from family life. According to a survey commissioned by the National Center for Fathering, approximately 70 percent of the U.S. population believes that the disappearing father is the most significant family problem facing America. Want corroboration? A 1997 Gallup Youth Survey found that 33 percent of American teens live away from their father, a figure that rises to 43 percent in urban areas. These figures represent a 400 percent increase since 1960.

Corporate executives are now rewarded for cutting headcount. Once upon a time, layoffs were a signal of a weak company. Now, Wall Street views reductions in force as a sign of good, proactive, necessary leadership. Leaders don't fight for their people; they fight to get rid of them. Is it any wonder that employees distrust their leaders? The phrase "cutting headcount" symbolizes the retreat of the Wise Leader from the corner office. The head of the personality and the Kingdom rests in the Wise Leader. When a leader is singularly focused on getting rid of people, he loses a vital connection with his staff and his moral compass.

To me, the most powerful evidence of the loss of connection with the Wise Leader coupling can be found in CEO compensation. In 1970, the average full-time worker earned about $32,000. In the same year, the average compensation among the top 100 CEOs was $1.25 million (according to data from Forbes magazine's annual survey). In 1999, the average worker's pay climbed to about $35,000 while the average compensation of the 100 top CEOs had increased more than 2,800 percent, to $37.5 million. In 2000, the average compensation of Business Week's top 20 CEOs averaged **$112.9 million**!

Seven Signs of Moral Weakness in an Organization
1. Does the boss refuse to stand behind his mistakes?
2. Has the boss hired incompetent friends or family and installed them in leadership positions?
3. Is the boss having a sexual affair with someone in the organization?
4. Does the boss launch leadership development programs and refuse to participate in them?
5. Does the boss still receive extraordinary bonuses in bad times?
6. Is the boss cheating the company?
7. Has the boss become disengaged from running and disciplining the organization (the Disappearing Parent Syndrome)?

Ethical Decision Making; The Secret to Moral Leadership

How do we coax the Wise Leader out of the shadows to confront selfishness and extremism? How do we remove the blinders from our leaders? When confronted with today's moral crisis, the rational leader reaches for such traditional fixes as: Establishing core values, measuring moral behavior, sending executives to seminars on ethics, installing "Ethics Officers" in the executive suite, and engaging consultants to perform moral audits. These fixes set a positive tone, but in general, they work around the edges of the problem, and some-times, they increase cynicism. For example, in 2004, Business Week reported that the Business Roundtable had initiated a new program to train executives in ethics. The **lead** for their story was: "**Don't laugh—plans are in the works**." (This cynical lead came from a business periodical, not the AFL-CIO newsletter.) Chaired by Henry A. McKinnell, CEO of Pfizer, the Business Roundtable program seeks to help leaders set and maintain the highest ethical standards. But the article reported that it wouldn't be an easy task. According to B. Espen Eckbo, founding director of the Center of Corporate Governance at Dartmouth College: "You can't teach ethics to a 55-year-old CEO with a big ego."

The secret to bringing the Wise Leader back into the light rests in learning how to make ethical decisions. Paradoxically, **moral strength** comes from learning how to choose between the good and good, not from choosing between the good and the bad. To the un-rational leader, an ethical decision **can** occur when two morals collide, like choosing between people and profits, or between individual glory and sharing credit with the team. If a leader runs away from difficult ethical decisions, sooner or later, he will lose the ability to see the difference between right and wrong because he loses the connection with his wise leader coupling. If the leader is willing and able to stand between a collision of values and arrive at a creative solution, he locates the roots of the ethical decision and finds the "essential quality" and "character" of himself. This confrontation brings courage and improves the moral vision of the leader. **It removes the blindfold**.

This positive resolution is depicted symbolically in the image of the Ethical Decision Device, where two morals hang in the balance. Obviously, the leader can't resolve a conflict between two rights by ignoring one of the rights and drawing a line in the sand. **The solution requires creative energy and it comes from tapping the unconscious**. Again and again, we see the vital role the irrational side of our personality plays in becoming a great leader.

The Bible provides a well-known example of ethical decision-making. Two women brought a conflict to Solomon, King of Israel and renowned throughout the ancient world for his wisdom. The women lived in the same house and had delivered babies at roughly the same time. Unfortunately, one of the babies died and both women claimed the remaining child. After hearing both sides of the story and seeing that neither woman would budge, Solomon commanded a servant to bring a sword, whereupon he announced that he would divide the baby in half and give each woman her portion. Upon hearing this decision, one woman begged Solomon to give the baby to the other woman so that it would live. Whereas the other woman said: "It shall be neither mine nor yours. Divide it." Solomon awarded the baby to the first woman, reasoning that the true mother would want her child to live, even if raised by another.

There are an infinite variety of moral collisions. The oncoming crashes often begin with the question of what comes first, my job or my loved ones? Do I take that plum job even though the travel will take me away from my children? Do I move to Chicago when I know my mother needs me to care for her? Do I fail to return that call from an old friend because I am too tired to call after another 14-hour day? Do I cancel that meeting with a troubled employee because I have to work on yet one more demand for a reformulation of the budget? Do I buy another company to satisfy Wall Street even though I know it will cause job loss and confusion for the employees I have pledged to protect and nurture?

What do we do when our morals collide like cars in a demolition derby? One of our first responses is to bargain with our moral codes as if we were children trying to get our bedtimes extended. We all know how this works! We say to ourselves (and I really do mean "we" for I am a world class petitioner at the feet of my dueling moral codes): "This is the last trip I will take for a while." . . . "I'll make it up to them on vacation." . . . "We will do a much better job on the next acquisition." . . . "I will start exercising after the holidays." . . . "I will give my employees an off-site at a great resort." . . . "I will go home early next week." . . . "I made the difference on this one!" These are the bonbons we serve to our inner self in order to still the tortuous voice that assaults us on the runway at O'Hare at 10 o'clock on a Friday night: *Why aren't you home with your family?* Bargaining gets exhausting, doesn't it?

My Professional Introduction to Ethical Decision Making

Until I left Comfortopia, I had a hard time recognizing moral collisions. I pretended that they didn't exist. I preferred black and white. If I did see the collision, I aligned myself with one side of the conflict and ignored the other side. This refusal to see the conflict produces a form of blindness and makes bad things happen. I am grateful to Pauline (my sponsor) for helping to remove some of the scales from my eyes. Not long after I met her, I hired her to present a workshop on Carl Jung to my staff. She read the following passage from Jung's autobiography, *Memories, Dreams, and Reflections:*

> But if a man faced with a conflict of duties undertakes to deal with them absolutely on his own responsibility, and before a judge who sits in judgment on him day and night, he may well find himself in an isolated position. There is now an authentic secret in his life which cannot be discussed—if only because he is involved in an endless inner trial in which he is his own counsel and ruthless examiner.

"As consultants, it's important to remember that the worst thing you can do is **ask** a client to share **his secret** with you," said Pauline.

"Pauline, you have to be kidding! You want us to stop listening to our clients. What are we supposed to do? Tell them not to share their secrets. We'd never get close to the truth of a situation," I replied.

"Are you telling me that you pull secrets out of your clients and use them?" she asked.

"No, it's not like that. We learn things about people and their conflicts. Then, we help leaders create solutions for the good of their organizations."

"And, nobody gets hurt?"

"Sometimes, but we do everything possible to minimize it."

"Charlie, don't you see the conflict of duties in your role? On one hand, the client has hired you to help his organization. On the other hand, his people tell you their secrets. What happens when the two conflict? What happens when someone tells you a dangerous secret? If you reveal the secret, the person who shared it will be hurt. If you don't reveal the secret, you may not succeed in helping the organization. This is the ethical dilemma of the consulting profession. I wouldn't want to be in your shoes."

"It is not as hard as you think. If we use good communication and feedback processes, nobody gets hurt too much."

"If you don't keep this conflict of duties front and center, your unconscious will do it for you. Whenever a person tells me that they want to help me, I walk the other way. And, if I feel bad enough about the person, I'll leave town. Seriously!"

Not long after the seminar with Pauline, a client hired me to interview his leadership team. He had purchased a company, but he lacked confidence in the executives he had inherited. He faced some serious personnel changes.

"I want to know if they will switch their loyalties," said my client.

While interviewing the team, I assured everyone that I would keep their comments confidential and that only major themes would be shared in a final report that everyone would see. My job was to identify important problems and then help the team solve them. I must confess that I have this ability to get people, even strangers, to trust me quickly with their secrets. (This skill is the dirty little secret of all good consultants.) One interviewee after another willingly volunteered their doubts, concerns and even suspicions about my client. After a few interviews, I began digging for the muck and began showing sympathy to the plight of my interviewees, which of course, made them divulge even more secrets. I jotted notes as fast as I could on my legal pad, and I still couldn't keep up.

At the end of the day (it was a Friday), I debriefed my client in his office and kept a poker face about what I had learned about how his people viewed him. He graciously offered me the use of his desk as I waited for my ride to the airport.

On Monday morning, I pulled out my papers to start writing the report. **I couldn't find the interview notes.** Where in the hell are those notes? I thought. I emptied my briefcase but to no avail. Then it hit me—I had left the notes on my client's desk in San Francisco. What if he looks through the notes and reads the crap everyone is saying about him? Oh my God!

No more than an hour later, my client called and informed me that his secretary had found the interview notes. He coldly assured me no one had read them and then he asked me, rather stiffly, what to do with them.

Did he look at the notes? Did his secretary look at the notes? I don't think so but the damage was done just the same. I had lost the confidence of my client and betrayed everyone I interviewed. When I told Pauline the story, she said that the important lesson was learning that I couldn't control my unconscious.

"But, why now?" I protested. "In all these years of interviewing I have never betrayed my client by leaving the interview notes. Maybe it was just a coincidence that it occurred after our workshop. I know I will never do it again."

"Charlie, you can ignore an ethical conflict, but your unconscious can't. Why do you think so many people get sick or have accidents when they cheat on their partners? Your unconscious has a will of its own and it will assert itself at the very moment you think you have everything under control. You can't wish away these problems. If you don't balance both sides, your unconscious will. You are not as **good** as you thought you were. Carry this **secret** with you and you will be less likely to betray your clients the next time."

Tapping Your Unconscious is Essential for Ethical Decision Making

Consulting your unconscious in the middle of a moral conflict is like conducting an experiment. The point of the consultation is to collect data. Carefully prepare by documenting the moral conflicts and your concerns about resolving them. Then ask: What do I want to learn? Like any experiment, you can never be sure of the outcome at the onset. This is especially true when tapping the unconscious. You don't know what will emerge or even how you will interpret the information. But, I guarantee you that the effort will always benefit you and will always shed a little light on the issue. Regardless of what you have been taught about your unconscious, it can support you. As in any good experiment, a little detachment will make it easier to see the results. Paradoxically, you should try to interpret the information rationally, even a little dispassionately.

Reading a description of the College of Augurs in Ancient Rome inspired me to create a process for tapping the unconscious that uses model airplanes. The College of Augurs consisted of a small group of men, appointed for life, who served the state as priests. Whenever Rome considered undertaking a great venture, such as declaring war or forming an alliance, the national leaders consulted the augurs who then consulted the birds. For centuries, the augurs had tracked and recorded the flight patterns of eagles that flew over the hills of Rome. They used this flight history to help them create an answer to the question of the moment. The augurs made simple reports of their readings: "The birds will allow it" or "Another day."

A few years ago, a client called me and said: "We are planning a crucial reorganization. Would you tell us what you think about it?" I met with the executive team and listened to their ideas. Since I didn't know very much about the people involved, I wouldn't comment on their personnel moves. I told them that their proposed organization structure looked sound. They wanted to know if they had considered all the risks and if it was the right time to go forward with such a momentous change. I asked them if they had consulted the irrational. Sensible engineers, they rolled their eyes and groaned, but since they knew me they were willing to experiment.

If you have ever experienced a reorganization, you know that the craziest things happen, most of them disguised under a thin blanket of rationality. During these times, leaders tend to run from meeting to meeting, brushing off concerns by saying: "Send me an e-mail and I'll try to mention it to the CEO at our next off-site." Reorganizations stimulate lots of moral conflicts, as people struggle to maintain their personal agenda (not to mention their jobs) in the face of a shifting and elastic organizational agenda.

Outside the client's staid offices, the Michigan autumn sky sparkled. I had asked them to bring paper, pen, and open minds. Under a tree next to their parking lot, I pulled seven gliders from a Project Innovations bag and said: "I have seven planes and I am going to throw each one into the air. Watch each flight and then ask yourself: 'What does this flight tell me about our decision to reorganize?' Then, document the answer. Each time you ask this question, your unconscious will respond with something. Try to capture it, no matter how weird it seems."

My first throw didn't go too well—the plane crashed onto the pavement. The guys joked about people watching them from the windows. "Now, they will think we have really lost our minds!" After each flight, I allowed them a few minutes to record their thoughts, images, and feelings. A couple of the flights had curly cues and daredevil dives with gentle landings. The guys chuckled, nodded knowingly, and wrote furiously, trying to capture as much energy as possible from their unconscious. The whole exercise took about thirty minutes. When we returned to the conference room, I drew a large circle on the white board and divided it in half. I reserved the top half of the circle for rational conclusions and the bottom half for irrational data that emerged during the flights.

"If you can acknowledge the unconscious has an impact on your plans, you can increase your chances of success. Tell me what ideas came to your mind as you watched the flights and let's see what they say about your reorganization."

I recorded their comments in the lower half of the circle, fascinated by their input. The crashing flights stimulated fears about failure; the soaring flights led to thoughts of challenge and glory and some flights led to thoughts from nowhere. Those were the ones I wanted the most. One of the guys said mysteriously: "Tom. His name came to mind during the flight and stuck there."

We began to discuss Tom and they all agreed (to their surprise) that his reaction to the reorganization would have a huge impact on its success. Tom was the manager of a critical department, and **they hadn't told him about their plans.** Obviously, the experiment raised into consciousness the need to involve Tom. This is how the unconscious helps you—not with a hammer, but with a name: "Tom." Once you have the name, it's your job to make meaning of the data. The thought of involving Tom energized the team, and they started to identify other managers that needed to be involved in the reorganization. This is another example of the power of the unconscious. It contains an infinite number of catalysts. At the end of the conversation one of the engineers summed up the experiment: "Two flights crashed, four landed safely, and one was hard to figure out. I think this reorganization is going to work."

Consulting the *I Ching*

Although I have strived to show how Unrational Leadership™ applies to organizational leadership, most people come to understand it through their personal lives. If they learn about personality types, they share the news with their families. If they incubate a dream, they discuss it with their wives or husbands. If they discover that they have fallen into the Swamps of Maturity, they turn to their families for help. People start their searches for Unrational Leadership™ at home because it is much easier for them to find their inner voice at home and because exploring their unconscious at work is rarely supported. (See Chapter Five, The Little Sea of the Voice that Defies Reason.)

A few years ago, an old friend asked me to lunch and began to talk about her marriage. It had been falling apart for a couple of years. "Divorce has always been unthinkable," she said. "It happens to other people. I never imagined it could happen to me."

"You are about to wander into a collision that you have never experienced before," I replied. "Just when you think you've found a path out of the danger, you will get hit again. When you think that it can't get any worse, it will. And just when your heart is five beats from stopping, your life will improve and improve until you become happy again. I know because I have been there."

For months, my friend couldn't think of anything but the ghastly question: Should I get a divorce? She conducted continuous debates. "Divorce is wrong." "You promised till death do us part." "The kids will never be the same." "Your mom wouldn't walk away." These voices hit her hard. But, the voices from the other side of the debate were no less insistent. "Life is not a dress rehearsal." "If you stay and suffer, what are you teaching the kids?" "You deserve a chance to be happy." "If you don't leave soon, you will die, then where will your kids be?"

I recommended she ask the *I Ching* for guidance about a divorce. *The I Ching or Book of Changes,* is a collection of ancient Chinese wisdom, presented in 64 short advisory chapters, also known as oracles. The chapters have names like: "The Power of the Great," "Pushing Upward," and "The Marrying Maiden." The advice is astonishingly general and can be read a bit like a horoscope. Yet, like a good horoscope, it can cut to the quick of one's dilemma.

To use the *I Ching,* an oracle is selected. Two forces drive this selection: chance and the unconscious. Chance comes into play with six throws of a set of three coins. Each throw results in a numerical value—6, 7, 8, or 9,—which is then correlated to a symbol. Six symbols (one for each throw) create a hexagram. At its simplest, one asks for advice about a certain problem, throws the coins, computes the values, creates the hexagram, finds it in the *I Ching* and reads the associated chapter.

In the process of selecting an oracle, the unconscious force comes into play quite mysteriously, just as it does in every ethical decision-making experiment. Though I'm quite sure it is triggered by the petitioner's question, I don't know how to fully explain it. I have turned to the *I Ching* a few times—only when my morals hit me like mad truck drivers. Each time I turn to it and throw the coins, I open my unconscious to my conflict. When I work with the *I Ching*, I use three pennies that have significant dates for me: 1909 (the first year of the Lincoln-head penny), 1930 (my mother's birth year), and 1953 (my birth year). While throwing the coins, I place pictures of my grandfathers on the table and I look at these as I shake the coins and ask for guidance. I believe that my unconscious creates an energy field that connects with a different energy field embedded in the oracle. In working with the *I Ching*, I believe the unconscious works in the same way as it does when I ask for a dream. It can give me clues about the future if I am willing to ask for them. Notice I said "clues." Just as a dream does not tell us what to do, the oracle does not give us a playbook.

Sitting back in my conference room, my friend did not tell me the question she asked the *I Ching*, and I didn't want to know it. **It was and is her secret.** When she finished casting her coins, I determined the hexagram and located the corresponding oracle. It was "The Army" (Shih in Chinese). As I read it to her aloud, her eyes widened. She held her breath. In broad, symbolic strokes it mapped out her divorce campaign.

It described the requirements for war and outlined the conditions for victory, one of which was justice. It said: "If justice and perseverance are the basis of action, all goes well." We talked about justice—for her, her children and even her husband.

The *I Ching* lifted the just warrior into my friend's consciousness. Its image revealed the essential quality of the moral collision. If she decided to get a divorce, she could become an angry killer and create a wasteland. If she proceeded with it, she had to go forward with mercy and justice in order to minimize her whole family's suffering. Before she left, she swore that she would stand guard for the feelings and rights of her children and her husband, especially her husband. If you have been through a divorce, you know how difficult it is to keep the other person's welfare in mind. It is so easy to fall into rage. The *I Ching* helped her see how she could be a **merciful** warrior. As she declared war and prosecuted it, I watched her exact justice without destroying her husband. Oh, she had many opportunities, but each time she found some quality of mercy and stayed her sword.

The Power of Prayer

In the long run, the unrational leader turns from self and looks for God. This has been my experience. In the beginning of my journey, I struggled to find my inner voice. Then, I discovered the energy of my unconscious in my dreams. Finally, I learned how to pray during my journey through the Swamps of Maturity when I went through divorce. Like many people, I had been taught to pray as a child, but these prayers had no power for me as an adult. I came to God not as a child and not as an equal but as an angry and disappointed partner. I carefully crafted my prayers to minimize misunderstanding. I wanted God to know what I wanted specifically. For example, I pray that my children grow up to be **healthy grandparents**. This prayer gives me strength to stand in the middle of many fires.

A friend was once president of a mid-sized company. During his tenure, he had brought the company through a difficult merger and acquisition and had worked hard to establish a culture based on mutual respect and a commitment to excellence. He is the kind of guy that will drink beer with you and talk about a biography of Alexander Hamilton or the philosophy of Thomas Aquinas. In other words, he can live in the here and now and he can go deep. Like all unrational leaders (though he would probably deny the label), he knows how to balance opposite forces.

After several years at the helm, the company became infected. Something was going on there and my friend didn't know exactly what it was. Turnover increased. Old customers left. He lost some energy for his job. He began to question his role as the leader. Should he move on? Should he stay until he had groomed a successor? Was he still the right guy for the job? The questions bounced around in his head. The moral issues of self-interest vs. the good of the company collided. He could have stayed for as long as he wanted. The company had never been more profitable. He wasn't sure what would happen if he left. No Crown Prince stood in the shadows.

He told me that he found a refuge in his church. He said that he regularly sat in quiet devotion, contemplating the image and wonder of the Divine. He never shared what occurred during his prayer, and I didn't ask. Not long ago, he resigned as president. A group of earnest men and women remained, inspired by a leader who had walked away to give the company a chance to build a new fire. I think he left for himself, for his company, and for his God. It was as if he had left the future of the company in God's hands.

Unrational Leader at Work

You could write a case study on Kathy's job hunt with my firm. She covered all the bases in her pursuit—patience, follow-up calls and notes, initiative and courage. No matter how many times I shrugged her off, she came back with another reason for hiring her. During our first interview (it took her a couple of months to get it), we chatted about her experience, and I answered the usual questions about our firm. Then, near the end of our pleasant little chat, I surprised her.

"Could you betray someone?"

"What did you ask me?" she stuttered.

"As a consultant will you be able to practice the art of betrayal?"

She must have been thinking: Everyone knows that betrayal is bad. Maybe he wants me to answer differently. Maybe he expects me to say: "Yes, as a matter of fact, I could betray someone for you." Could I say that?

"Of course, I couldn't betray anybody," Kathy said sternly. "It goes against my values." If she would've squeezed her legs and straightened her dress, it wouldn't have surprised me. Then, her prim and proper expression changed. Everything that was clear turned to mud. The towers of predictability and political correctness crumbled. Morals collided. Doubts flashed across her face.

"Thanks for responding to such a difficult question. I'll bet it's the first time you have heard that one."

"Yes, it certainly is," she replied with some relief. I wrapped up the interview and told her to keep in touch. As she left, I crossed her off my list of eligible employees. Betrayal may be immoral, but it certainly can be ethical, and it is always possible in consulting, as the following story will show.

Patty was on the executive team. During my engagement with her organization, we became good friends. She thought I was brilliant; I thought she was filled with vision. For her, I breached my personal wall between client and family, and invited her home for dinner. But, the rain always follows the sun. Her behavior became erratic as the project became more difficult. She fought with the other executive team members. I waded into the middle of conflict after conflict for her, counseling her repeatedly about the negative impact of her behavior.

As the consultant, the other employees looked to me for objectivity, but after several rescues, they began to doubt me. The worst thing was no one—not even the vice president (her boss)—wanted to pull the trigger.

I stood in the middle of this collision and flinched at the thought of betraying her. When I see a danger to the organization (and my friend had become a major liability), my duty as a consultant requires me to act decisively and protect my client. On the other hand, I befriended her. She trusted me. Didn't I owe her one last warning? I fought with these morals until I watched her blow up in yet one more meeting. That afternoon, after deciding against a warning, I called the vice president and told him that he needed to fire her. The dam broke, and within the week, she was gone.

I talked to Pauline after the blood had been mopped up. "While you made your decision, were you conscious of your betrayal?" she asked.

"Yes."

"Did you maintain a feeling of compassion for her or did you blame her and assume that it was her fault," Pauline asked, digging deeper.

"More of the former than the latter," I confessed. "I went into the decision *conscious* of my role as a betrayer. I saw the collision, I stepped into the middle, and I held the suffering until a decision emerged."

"If you think about your contract with the client, did you make the right decision for their organization?"

"Definitely," I replied. "They are most relieved, and it is easier for them to look into the future."

"To survive this new age, we all need to take a little evil onto ourselves," concluded Pauline.

Could you betray someone consciously? That is the question, and you might be surprised to learn that Kathy called me from her cell phone about ten minutes after she left the interview. "I have been thinking about your betrayal question," she said. "I can see that there would be some cases where I might have to betray someone to protect my client. But, I sure hope that I don't have to do it very often at Project Innovations." Not long thereafter, I hired her.

Notes

1. United States, Russia, China, Great Britain, France, India, Pakistan, Israel, and North Korea.
2. This story had a mixed ending. Several employees stepped forward and reported similar abuse situations. The bully was forced to apologize and to attend anger management classes. Then a few years later, I heard that he had resumed abusing his team members.

Important Concepts for the Unrational Leader

- Morals and ethics are not the same.
- Our moral compass has shifted.
- A leader must act decisively to stop immorality.
- The retreat of the Wise Leader coupling is creating a moral crisis.
- Ethical Decision Making is the secret of moral leadership.
- Tapping your unconscious is essential for ethical decision making.

14 The Treasure of Unrational Leadership™

" **I** called a hero and one has arrived. Blessed be."

Brigid's voice teased TrueHeart as he stepped through the magical door into the King's private courtyard. Robed in black as always, Brigid lounged against an ancient oak tree. This was the King Tree, planted long before Covey arrived with his habits; the same tree that TrueHeart's father had painted in his tower at Snow White's manor.

"What are you doing here?" asked a startled TrueHeart. "Don't you have some shadows to tend to?"

"Ah, TrueHeart. I came to help you, but your face is dark. Are you still angry with me? Come. Was my advice worth 300 crowns?"

"I survived."

"Ah. Don't worry. The rain always follows the sun!" She cackled and the wrinkles fell off her face.

"If you want to charge me another fee, be forewarned: I have no gold."

"TrueHeart, do you still want to break the spell?" she asked suddenly.

"There is only one candle that still burns. I came for the Princess."

"Meet me here tonight when the moon is high. I will show you the way to awaken her."

The Challenge is Drawn[1]

The moon ruled full from its throne in the black sky. The wind howled and the cold air chilled TrueHeart's bones. Again, he found Brigid relaxing against the King Tree. Damn these magicians, TrueHeart thought. They always look like they have swallowed the cat.

"Good evening, TrueHeart."

"And what is good about yet another gloomy night?" TrueHeart inquired. "Does your kind ever work in the sun? Great God, save me from your bleak bones!"

"Quickly, for we have little time," insisted Brigid. "This magic requires the hero to surmount three challenges. He has to find the Crown Prince, the Prince and Moira. If the hero overcomes these challenges, the Royal Family and the Princess will be roused tonight." She looked at TrueHeart keenly.

"Moira lives?"

"After you left the battlefield, the spell worked its will upon her. Only you escaped the sleep."

"How so? I thought witches were immune from their own spells."

"No one is immune from the shadow. Have you not learned that yet?" declared Brigid, waving away the discussion. "Hear me well, TrueHeart. If your heroism fails, your pretty Princess and the rest of this Kingdom will sleep forever."

"If you are trying to inspire me, it's not working."

"Hush. Here is your first challenge: Within the hour, you must bring me the body of the King's youngest son, the Prince."

"Is there no other path to the Princess?" TrueHeart asked.

Brigid responded by handing TrueHeart a torch and told him to look for the Prince in the castle dungeon. Glumly, TrueHeart took the torch, made his way to the dungeons and descended into an eerie choir of ghosts—victims of the Ninth Habit. He took courage from the torch; the deeper he fell, the brighter it burned. In the last cell he found the Prince's corpse looking not a minute older from the day he had charged on to the field against Moira's black warriors.

What dark magic, thought TrueHeart, as he picked up the body and began the long, heavy climb back to the courtyard.

"Put me down, foolish Knight," screeched the Prince. True-Heart started and dropped the body with a thud. He immediately saw that a ghost occupied the body. With more than a little trepidation, he cradled the dead body again. "If you must carry me, Young Knight, then I must tell you a story to lighten your journey.

The Tale of the Captain Who Drank Too Much

Once upon a time, a young captain and his loyal sergeant walked home from the wars. On the way, they entered an unhappy port. They went straightaway to a tavern by the sea, where they met the beautiful daughter of the innkeeper. The girl merrily served them food and drink. The young captain, in search of a wife, fell instantly in love with her, and his sergeant, long married with many children, willingly played the matchmaker. While the moonless night was young, the captain declared his love to the beautiful maiden, who had often dreamt of rescue from the clutches of the suffocating village and her father.

"Visit my room tonight and I will prove my love to you," whispered the maiden. "My father is very jealous and watches me like a hawk. Provide this secret knock to my door."

She rapped a code on the table and proceeded up the stairs to her chambers. Overwhelmed by his good fortune, the luckless captain drank too much, whereupon the loyal sergeant carried him to his quarters. Soon thereafter, having heard the secret code, the sergeant easily gained entry to the girl's bed, and he made passionate love to her through the pitch-black night.

The next morning, the maiden discovered her error when the sergeant brazenly winked at her and rapped the secret code on the tabletop. The enraged girl plotted to have him arrested. She stole five gold pieces from her family's strongbox and prepared to transfer it to the sergeant's room in order to accuse him of robbery. But the sergeant, cleverly foreseeing this possibility, alerted the girl's father, and they were hiding in the closet when the girl entered with the gold.

Beside himself with anger at his daughter, the father paced back and forth in the little tavern. The girl's mother pleaded and begged for him to stay his anger. But her words were useless. He banished the girl far beyond the outskirts of the desolate village, leaving her to fend for herself among the prowling marauders and wild animals. In the meantime, the sergeant roused the drowsy captain and told him where he could find the girl.

"When you rescue her, she will cry and shout any number of lies in order to return to her mother," the sergeant said. "Ignore them all, and on the pain of your own death, ride home and marry the wench." The good captain followed the sergeant's instructions to the letter, even as the girl screamed and cried that the sergeant had despoiled her. Back at the village, everyone gave up the girl for dead and the mother soon died from heartbreak.

"Answer quickly Young Knight, or all your plans to love my sister will end in this rat-infested dungeon," said the ghost. "Who is responsible for the mother's death?"

TrueHeart's mind whirled for the right solution to the conflict. He longed to lay down the heavy corpse and think. But he knew he had no time to spare. He shut his eyes and strained for a vision of the Princess. The answer came unexpectedly from his inner voice.

"The girl and the captain can be excused for they acted out of natural urges and love," said TrueHeart. "Of course, we can't blame the mother for her own death; she begged her husband to spare the daughter. As for the sergeant, he is partly guilty for he had no business going to the girl's bedroom. But, overall, the primary guilt rests with the father. He refused to examine the girl's reasons for taking the gold, refused to listen to his wife and refused to wrestle with his own anger."

With a flash of light, TrueHeart found himself in the courtyard. Nearby, the Prince's body rested peacefully. The ghost had been banished. Brigid sat against the King Tree smoking a briar pipe.

"Are you ready for your next challenge?"

The Tale of the Crossroads

With a new torch, TrueHeart begrudgingly picked his way through the sleeping bodies in the corridors leading to the

Great Hall, where he would find the Crown Prince. Only a vision of the Princess kept him going on his gruesome mission. Most suitably, he found his prize slumped across his father's throne, looking not one day older than the day TrueHeart watched him charge Moira's Knights. After carrying the body for a hundred paces, it twitched and threw itself to the floor. To TrueHeart's dismay, it started to talk.

Ah, my old friend the Young Knight! Perhaps you have heard the tale of the Heavenly Crossroads? Once upon a time, the son of the mayor of a small Protestant village fell in love with a Catholic girl from a nearby town. Their love swiftly conquered their moral fiber, and new life soon appeared in the girl's belly. She married and moved from the town to the village, where her husband forced her to convert to Protestantism—an act that she resented greatly for she believed it doomed her soul. After her son was born, she secretly took him to her Catholic priest for baptizing. Meanwhile, after some years, her husband became the mayor of the little village and made sure that his son was duly confirmed into the Protestant faith at the age of 12.

When the boy was 13, his father launched a pogrom against the Jews who lived on the outskirts of the village. The mother, who had a nightmare of bad tidings, contrived an illness for the boy on the scheduled night of the slaughter and revealed her secret to her son: "You are really a Catholic." When the father and the good villagers set fire to the synagogue, the roof suddenly collapsed and killed them all.

The surviving villagers responded by murdering every Jew in sight, except for one woman who managed to escape to the mayor's home where she begged the widow for mercy. Relieved that her husband perished, the widow hid the Jewish woman and cared for her.

Shortly thereafter, the villagers, who had always distrusted the Catholic wife from the town, contrived a fatal accident for her on the footbridge over the nearby river. Fearing for the boy's safety, the Jewish woman took him and fled to a faraway city, settled in the ghetto, opened a bakery and raised the boy as her own. Several years later, she became mortally ill. She begged the boy, now a young man, to convert to Judaism. Not wanting to disappoint his benefactress, he studied with the rabbi and converted.

On her deathbed, the woman told him of a secret treasure that was buried on the outskirts of the Protestant village. After the woman's funeral, the young man returned to his village, and as instructed, joyfully unearthed a great treasure.

Now rich, he decided to travel. Near the end of his journey, which took him to the three corners of the world, he entered a Kingdom beset with a terrible dragon. The King had promised his beautiful daughter to the man who killed the beast. Although many men had already failed, our hero took on the challenge and outwitted the dragon to win the hand of the ravishing Princess. The girl's father insisted on one small favor before the wedding. He asked our hero to convert to Islam, to ensure that his grandchildren would join him in Heaven when they died.

Desperately in love, our hero readily agreed to adopt yet another religion. A month after the wedding, the King asked the man to lead a fleet to attack his Christian enemies to the north. During the voyage, a great storm destroyed the fleet and all its sailors, including our hero. On the way to Heaven, he found himself at the crossroads.

This day, Satan himself guarded the intersection and said: "Young man, you stand in the middle of a crossroads with one direction each for your four religions. Only one road leads to Heaven. The others take you to Hell and my everlasting fires. Choose quickly and correctly, before I strike you five fathoms deep into the furnace of Hell."

"TrueHeart, which direction takes our hero to Heaven?" asked the Crown Prince. "Answer quick and true or you will find your own soul burning in Hell." TrueHeart's mind contracted into a noose. How could he decide? His soul spoke for him.

"When the man obeyed the woman's wish and converted to Judaism, he rescinded his Protestant faith. He nullified his Jewish beliefs when he became a Muslim. Even Satan knows that the Jews don't believe in Hell. He chose Islam because he wanted the girl. But, did his faith outlast his honeymoon? Only his mother gave him the energy required to sustain a true faith. She betrayed her husband to have the boy secretly baptized, kept him away from the pogrom and saved the Jewish woman. Therefore, he carries his mother's faith. He is a Catholic."

There was an explosion of light, and when TrueHeart opened his eyes he stood next to the King Tree. The Crown Prince's body was next to his brother, the Prince.

The Donkey's Tale

Brigid reminded TrueHeart that he had to enter the Dark Forest near the castle to find Moira. A torch lit a dim path between trees that stood like sentinels in the shadows. Within minutes, even with the light of a full moon, he was lost. Then, he heard a strange sound. He stopped and listened to the woods speak. Again, the sound.

"For whom do you search?" It was the snake! TrueHeart bent the torch to the earth and saw it.

"The answer is the same as the first time we met. I seek Moira."

"And, what has been given since that fateful day?" asked the Snake.

"Love and suffering."

"Those twins still rule the race of men. Yet, I suspect some greater power carries you into this bewitched forest. Come. I will take you to the woman you seek."

Following the sounds of the slithering snake, a light in the

woods soon appeared. He hurried and stumbled into a clearing. In purple, Moira lay on a bed of green leaves, surrounded by watchful flames. He almost gasped. As a youth he had not recognized her ripe beauty. Now, it reached for the most private places in his heart. Ever so gently, he raised her into his arms and slowly picked his way through the trees. With the walls of the castle looming ahead, Moira opened her eyes and spoke.

"TrueHeart, you must solve one more puzzle to awaken your Princess." Her voice aroused dead memories of the day he had saved her dog in the rushing river on the way to Snow White's manor. A lifetime ago, he thought. He refused to look at her as she clasped her hands around his neck.

One day a farmer's donkey fell down a well. The animal cried piteously for hours. The farmer and his friends couldn't figure out how to rescue it. Although the donkey and the farmer had been partners through many seasons of famine and plenty, the farmer decided the animal's time to die had arrived. Besides, the well needed to be covered, as it wasn't producing much water.

The farmer gathered some friends, opened a jug of whiskey for them and provided them with shovels. They began throwing dirt into the well. The poor donkey realized what was happening and cried horribly. The men easily pushed the sounds of the animal away from their ears. They drank heartily and forgot about the donkey as they told jokes and teased each other.

Late in the afternoon, the farmer looked down the well and was astonished at what he saw. Each time the dirt hit the donkey's back, the animal shook off the dirt and stepped on it. The farmer got excited and encouraged his friends to shovel harder. With each load of dirt, the donkey climbed higher and higher. Soon, everyone cheered as the donkey stepped over the edge of the well.

"Look friends! Our hard work has saved my donkey!" exclaimed the farmer.

"Farmers are the most stupid people in the world!" answered the donkey and to the amazement of all, the animal turned around and kicked the farmer. Then, it grabbed the jug of whiskey in its teeth and ran off into the woods.

Moira laughed and then said to TrueHeart, "What is the moral of this tale? Answer quickly or you may fall asleep for eternity."

"When you try to cover your ass, it always comes back to get you!" said TrueHeart.

As with the Prince and Crown Prince, there was a burst of light, and TrueHeart was transported back to the King's private courtyard.

TrueHeart's Judgment

When TrueHeart opened his eyes, the scene startled him. Instead of Brigid, he found an old man in a black robe. Crowned in a magician's hat, the old man stood against the King Tree.

"Welcome, Young Knight," said the old man. "Thank you for doing the hero's job."

"Rich in Wisdom?" The old man moved into the center of a smoky circle of torches.

"One and the same." It was the ancient court magician, Rich in Wisdom. On the south, west and east points of the circle of fire, TrueHeart saw the King, the Prince and the Crown Prince respectively. Some dark magic forced them to stand guard for the magician. In the center of the circle, behind Rich in Wisdom, sat four mute women on thrones: the Queen, the Princess, Brigid, and Moira. TrueHeart looked deeply at the Princess, but there was no time for any feeling.

"As you can see, Young Knight, my magic is much stronger than the magic of your feeble teacher from the Dark Forest. I have waited many years for your return. Now, the final spell can be spun. Come into this center," commanded Rich in Wisdom.

"I will stay on this northern point," said TrueHeart, surprising himself with his firmness.

"**You will enter this unholy circle.** Your dark destiny is to complete mine," said Rich in Wisdom, pounding a staff with a snake curling around it. "Your future and mine are one."

"I cannot join your black spell until your wisdom is proved," replied TrueHeart.

"What say you, little man?" demanded Rich in Wisdom.

"I have three simple questions," replied TrueHeart. "A man of your great wisdom will answer them with ease. Satisfy me with these small favors and I will help you gain this unholy power that you seek."

"Be quick," snapped the old man.

"Can two wrongs make a right?"

"Humph!" The magician stabbed the ground with his staff. The snake's eyes glittered at TrueHeart. "In all wrongs, some right exists, no matter how small, just as in all cold, some heat exists. Therefore, two wrongs will always yield some right."

"A clever response," replied TrueHeart. "Here is my second question. Did George W. Bush steal the 2000 Presidential Election from Al Gore?"

At that moment, a sharp wind blew into the courtyard, raising even more smoke to swirl between the two men.

"In May 2001, *USA Today* reported that George W. Bush carried Florida by 537 votes. Bush won fairly."

"Your wisdom is most impressive and in a few short minutes, my heart will be yours," replied TrueHeart. "You will have three chances on your final question, but I am sure you will not need them. Tell me this—how did God get to be God?"

"He was the Son of an even greater God," said Rich in Wisdom without thinking. TrueHeart could see that the question had jolted him.

"No."

"As the all-knowing, He of course created Himself from the all-nothing," the magician said a little more thoughtfully.

Again, TrueHeart shook his head. "No."

Rich in Wisdom left the center of the circle and began pacing its circumference. Patiently, TrueHeart watched him walk with increasing agitation until the light broke through his eyes. He stopped next to TrueHeart and glared. The Crown Prince, Prince and the King all began to howl piteously. The women found their tongues and wailed. TrueHeart trembled at the chorus but the fear did not overcome him. He stood his ground.

"After the Queen sent your father to his death, I begged the King to kill you," said Rich in Wisdom. "He refused out of loyalty to your father's memory. I saw your black heart even when you were a babe. Indeed, it's blacker than mine. Your question is a trick. **God is dead**. He died on December 8, 1980 in Manhattan, when Mark Chapman assassinated John Lennon in front of the Dakota Apartments." The howling and wailing increased to a roar.

"You are wrong on three counts," TrueHeart replied solemnly. "First, my father died in my arms. Second, God is alive. He is here, bidden or not. And third, as even the smallest child knows, **the first person to die became God**."

Upon the final mention of God, the Heavens opened and Rich in Wisdom flew out of the circle and this world. Lights exploded, and then, darkness fell.

Note

1. These fairy tales were inspired by, "The King and the Corpse," an ancient Indian tale, retold by Heinrich R. Zimmer in the book: *The King and the Corpse.*

15 The Sea of the Great Heroes

The Sea of the Great Heroes has a placid surface, but its depths are filled with doubt. As you sail from Unrational Island, laden with treasure, on the distant horizon off the port side, you can see the shoreline of Decision Island. The island presents you with a choice: You can sail back to Comfortopia and make a triumphant return or drift into Selfish Bay, where you can rest for a day or an eternity in Solo Town. It may seem astonishing for our hero, after all he or she has endured, to choose an option dedicated to him or herself, but it happens. In fact, it happens a lot. Do you know someone who made a killing on the stock market and took a few years off to satisfy his or her wanderlust? Or maybe you have friends who plan to sail around the world when their last child graduates from college.

In this chapter you will meet six great heroes. Each one of these heroes has answered a call to action, sailed into the unknown of their own hidden depths, discovered a treasure, brought it back to Comfortopia and shared it. Heroes are role models. Heroes are admired for their qualities and achievements, and I have learned much from these six heroes. The best thing I have learned from them is courage. I hope that they inspire you as much as they have inspired me.

I Was Great at Being a Guy

At the top of her resume, Kimberly (Kim) Lehrman of Cedar Rapids, Iowa, describes herself as a "strategic, passionate leader with a talent in creative business planning, market development and execution of profitable, sustainable models." I would describe her as Superwoman. She is the mother of three children and devoted wife to her husband, Bruce. Kim is one of those people you meet and say: "Whoa. This lady is smart." If you are lucky enough to have dinner with her and her family, you will say: "This is a person who knows the true definition of balance." Kim graduated Magna Cum Laude from the University of Iowa and has over 20 years of marketing and sales experience, including 15 years in P&L management. With her husband, she started and sold a successful company and has moved through the infamous glass ceiling with grace, smarts, and results.

I met Kim in Cedar Rapids in 1999, just before she sold her company to an Iowa-based client. Shortly thereafter she was selected to participate in one of the first renditions of Unrational Leadership™. I caught up with her recently and she talked about her participation in the program and the long-range impacts.

How did this heroic journey begin?

My husband, Bruce, and I sold our cozy little technology company to a telecommunications company on an acquisition spree. It seemed like the right thing to do, but we had to work for the buying company to make the deal pay off financially. We had our fortunes at stake. But, I had a lot of trouble adapting to a big organization. It seemed to sit on me and blocked my energy. I couldn't get anything done and the politics turned me off. I struggled mightily with the question of whether or not I wanted to stay in the business world.

Then out of nowhere one of my colleagues threw me a life jacket called "LeaderEase." (Note: LeaderEase was the predecessor program of Unrational Leadership™.) The program was such an unexpected relief in the middle of the huge bureaucratic ocean that Bruce and I had fallen into. The aim of the program was to turn us inward, which was strange in this fast-paced extroverted company that only cared about results.

I am truly grateful to the leaders of the company for funding LeaderEase. It became a turning point in my life. It taught me that my angst about my career was coming from my transition into the second half of life.

IIow did you know that you had entered the second half of life?

I knew that something was changing inside of me. I had sold my company. Suddenly, I became uncomfortable in a culture where success and achievement were the most important values. I lost my desire to be a high-powered businesswoman. I looked for this desire in the usual places, but I couldn't find it! I had been the VP of Marketing and Sales for too long in too many companies. I wanted to get a different balance and the corporate success route was not doing it for me.

I had myself all wrapped up into this internal conflict so I went to a shrink. He said: "Here's your medication. Go and have a happy life." That didn't do it for me, so I started reading on my own about balancing life and finding meaning in places other than work. Then the LeaderEase program appeared, and I found myself on the map, flailing away in the Swamps of Maturity.

What happened on your journey?

I realized that I could stay in business and stay connected to my true self. Like most businesswomen I know, I had sacrificed my true self in order to become an alpha woman. In the LeaderEase journey, even though it wasn't specifically about gender, I learned to listen to a deeper feminine voice and to differentiate between my feminine and masculine voices. At first, I had trouble tuning into my deeper voice. I was great at being a guy! When I did listen, it told me: "Take care of your self so you can give back." It took me a while to understand this concept. I had been trained to see people as things. I had been handsomely compensated to arrange these things and give them instructions. And it didn't matter if the things were male or female.

I went from seeing people as bundles of resources to seeing people on their own journeys. I started to see work as a piece of my journey. I stopped defining myself by my job title and my parking spot. Suddenly, the word "holistically" meant something to me.

Did you have to use the Mysterious Shadow Energy Converter?

(Laughter). I had to stick two shadows in your converter. One is my secret desire to control everything. Everything has to be my way. The other shadow is taking other people's energy and not giving it back. I hold it for myself and put it under the bed. This is symbolic, of course. But it shows up in my dreams. Slovenliness is an example. I have all these dreams where I am living in this house that is a complete disaster. I don't throw anything away. In these dreams, I never graduated from college. I live in total chaos. That dark side energy is hidden in my psyche and I am still working with it—years after I finished the program.

How do I wrestle with my shadow? I write in my journal constantly. When my shadow comes out I try to say: "Why are you coming out?" Sometimes it is enough to acknowledge it is **there**. But, I don't want to mislead you. I don't have a three-step plan for eliminating the shadow. That's the other thing that I thought was really interesting. Once you start the inner journey, it just never ends. Making it happen takes energy. Sometimes you just have to say to your unconscious: "I can't do it right now. Give me a break."

Did the changes stick?

Oh yeah. The company that I'm with right now had 60 years of matriarchal tradition. A male friend of mine bought the company, and I helped him understand how the masculine and the feminine energy coming together would make the company much stronger. It was a struggle. Not everyone saw that change as symbolically or consciously as I did!

Just the other day I did a PowerPoint presentation where I had inserted a lot of symbols, including two red paper clips. The president of the company sent me an email telling me that I had to take the paper clips out because they look too much like a uterus! Something that really energizes me now is the feminine energy. I am seeing mothers everywhere. I spent so much of my life being applauded for male things. In this stage of my life, I truly need to balance that outer masculine voice with my inner feminine self.

I do a lot of storytelling. I love the concept of symbols, of finding images that tap our unconscious. We're a small company that competes with a huge greeting card company. One of our sales managers was telling the story of fighting valiantly for a sale. I had an inspiration to link our value proposition to the biblical story of David and Goliath. This helped everyone see that our journey is bigger than any single sale and that we can embed this energizing symbol of the underdog into our sales process.

I am not willing to change my life for money. If I have issues with people in places of power, I don't have to sacrifice my self to further my career. Maybe they have something to learn from me just like I have something to learn from them. I won't trade off time for money like I used to. I have a bigger role to play in the community in general, a role far beyond giving somebody a job. I am much calmer and content with life!

Any words of wisdom for fellow travelers?

We don't take time to listen when we're motivated to produce, produce, produce. We are programmed and rewarded for being the center of attention. It's not possible for everyone to stand in the center of the room and receive all that dynamic and extroverted energy. Stop talking and listen. Please.

The Light Seems Brighter at the Finish

Russ Gronevelt is the President of Orchard, Hiltz and McCliment, Inc. (OHM), a civil engineering consulting firm headquartered in Livonia, Michigan. OHM employs over 185 engineers and technicians who help communities throughout Southeast Michigan build and maintain their roads, bridges, and communities. OHM's mission statement is: *We team with clients to provide infrastructure solutions.*

Russ earned his Master of Science degree in Civil Engineering from Wayne State University in 1982, and his Bachelor of Science degree in Civil Engineering from Michigan Technological University (Michigan Tech) in 1969. He is on the Board of Control for Michigan Tech. And he is active in the American Consulting Engineering Council, American Public Works Association, and American Society of Civil Engineers. Russ has been acknowledged as one of America's Top Ten Public Works Administrators and has been inducted into Michigan Tech's Academy of Civil and Environmental Engineers.

OHM and Project Innovations have experienced a long and fruitful partnership. Over 50 OHM team members have participated in Unrational Leadership™ programs since 2001. I talked with Russ about the impact of the programs on himself and his company.

What's your story in a nutshell?

I've been president of this engineering company for five years. Prior to that I worked in government for 29 years. Directly out of college, I worked as an engineer for a large suburban city outside of Detroit. After five years, Mayor Ed McNamara appointed me to the position of Director of Public Works and I did that for 13 years. When McNamara was elected as Wayne County Executive, he appointed me Assistant County Executive. I was responsible for the county's infrastructure and had a budget of hundreds of millions of dollars. I enjoyed it immensely.

What are you doing in these sunset years of your career?

I'm giving back! Governor Jennifer Granholm recently appointed me to the Board of Control at Michigan Tech in Houghton. It really energizes me to help my alma mater develop the next crop of engineers. I would not be where I am today without the basic training and educational experiences that I received from Michigan Tech.

In my role as president of OHM, I spend a lot of time working with young, eager engineers. I especially enjoy the ones who are devoted to helping the public sector. They know the technical stuff, but they want to learn about politics and relationships. I can tell you one thing—this next generation of engineers is more well-rounded than mine was. These young professionals take the time to hear our stories. They are not solely focused on the technical side of the business. They are energized by self-knowledge and how their personalities play into personal and professional relationships. They keep asking for more. I asked the OHM Board for money to continue individual coaching with this group after our second

Unrational Leadership™ program. The Board approved. In our industry this type of investment is nearly unheard of!

I like watching my son, Rhett. He works at OHM and the only thing that worries me is that he is so good it's scary. I once asked him how he dealt with failure and he said he couldn't think of anything that he's failed at. He excelled in school—Michigan Tech, of course. As a young kid, he built model cars with electric motors and raced them. Then, he built a computer to track the performance of the cars. At the age of 12, he competed with adults. Will he be able to deal with failure when he experiences it? I've tried to trip him up but he hasn't taken the bait.

What does Comfortopia mean to you?

At age fifty, I decided that I wanted to take my career to a different place and left government to accept a position with my current firm. I am a true "ST", a warrior/doer/hunter. I like controlling the world around me. It's in my nature. Even as a young manager, I wrestled for control. Comfortopia for me was being confident, sure of myself, knowing that I met everyone's expectations. OHM initially hired me to develop a new piece of business for the company and I accomplished it in 18 months. I hit an out-of-the-park home run. In that short period I developed a close working relationship with the company president and felt that I had a good handle on what the company needed. A little later, I was asked to assume the role of president after our president stepped down. That was when I jumped off the shores of Comfortopia! I had spent my whole career in government, and now I was taking on the leadership of an engineering company. It exhilarated me, and it stretched me.

Are you an unrational leader?

Sometimes. My leadership style has changed in recent years. I have learned more about myself and the other parts of my personality that I really didn't trust. I see that I must use my Wise Leader coupling as president. Now, I know the meaning of: "It's lonely at the top." It means that you have to make decisions that may not be popular, but are necessary. Loneliness is the price you have to pay for the privilege of leadership.

As I have become conscious of my inferior coupling, the Creative Facilitator, I have learned to let go of things and let people make their own mistakes. I have definitely learned more from failure than I have from success. I now understand that another individual's way of doing things is just fine. They don't have to do it my way anymore! I have let loose of my dominant coupling, and I am an engineer who is living to tell about it.

One Unrational Leadership™ exercise had a big impact on me. In one workshop, I picked up a photo and pretended that I was that person. I talked like that person and thought like that person. Then, I wrote a letter about the experience and I couldn't stop writing. In the process of reviewing the letter, I realized that I no longer felt like I had to please my father. What a strange and unexpected result. I guess that is the benefit of Unrational Leadership™—it opens your unconscious to help you.

I am much calmer than I used to be. I meditate every day. Every morning I sit silently for 10 to 15 minutes and try not to think about anything and listen to my breathing. If, in the course of a day, I feel internal stress, I'll look away and count three breathes to not let my emotions lead me and that has been very helpful. I tell my engineering buddies that I do this and they think I'm crazy.

And, I do pay attention to my dreams when the Creative Facilitator asks me to. Funny, you (Charlie) have been in my dreams. I go into airport bookstores and see an **audio** version of your book. (So Charlie, do I get royalties from the audio book sales?)

Have you made a triumphant return to Comfortopia?

When I became President, our revenues were about $11 million. Now, we run about $20 million and have been as high as $24 million. I'm proud of this growth and the role that I have had in making it happen. I love my life, my family, my home in the UP, my friends and Char—my wonderful wife. The light is brighter at the finish of my career, but honestly, I don't think of myself as a hero. I think of myself as a leader and maybe there are moments where a leader appears to be a hero because he did the right thing. I always figured that's what you're supposed to be doing. Now I am working on taking that knowledge of growing your personality to the next generation. At OHM, they will get the strong foundation they need to become phenomenal leaders.

What advice do you have for young leaders?

I think there are three keys to good leadership:

1. A personal friend and great leader gave me the best definition I have of a leader. He said: "Leadership is taking people where they want to go. So, the first key is to listen."
2. The second key is being decisive and having a good batting average at making decisions. The decisions that leaders make always have positive and negative elements. I have discovered that taking a moment of time, whenever possible, to listen to my own feelings about the decision, promotes better decisions.
3. The number three key is simple. Be honest and ethical in every thing you do. Without the respect of others, leaders fail in a free society.

Stranger in a Strange Land

Teresa Weed Newman (age 46) has a challenge. Her dominant personality coupling is the Creative Facilitator. Not only has she spent her career working with Committed Managers—the personality on the other side of the Clouds of the Unknown from hers—she has also been an engineering analyst, accountant, human resources manager and a process improvement specialist. In her journey to the left side of her mind, she has worked with and for companies like General Motors, Daimler-Chrysler, Detroit Edison, and Fujitsu. Entering the second half of life and looking for a change, Teresa joined Project Innovations three years ago as a human resources consultant.

Teresa and her husband Bill are the proud parents of four children. A mother to the core, she presents an unselfish role model to her children. She chairs her church board and the Women's Automotive Alliance Professional Development Committee. She is a graduate of the Walsh College School of Business Management and is on the path to a doctorate degree in Depth Psychology. True to her dominant coupling, she loves people and still finds time to entertain friends and family in a modest but lovely home. I talked to her about how Unrational Leadership™ had helped her accept her true self.

When did you realize that you were different?

I took a Myers Briggs Personality Type Indicator (MBTI) in my first week at Project Innovations. I found my type and I read it and I read it and I read it and I thought, my god, this explains so much! I thought: Here I am 43 years old and I am just figuring out how I am wired. It was just a huge lightening bolt. Now I am proud to say that I am an intuitive feeling type (Creative Facilitator) and my core strength revolves around working with people—not numbers. Can you believe I worked at General Motors as an engineering analyst for 10 years? In the years since I have graduated from college, I worked entirely through my inferior coupling. No wonder I was so frustrated.

What has changed for you?

Professionally, everything has changed. As you know, I went from exploring my own type to obtaining my certification as a MBTI practitioner. This was really a turning point for me. Once I understood how to manage my way through the Clouds of the Unknown, I learned how to help other people make the same trip. In less than two years, I found a vocation that must have been dormant in me since the day I was born—helping people and organizations grow. Nothing gives me more energy or a better feeling than making a difference in people's lives.

Another major change has occurred with my creativity. Prior to learning my type, I didn't think I could write. When I attended my first Unrational Leadership™ workshop, the facilitator encouraged me to keep a journal and practice stream-of-consciousness writing. Now, I know this is an ideal way to tap the unconscious, but three years ago, the process seemed weird. It lacked structure and purpose, but I kept at it and soon, amazing ideas and energy emerged. When I reread my journal, I realized that I had never been able to assimilate so much information so quickly. I saw where I had come from and where I wanted to go. For the first time, I was working out of my dominant coupling, the Creative Facilitator. My artistic side blossomed and I kept writing and writing. Today, I have published four articles, including two in the Association for Psychological Type Bulletin. This accomplishment has been one of my personal treasures.

How have you learned to thrive as a Creative Facilitator in a land dominated by Committed Managers?

It is definitely a constant search for balance. My husband runs a hi-tech consulting practice. In his group, he had an intuitive feeling type sales guy who built great relationships but was not able to disengage from these relationships and grow new clients. He couldn't get to the next level of success. The lesson is obvious. To be successful in this world, you've got to build relationships **and** deliver.

I still don't execute well. It's a struggle for me and not just on the work front. As an intuitive type, I don't fit well into the mainstream. My success depends on my ability to roll in this linear logical culture that says I'm not going to listen to you, I'm not going to take you seriously unless you can speak my language.

You (Charlie) probably don't know it, but the best thing you did for me at Project Innovations was to force me to learn rainmaking. In the process, I learned to disengage myself from suspects, to not get sucked into the relationship side instead of focusing on making the sale. As a Creative Facilitator, I am prone to giving away my energy to people because it feels good. And as this intuitive feeling energy has blossomed at my work, I have to make sure I don't overdo it and try to save people from themselves. What I had to learn, in order to stay in the company, was to walk away from a **suspect** and move on to a **real prospect**. This has put some structure in my work and has helped me to stay balanced.

When did you leave Comfortopia?

You know, I think we come and go from Comfortopia many times in our lives, but I still haven't forgotten my first meeting with you. As you may remember, I met you in July of 2001 in a bar in Royal Oak with my friend Linda. After listening to my story about starting a consulting business, you immediately threw dirt in my face. You said: "You mean you quit your job to go out and do something you don't even really like doing?" It was a slap on both cheeks! Then, I did not have the ego strength to take you on and besides, you seemed strange to me. But you piqued my interest and I went back to you and said; "You're right. I don't want to stay on this path. What can you do to help me?" You told me to write about the things I loved doing and the things that gave me energy. You suggested that I identify what I do well that drains my energy. Then, you gave me some Jungian stuff to read and some videos and I sucked it in like a sponge that hadn't had water in so long.

On September 10, 2001 you offered me a job and I hemmed and hawed. Then September 11 came and my husband Bill and I couldn't get back from Florida. We rented a car and during the long, sad and anxious drive in which every word seemed to have weight, Bill and I talked about your job offer. I said: "Charlie's job offer looks more attractive today than it did yesterday. The economy will tank and our nation will freeze." We went back and forth. I had managed to sell a couple of clients and had half a mind to give my business a try, but then I said to Bill: "My whole life I've had great ideas for business and three or four years later, they are mainstream. I think Charlie's onto something. My gut says jump!" So, on 9/11, like so many Americans, I too left Comfortopia.

The Long and Winding Road

Once upon a time, there was a mighty city named Flint. A Michigan town, 80 miles north of the Motor City, it beat the Great Depression with strong factories and helped our soldiers win World War II. Flint was home to many successful families, including the Motts, Durands, Ketterings, and Collards, to name a few. My featured hero in this story is a third generation "Flint-ite" named Ken Collard.

Ken's father was an electrical engineer, and Ken followed in his footsteps by earning his Bachelor's Degree in Geology, his Master's Degree in Engineering Management and becoming a registered Professional Engineer. Prior to college, with the aid of a scholarship, Ken attended Cranbrook School, a prestigious Michigan prep school. After college, he returned to Flint, to work in city government. He married Marion (his beloved wife), and raised two sons and a daughter. Ken has spent most of his career in public service—planning, engineering and maintaining roads, utilities, parks, etc.

He has invested many years of time and talent into his birthplace. As many readers know, Flint, Michigan has suffered more than most cities. Ken did not sit on the sidelines during the crisis. He stepped into the middle of the fire as Flint's Public Works Utilities Director, but after years of effort, Ken and his family moved on to new challenges and opportunities. In 1992, he became the Public Services Director for Kalamazoo and recently accepted the role of Deputy City Manager. Like Flint, Kalamazoo faces a challenge of reinventing itself and its economy, but unlike Flint, Kalamazoo is poised for a rebound, thanks in part to Ken's hard work.

I met Ken in 2001, when he hired me to help Kalamazoo resolve a conflict with its suburban communities (see Chapter 16, Give Back Bay). In these cynical times, it is hard to envision that we still have people of integrity in our communities who are thoroughly devoted to the public good. Ken defines the term: Public Servant. When I asked him to characterize his journey from Flint to Cranbrook, back to Flint and then to Kalamazoo, he said it reminded him of the old Beatles song: *The Long and Winding Road*. Here is what he had to say about his journey.

Do you have a calling?

I don't know. I **am** committed to fighting for my family and my community. In my early years, personally and professionally, I was Mr. Do Right—the pragmatic doer trying to keep everyone safe. That role began early, when my parents divorced and I had to keep my mom and brother safe. When I married, I tried to be the warrior and the project manager. My wife tended to the affairs of the heart, and I handled the analytical hands-on stuff. As you know, these male and female archetypes must integrate if you want to grow, and there is no better place to do it than within the family. I remember how I felt when my first child was born and I picked him up from my wife's arms. That little bundle weighed next to nothing but I felt like I had the weight of the world in my arms. His birth laid the intellectual foundation for all that I care for today!

Your kids are grown now—is it easier?

No way! I tell the story that everybody lies to parents. The lies always start with this: Everything will be better **after**—after the first one sleeps through the night; after they eat solid foods; after they're potty trained; after they go to school; after they can drive; after they go to high school; after they graduate from college; and after they get married. And you know the story is a lie. Parenting doesn't start and stop. Don't get me wrong. I relish my role as a parent. In fact, I feel exactly the same way about my grandson (shown in picture with Ken). The instinct to protect him is the same.

When did you leave Comfortopia?

I left, personally, when my dad died and I had to get my act together to fill an uncomfortable role as patriarch of my family. Family members were asking me tough questions that should have been answered by my father and grandfather.

Professionally, my call occurred while working for Flint. The city was going down for the last time, and I wanted to make a difference. There is a recognizable pattern of destruction in our urban communities. I fought against that pattern with an outstanding team but we couldn't beat the dynamics of racial politics and corporate economics. In 1992, I carried the fight to Kalamazoo.

Then, when I met you and you introduced me to the IOPD model (see Chapter Eight), I felt as though I had left Comfortopia again. The model was compelling to me because it helped me see how Americans can rationalize decay and ghetto conditions away. Also, as I followed the model on a personal level, it drew out some issues. It helped me stop making myself into something that I wasn't. It released lots of energy and set me on a quest to learn about Carl Jung and how the personality works.

You mentioned the IOPD—where do you fit?

Most of my friends would be surprised to know that this pragmatic doer is really more comfortable and energized by the Creative Facilitator role. In my early years, I forced myself into the warrior/protector roles. I would argue that our society, even beyond the education system, forces you to go to the "ST" Warrior/Committed Manager place because that's where the gold is. Learning about the IOPD helped me see that I was out of balance and a new world opened up for me. I am now very involved in the people side of business and am definitely a better leader than before. I was the engineer with reams of data trying to get buy-in and just making people angry because I wasn't listening to their opinions. I realize now they just wanted to be engaged and have their perspectives and concerns heard. You know, I've got information. You've got information. Let's share it. I broke out of a mold that wasn't me in the first place, the old hierarchal and autocratic way of doing business.

Have you made the IOPD work in real-time?

The big breakthrough came when I dealt with the recent financial cutbacks in Kalamazoo. Then, I was the department head with 300 employees. It is difficult to interface with all of them, but as the cutbacks loomed, I knew I had to engage my staff or risk losing their energy. Based on the IOPD, I generated a list of questions—all focused on change. Questions like: How many jobs have you had? How many homes have you lived in? Have you ever watched a baby being born? Then, I planned a series of meetings. At the beginning of each meeting, I presented these 15 questions dealing with change. You would call it an icebreaker. The tone of the meeting was totally different and the people absorbed the news about layoffs and cutbacks with sad, yet open hearts. I got extraordinary feedback and all of the sudden I became human in their eyes. We pulled down the fences between management and the workforce and focused on the goal at hand, trying to save Kalamazoo by providing excellent public services.

Who were your monsters and allies?

Probably the biggest monster was me—that voice inside of me saying: "What right do you have to suppose that you can have an impact? After all, you are just a normal guy." It's probably not true. I do have some special insight and maybe special abilities but the monster was always lurking around the corner saying: "You haven't done anything yet; you're not really special so shut up and sit down." The words from the Beatles song *Long and Winding Road* come to mind: "You left me standing here." To me it means not a significant other but yourself—like you and the dreams of what you could do or become.

My allies are the great people who have helped me keep pushing. These are simply the heartfelt kinships that I built on this long and winding road. I am fortunate to have received a good education and have met great people. I have been able to draw on enough talent, resources and authority to believe that this world is going to get better.

So, how is the world going to get better?

First, we can't lose the basics. Lou Holtz made a motivational tape called *Do Right* and in it he says that you can gauge the health of a relationship by three questions: "Are you committed? Can I trust you? Do you care about me?" These questions are the foundation of the Golden Rule and I think we should spend more time asking and answering them.

Second, our young leaders need to be exposed to this sequential reality of life, the first and second-half stages. You can't force it on them but you can show them the fertile ground and see the greatness in it. About four years ago, my eldest son said that he was concerned about his generation. Now he is a great young leader, an outstanding police officer and about to finish his master's degree. He said that he was afraid that his generation wasn't up to the task of something on the scale of World War II. I couldn't have disagreed with him more. Yes, they are confused and less focused, but they didn't have anything to focus on—nothing to challenge them or provide an opportunity to demonstrate their greatness. On 9/11 these young people—20 and 30-year-old police officers, firefighters, and emergency workers-stepped up and stood proud. Here is my advice for young leaders: First, you need to know that you are great and second, you need to understand how your personality changes and grows over time.

Third, I hope that your Map to Unrational Leadership™ takes off. It could make a difference in communities that are decaying. It works from a personal point to a community plane. Thanks for bringing it to Kalamazoo.

Together at Last

Chuck Daniels graduated from the New Jersey Institute of Technology in December 1980 with a Bachelor's Degree in Engineering

Science and a minor in Nuclear Engineering. Little did he know then, but he was about to embark on a 20-year journey in which he would move seven times, work for six companies, and live in major metropolitan areas in California, Colorado, New Jersey, New York, Texas and Washington.

Daniels (48 years old) is a bright, energetic and successful executive who muscled his way through the '90s telecom boom. He spent the first 15 years of his career building success after success with his quick wit, sharp mind and take-no-prisoner attitude. I first met Chuck as he was moving from MCI to a new telecom start-up called NextLink Communications (now XO Communications). At NextLink, one of the hottest Competitive Local Exchange companies (CLEC's) of the "dot com" days, Chuck served as Chief Technical Officer and President of the Technology Services. Starting with nine employees, Chuck built an organization of more than 600 techies to support the launch of a national telecommunications company. He has been in at the ground level of several start-ups since NextLink and is currently working on a business plan for yet another hi-tech venture. Chuck is one of the flat-out smartest guys I know. I asked him to talk about his inner journey.

What was your Comfortopia like for you?

It was filled with dreams and nightmares, and I kept them on opposite sides of a heavily guarded wall. I reached my peak in Comfortopia when NextLink offered me a ground-floor opportunity. I had been in several start-ups but this was the best—the best funded, the best team, and the best plan. I had arrived! I was at the top of my game and thought that I was infallible. I had the self-assuredness that most people would call cocky. God blessed me with a quick mind that could shred you in a heartbeat if you crossed me. It didn't hurt that I am 6'4" tall and 240 pounds of intensity. In those days, I was your typical type-A, an incredibly successful go-getter and on my way to riches and fame.

On the dark side, I came from the typical broken childhood. I had an alcoholic, abusive father who beat the crap out of my brothers, sisters, my mom and me. Needless to say, I developed a very thick skin. I was like a bulldog. If you pushed against me, I leaned right back into you. There was no reverse or retreat on my gearshift column. It was always **fight or fight**.

I worked 80 hours a week and knew how to please my bosses in order to get the things I wanted: top bonuses; extraordinary vacations; a dream car; and a huge house for my lovely wife, Linda. (Note—Chuck has two children, Fred and Adeline. His son was born the day he signed on with NextLink.) Before NextLink, I worked for MCI. I succeeded at MCI. If you're very successful there, you're a ruthless bastard by definition. At MCI, we left a lot of dead bodies in the road. But, secretly, I really didn't like all the conflict. What good is success if you have to go home and argue with yourself, and second-guess your behavior? I was on a path to a nervous breakdown or a heart attack, but I didn't really want or know how to get off the merry-go-round.

When did you know that you had to leave Comfortopia?

My wake-up call came when I realized that I was losing my job and my dream at NextLink. The job was a pressure cooker. The Wall Street expectations were enormous and the stakes were high. I set myself up as the watchdog and became very vocal about team members who were not focused on the best interests of the company. I was at war with one of them. The company terminated him, but I looked bad in the process and caused the executive team great concern. I didn't worry about hurt feelings or devastated lives; I just wanted people to stop playing their petty games. I was fighting against all the crap you see going on in corporate America—the backstabbing, politics, gossip, and secrets that are detrimental to a company's success. In short, I had tons of righteous anger.

A fellow executive warned me that my career was at risk and as I absorbed this unpleasant information, I saw that I kept hitting the same speed bumps in life. Once again, I had found myself on the wrong side of a successful proposition. Even though I beat expectations and exceeded my objectives, I polarized people with my anger. I finally realized that under pressure, when I need to be the most effective, my personality turned inside out. In these times when I needed to accelerate, I slowed myself down by spending too much time focused on what somebody was doing to me.

How did you change yourself?

I made a commitment to change. And, I did three important things: I got help from a wise counselor, I took a couple of years off and immersed myself in my family, and I built my dream house in New Jersey, my home state. Doing these things helped me get the insights and the feelings that I needed to confront my inner demons. When you're forced to look at yourself and acknowledge that you are the source—not only for all the good in your life, but pretty much for all the disasters—it changes your way of acting. When I learned that I had an unconscious that drove me into the ditch, I had to accept that fact that my so-called enemies had their own unconscious. Before I started my journey, I honestly did not believe the unconscious was really unconscious. I believed that these people were "consciously" screwing me. They knew exactly what they were doing. Everything was on the surface to me. The biggest thing I had to face was that the people who made me angry were just like me. They acted the same way that I did. Here is another way of putting it: When you get mad at somebody else, it's really because you're mad at yourself because they represent something you don't like about yourself. You would call it the shadow.

I had one more epiphany that I want to share. I realized that all my strengths: Incredible intuition, great problem solving skills, and my technical prowess had also become my greatest weakness. It blinded me to how I responded to people, how I interacted with them and how I evaluated them. It was easy for me to envision the enterprise technology model and how to break it into specific functions and processes. But on my inner journey, I learned that you couldn't put the human challenge in a computer program. The technical challenge is really all about people. It's always about the people. In the role I'm in now and in my last couple of roles, all my focus has been on the people because I know the technical stuff will work itself out.

How do you know that you've really changed?

My thinking has changed substantially. For the longest time (my first 21 years) I felt the world was black or white. For the next 20 years, I was taught that the world was gray. What I now realize is that the world is black and white at the same time! Now, I can hold my anger. I have a five-step process that really works. First, I acknowledge the anger: "Yes, I'm angry. Okay? I'm not going to hide it. I'm angry." Second, I honor the anger: "I'm not a bad person. If I'm angry, there's got to be a reason why I'm angry." Third, I get into why: "Why am I angry?" Fourth, I start considering the important question: "Is this anger related to rejection? What is going on here? Why does this person make me so angry? And then fifth: "What is it about them that reminds me of something that I dislike about myself?" If I tackle these five questions sincerely, I can see and integrate the black and white sides of conflict.

Something happened to me on my last job. Somehow, I turned into the conflict facilitator for the executive team. I became a catalyst for helping them resolve their group issues. One of the senior executives, an incredibly talented lady, pulled me aside after a meeting and said: "Chuck, you are the calmest, most thoughtful executive I have ever worked with." That comment was Nirvana.

Chaos Man

Don Trim is the co-founder, builder, and now, resident elder of Wade-Trim, Inc. a surprisingly progressive engineering firm in a sector known for conservative leadership that has an almost genetic aversion to risk. For those of you who don't know, engineering consulting firms service almost every community in this country, surveying, designing and engineering the roads, water plants, sewer lines, tunnels, ports, subway stations, subdivisions, skyscrapers, airports and the rest of the infrastructure that supports our civilization. A 1959 graduate of the University of Michigan, Don went on to use his degree in Civil Engineering to change the landscape of Metropolitan Detroit through the design and management of large-scale water resource projects. In 1968, he and co-worker Bob Wade, bought out their boss, and founded Wade-Trim, Inc.

Don and Bob grew the firm from a staff of 22 to more than 400, with 11 offices in Michigan, Ohio, Pennsylvania, and Florida. While making his journey, Don served as president of the American Consulting Engineering Council, a 5,700-member organization devoted exclusively to the business and advocacy interests of engineering companies. Although Don no longer leads the firm that he built, he keeps his Professional License current, and he is justly proud of the company's mission statement: *Trusted Professionals Building America's Infrastructure.*

Recently, I talked to Don about his confrontation with the irrational side of his personality. His story illustrates the great shift in our culture from command and control to gut and intuition.

How did you get the name Chaos Man?

It all started because Bob Wade (my partner) and I had an office without walls. It was around 1990 and Bob had discovered strategic planning. Our company had grown a lot and Bob and I needed to give the company long-term direction. I heard Bob discussing how to handle a strategic planning meeting. Now, Bob didn't know it, but a few weeks before, I had read Margaret Wheatley's book: *Leadership and the New Science*. The main point of the book is that command and control doesn't work in the long run. Why? Because our world is filled with chaos. Wheatley's point is that a leader needs to provide order instead of beating his head against the wall trying to control what he can't control. Organizations will organize themselves effectively if we can only learn how to tolerate a little chaos.

As I listened to Bob talk, I made a gut decision to disrupt the strategic planning meeting—to introduce some chaos into the minds of our very command-and-control leadership team. Strategic planning meetings only happened once a year and we treated them very seriously so my decision to disrupt the meeting wouldn't be taken lightly.

Our strategic planner started the meeting by talking about how the plan would take us from Point A to Point B. He gave me the perfect opening when he said that we would travel a straight line between the points. I interrupted him and said: "It's only a straight line if you are really sure that Point B is where you want to end up." I walked up to the flip chart and drew squiggly lines between A and B, and then I finally moved Point B off the chart. I shocked that room of logical engineers into silence. They had spent their whole career drawing straight lines and I was telling them that it was okay to be squiggly. I spent an hour talking about chaos and the limitations of a command and control attitude. Needless to say, I got a lot of blank stares and I know I ticked off a lot of my team members. I had violated the agenda and at that time, agendas were a sacred thing at Wade-Trim.

After that meeting, I became known as "Chaos Man," and people never knew when he might appear at meetings. In fact, I never exactly knew when my gut would rear up and say: "There's too much command-and-control thinking in this room!"

Fortunately, in the strategic planning session, I got through to some of the younger people and they decided to get on board and see what this chaos thing was all about. We concluded that we needed a corporate vision and that we had to involve everyone in the company in the process of creating it. Today, involving the whole company in a visioning process may seem old hat, but 15 years ago it was revolutionary. People said: "We won't have enough time. There will be too many arguments. We can't satisfy everyone." But, I told them that the company would organize itself around a vision statement if we were patient enough to let it emerge from the chaos of lots and lots of staff meetings. As I predicted, it took us a while and the process frustrated the command-and-control types, but we created a vision statement that has been the company's foundation for more than ten years: *Building Relationships Upon a Foundation of Excellence.*

What advice do you give young leaders?

The most important thing they can do is to learn how to listen. As engineers we come into the world thinking that we have to be right, so we tend to block out any information contrary to our chosen point of view. Too many young leaders have decided how they want to get somewhere when they don't even really know where they are going. They need a vision. I tell them to seek out people who have different opinions and develop relationships. As a young leader, I was very command-and-control. I was heavy into math and science and I thought there was an exact answer for every problem. As I have grown older, I have learned how to pull myself back from my own urges to fix everything with logic. I have learned how to seek out people who disagree with me. Sometimes, it's hard to beat back all of my engineering training, which says: "There must be a linear process to solve this problem." But, then I find that, with patience, I can feel my emotions coming into the forefront and I use them to make better decisions.

What does the future hold for Chaos Man?

I am still leaving Comfortopia. Dorothy (my wonderful wife) and I recently bought a large piece of property in Northern Michigan. We are busy developing it into a combination of a natural preserve, a retreat for my family, and a tree farm.

I serve in the American Consulting Engineering Council. I am leading the Trusted Advisor Committee. We are developing a plan to educate our members on the benefits of becoming a trusted advisor to their clients. Lots of engineering consultants don't want to mess around with words like trust. They can't measure them or put them in a spreadsheet. But, I know we have to move that way if we want to stay competitive, and in the process, I will create as much Chaos as I can.

16 Give Back Bay

I'd driven through Kalamazoo many times, but I had never truly been there until I met Ken Collard, the city's Director of Public Services and Bruce Minsley, Deputy Director, in May 2001. You met Ken in Chapter 15, The Sea of the Great Heroes. He plays a starring role in this story and also provides a running commentary on how he felt about the introduction of Unrational Leadership™ into his community.

Ken and Bruce asked me to come to Kalamazoo to talk about a mess. Not that they called it a mess when they started telling me their story.

Here is the basic plot that can be found in any city of size in Michigan. The City of Kalamazoo, through its Department of Public Services, provides sewage collection, transport, treatment and disposal services to the city and many surrounding suburban communities (customers). In 1988, several customers sued the city because they thought the rates were too high and that the city was mismanaging the wastewater system. The lawsuit resulted in an agreement to form a regional authority by 1993 to manage the system. Obviously, an authority would require Kalamazoo to give up sole control of their wastewater system. The agreement gave them five years to create the authority or face long-term financial penalties. Due to mistrust and political positioning, the authority fell through and Kalamazoo was penalized.

"Charlie, we've started our regional master plan and it's supposed to identify the customer's needs for the next 20 years," said Ken. "We want to get the customers to cooperate with us. We don't want any more lawsuits."

"Yeah, Dick Hinshon gave your process a great reference," added Bruce, a short, intense guy. "He said, 'It sucks but it works.'"

"With friends like Dick, I don't need enemies!" I said, laughing. "Tell me your story, guys, and I'll tell you what I think. For free." They made an "oh, sure" grunt and started their story, taking turns, trading roles and supporting one another with asides and grunts. They talked like musicians who had been playing together for ten years. After listening to them for a while without interrupting, I said, "You know what you have here—you have a mess."

"Is that a technical term?" replied Ken with a little sarcasm.

"As a matter of fact it is," I answered seriously.

Pausing for a moment, I said: "If you want to solve an irrational problem, you have to use irrational methods. I have a proposal. Give me $5,000 and a list of people to interview and I will show

---

Ken Collard's Perspective on Messes:
When Charlie called it a mess, I thought it was funnier than hell. Here, we had brought in this real successful guy based on good references and what he said was: "You got a mess." Then he says the word irrational. To me, the word has bad connotations. I have an engineer's way of thinking, and I can't stand irrational. See, when you make things rational you make things better. Obviously, at that point, I didn't understand what Charlie meant by irrational solutions, but I became fascinated with the incongruity between rational and irrational. Yeah, I bought his rhetoric.

---

you how an irrational method can help solve your problem. If you don't like my results, you haven't wasted much money."

They looked at each other and said: "What have we got to lose?"

What is the Setting and Why is it Important?

The regional master plan would address one of the major sources of conflict between the city and its customers: contract limits. In the mid '70s, a study established the maximum sewage flow each customer could send to the Kalamazoo Water Reclamation Plant. These flow limits were embedded in individual customer contracts. Through the '80s and '90s, the city's economy declined, while the suburbs grew—a classic tale of a declining city surrounded by growing sprawl. The city felt abandoned by the suburbs and talked openly about restricting the growth that seemed to hurt their city.

As for the suburbs, they were still unhappy with their relationship with the city. They formed a Regional Commission in 1997 to defend themselves. Although invited, the city quite naturally refused to join the group. By 2001, some customers had exceeded the flow limits in their contracts. They were sending more flow than they should have to the city's reclamation plant. The customers were anxious. They thought Kalamazoo might enforce the contract, stop sewer construction, and choke their growth.

Ken and Bruce sent me a list of nine interviewees, community leaders with deep insight into the mess. I responded with a list of interview questions. The first question was: "What movie or book does this relationship bring to mind?" The second question was: "What is the setting and why is it important?" I think you get the irrational drift of a set of questions that didn't seem to have any bearing on the problem at hand.

I called Bruce and asked him if he had gotten the questions.

"Yeah, I got them, Charlie," said Bruce. "But you have to know that Ken hated them. Just hated them."

"I can't tackle an irrational problem without irrational questions," I replied.

> **Ken's Perspective on the Irrational Questions:**
> When I got the questions, I said to myself: "I'm not going to answer them. Not only did I get duped with his proposal, I have to play a game and remember stuff." Then, I developed a conviction that I couldn't remember enough about a movie or a book to do a decent job. I kept reminding myself that Dick swore that Charlie's process worked. Then, the movies came to mind; *The Sons of Katie Elder* and *Slapshot.* Damned if they didn't describe things in our situation. Oddly enough, by the time he interviewed me, I really wanted to talk to him, but I was afraid of looking foolish and too linear.

Raise the Irrationality to the Surface

I started my interviews from the movie angle because I was convinced that fiction had trumped fact. I have learned that fiction is stronger than fact—even in the most rational of people. One rational leader might say that my only job was to get the facts straight and another might say that my first task was to separate fiction from fact. But I thought my job was to raise the fiction to the surface so the clients could look at it and absorb it.

The conversations about movies led me to the red herring in this mess—the "Threatening Letter." I kept hearing about a letter that Kalamazoo had written to the customers threatening to shut off sewage service because they had exceeded their contract limits. I asked: "Could I get a copy?" "Do you remember writing it?" "Do you know who wrote it?" "Did you actually receive a copy?" I must have been the first person to ask for an actual copy of the letter. Everyone knew about it, but no one could produce it. I gave up searching for the letter. This is what happens when irrationality captures a group.

When I finished the interviews, I decided to portray the results in a mandala. (See Chapter Five, The Little Sea of the Voice that Defies

The Light Before the Dawn

Reason for information on drawing mandalas). "The Light Before the Dawn" was the first mandala I had drawn to portray a client's mess. My inner voice told me it was a good thing to do. I have written hundreds of interview reports and filled them with negative comments. When my clients get these reports, their faces often sink into despair. Sometimes, they even cry. I wanted something different for Kalamazoo. I wanted to lift them above their mess without hiding it. My toughest decision was mailing it to Ken and Bruce. I couldn't imagine their response, and I waited a week before calling them. I asked Bruce if they had received my picture.

"Yes, and boy is Ken weird about it."

"Oh." My heart sank.

"But, he showed it to some customers and they really liked it," Bruce added. "And, now I think Ken likes it. In fact, he wants you to come and meet with us as soon as possible to discuss the next steps."

Ken's Perspective on the Mandala:

When I opened up the package, I thought, "What the hell is this? How do you take nine interviews and turn them into anything other than a report?" I didn't like it or dislike it but I knew it was something special. My grandfather, who worked in a casting foundry for 40 years, was a great carver. He was an artist, and I respected him as such. You couldn't pay me enough or make me work often enough to create what he created. I just don't have those talents. I felt the same way about the mandala. It was art. I showed it around to people in the office. "I got this unique thing. Have you ever seen anything like this before?" In the end, I decided it didn't belong here. That's why I framed it and gave it back to Charlie at the end of the job. It belonged to the artist.

Drain the Irrationality from the Swamp

Ken and Bruce wanted me to take the next step and facilitate a resolution of the conflict. My first meeting with the community leaders occurred at the Kalamazoo Water Reclamation Plant, a facility nestled on the banks of the Kalamazoo River in a peaceful, park-like setting, with a lobby filled with greenery and flowers. There were about a dozen players—township supervisors, city commissioners, and various advisors and administrative managers.

"I am going to help you think differently about your conflict," I said, pointing at the mandala.

"That's nice, Charlie. We will do anything you want, but you have to finish by Christmas," someone said.

"It's November," I said. "You have had this problem for 14 years and you want me to get you out of the woods in three meetings?"

"You got it, mister!" they exclaimed.

"Okay, then," I said, rubbing my hands together. "Let's get to it. Task number one is to get irrational."

For the first irrational exercise, I asked the group to draw pictures of the wastewater negotiation process. I told them to depict it as a long sea voyage. I asked them to think about the kind of ship they had been sailing, what the weather had been like and whether there were monsters in the water. Most people looked at me dumbfounded. (Note: This is one of the most practical exercises for tapping the unconscious.)

"I'm no artist," some complained. Others laughed uncomfortably as they began the exercise. One guy said angrily: "Is this kindergarten?" A few people drew squares and lines, and flat out refused to create an image. But, many of the pictures did convey the unconscious situation. They were caught alone in the ocean in the midst of their enemies and the elements. I asked them to trade pictures and to make changes. "Find something that is missing and add it," I instructed. They responded with more groans but complied. Then, I taped the pictures on the wall and the reluctant artists explained their creations. (See samples on next page.)

After the drawing exercise, we had breakout sessions that resulted in the outline of a solution. Yes, that's right, within a couple of hours the group had the concept. It wasn't really new—the city would trade some control over the system for an increase in revenues. But, the drawing exercise had drained enough irrationality from the swamp to make them believe they could make it happen.

For the next two months, the group fleshed out their concept. Whenever we got together, I put them through an irrational exercise—drawing pictures, writing poetry, telling childhood stories. They had a massive irrational swamp! Even though most people whined and complained, they followed instructions. I knew I was making progress when Rich Pierson, the Director of the Regional Commission, said that the process helped him look at himself. The first principle of Unrational Leadership™ was on the move: Start all problem solving by taking personal responsibility.

> **Ken's Perspective on draining the Swamp:**
> I absolutely hated the irrational exercises and I didn't look forward to
> them. The creative or artistic piece of myself is something that I had never
> explored. Also, there was the shyness piece—I didn't want people to see
> how incompetent I am. But again, I experienced a fascination with the ef-
> fectiveness of the technique. All of us were awful artists and poets, but
> during the exercises we always smiled and laughed at each other without
> being hurtful. We ended up laughing with—not at each other. By the
> end, we weren't comfortable until we did one of those dratted exercises.

The Closer We Get to a Decision, the More Irrational We Become

Christmas came and went and the group kept working on a solution.
There were two big obstacles to trading control for revenue. If the
suburbs raised their rates in order to buy out Kalamazoo, it might be
construed as a tax increase. If the city gave away control of the system
it would violate covenants in utility bonds that the city had issued.
Despite these monsters, the group crafted a Memorandum of Understanding (MOU) for creating a new authority. I told the group that
the closer they got to a decision, the more irrational they would become. I had seen this pattern over and over in groups. At the point of
making an ethical decision, we stand at the cliffs of the Sea of the Dark
Side and get overwhelmed by fears, anxieties, and betrayals. It is the
place where a retreat can quickly turn into a rout.

Kalamazoo asked for input on the MOU from its political friends
and received a blistering condemnation from one of its most respected public relations consultants, which translated into something like: "ARE YOU CRAZY? Do you think the voters are going to
accept a rate increase in these days and times because your customers want a say in the system?" This critique shook the city's leadership, and people talked of not only abandoning the MOU but the
entire process. The ship was dead in the water and slowly sinking. I
wasn't surprised. Don Schmidt, our legal advisor who had been

involved in the 1988 case, told us from the beginning that a citizen uprising could hammer a revenue increase.

In 14 years of conflict, they had never gotten this close to a solution. They were in the coastal waters of the Sea of the Dark Side, **unconsciously** searching for an ethical decision. Naturally it was easy for them to start finger-pointing. I received some angry phone calls and e-mails. But, I stayed confident. I didn't know how the lucky break was going to unfold, but I knew it would come because they had explored the irrational side of their mess. Whenever people go in and wrestle with the dark side, something good usually happens. This is the most important lesson of the search for Unrational Leadership™.

Move Toward the Irrational to Make Ethical Decisions

Time passed and from my home base in Farmington Hills, I wondered if anything was happening. Then, Ken invited me to Kalamazoo to meet with the two key protagonists: Pat DiGiovanni, the City Manager of Kalamazoo, and Gary Cramer, the Chairman of the Regional Commission. "Oddly enough they have been talking by themselves," declared Ken. "They have something to say to the group."

Pat is an intense East Coast guy with sharp humor and incredible decisiveness. He is responsible for facilitating the redevelopment of Kalamazoo's inner city. He's the type of person you'd expect to find running a large corporation in New York City. Gary, on the other hand, is the supervisor for Kalamazoo Township—a middle-aged community whose growing days are behind it. He is a laid-back ex-educator, dedicated administrator and ideally suited for steering customers out of the storm. To me, Pat and Gary seemed like oil and water, but something made them mix because they broke through the 14 years of irrational conflict and delivered the solution.

I started the March 2002 meeting with a clip from the 1996 movie

Tin Cup. The movie's hero, Roy "Tin Cup" McAvoy, played by Kevin Costner, is a washed-up golf pro from the dust bowl of West Texas, who achieves his life dream of competing for the U.S. Open Golf Championship. He plays over his head in the first three rounds. On the tournament's 72nd hole, a long par 5, he confronts a water hazard in front of the green. In the first three rounds of the tournament he dumped the ball in the water instead of playing safe and laying up short. Against all odds and most especially his own character, he is leading the tournament by a stroke.

He hits a fine drive and is about 225 yards from the green. He can play safe for a par and guarantee at least a tie or fly the ball over the water hazard and seize a certain and heroic victory. Against all rational advice from his caddy and his girlfriend in the gallery, Tin Cup decides to go for the green. He hits four balls in a row into the water and loses all hope of winning golf's most prestigious championship. Then, he fires the last ball in his bag over the water and it goes in the hole. The crowd goes nuts along with his caddy and of course, his girlfriend. Paradoxically, his irrational decisions lead him to his deepest desires—a hero's welcome and complete acceptance from the crowd and his girlfriend. The movie fulfills our hidden irrational dreams of sticking to our guns in the face of all rational advice.

I asked the group to compare themselves to "Tin Cup," and they concluded they were sick of playing safe. "Playing safe" meant worrying about lawyers, public relations spinners and everyone with a grudge against the city. All those other people seemed to be saying: "Play it safe. Don't do anything wrong. Don't do anything unless you are sure it will be perfect." I saw an opportunity to concentrate this defiant energy and turn it into action so I told them to sit in a circle for a dialogue (see Chapter Two). I pulled out my magic rock.

"Just remember, folks," I said. "This magic rock is from the bottom of the Ganges River." I received a chorus of groans and sarcasm.

But, sometimes, the rock has a magic that cannot be denied. Not too far into the dialogue, Pat DiGiovanni asked for it and after cradling it for a minute, made a stunning offer: "The city will assign extra capacity to customers who are nearing or are above their contract limits—without requiring compensation or a new contract. In other words, we will give you what you want for nothing." Then, Gary Cramer asked for the rock and said: "I am with Pat. **I think we should go for the green.** We need to quit worrying about what everyone else is going to think and do what's right for this community. Let's take Pat's offer and work for it. On my part, I pledge that the Regional Commission will work with the city to prevent decay and make the city an attractive place to live and visit. We must not abandon the city."

> **Ken's Perspective on the Offer of Capacity:**
> When I heard the idea of giving the customers three million gallons a day, I thought it was wrong. But, I had worked with the mess long enough to know that we had to get on a plateau that we could operate on. The real value was what the solution symbolized—a New Day.

The Best Journey Ends with Sharing the Treasure

Kalamazoo stepped into the center of the Clouds of the Unknown when it offered to give away the capacity that it had so closely guarded. How would the customers take the offer? Would it spark a similar gift in kind? After the March meeting, the answer came quickly as the customers pledged to focus their energies on helping the city revitalize itself. Both sides gave to each other for the overall good of the community. A revolutionary agreement for collaborative management and leadership, a sterling example of giving back, soon emerged.

- The Regional Commission agreed to facilitate the removal of the financial penalties that had been assigned to the city in 1993.
- The city agreed to join the Regional Commission and contribute only one vote to the decision-making. (Note: in 2002, customers outnumbered Kalamazoo 13 to 1.)
- The city gave the Regional Commission first-level decision-

making over the most important functions—rate setting, budget development and capital investment planning.

- The city agreed to give the Regional Commission three million gallons a day of treatment capacity.
- The Regional Commission agreed to work with the city on urban decay by hosting an annual conference on urban issues.

Landing this ship wasn't all fun and games. The group had been in conflict so long that conflict was more comfortable than peace. The closer they got to success, the more danger they faced from irrational forces. I brought the mandala to each meeting and tacked it on the wall as a good luck talisman. I didn't talk about it; I just hoped its mere presence would have a positive impact as they floundered in their uneasy seas. In an attempt to help ease the group and eliminate their visions of political disaster, I facilitated a mandala drawing exercise. I wasn't sure if it had any impact until Pat gave us a pleasant surprise. He started one meeting by passing out paper bags that contained an object. Next, he played the Carly Simon song *Anticipation* and asked people to open the bag. We each found a bottle of ketchup. Pat said: "Look at the label!" He had removed the manufacturer's label and replaced it with the mandala. Within 90 days, the communities throughout the region ratified the agreement without a single negative vote.

17 The Triumphant Return

They sat holding hands on a bench overlooking a meadow in the Dark Forest. The sun was a few hours away from dropping under the top of the Earth. The setting heat warmed their bones.

"How did he live so long?" asked TrueHeart, as he watched a three-legged dog hop towards them.

"Magic," said Moira. She gazed into his eyes. A deep lover's gaze. "Answer me this, my dear TrueHeart. Now that your great adventure is finished, what's next?"

"And if I don't answer, my head will spin like a top and explode?"

"I better kiss you before it happens."

"Mmmmmmm."

"Darling," he said, keeping her close, "I will write a book about my search for Unrational Leadership™. After it lands on the best seller list, I might open a school."

"The Academy of Unrational Leadership™?"

"And, the frog turned into a professor," laughed TrueHeart. "What are your plans, my Queen?"

Moira smiled lazily. "Now that Brigid[1] abdicated her throne to me, my first task is to change the name of this shadowy realm."

"Too uncomfortable," he chuckled.

"Too depressing! I want to reform everything. I want to introduce democracy, public education, prenatal health care for expectant mothers, and free high-speed broadband."

"Unrational Leadership™ will be compulsory, along with dream circles?"

"Yes, my dear," said Moira.

"Before dawn, the darkest hour passed! As your most loyal subject, I support your plans."

"Oh, I almost forgot to tell you. The Princess called early this morning."

"And?"

Moira paused for effect. "She's engaged!"

"Great news! She is a sweetheart. I knew she would find someone quickly."

"Indeed. A week after our departure, she was walking in the woods and met our dear friend the snake, who asked her: "For whom do you search?" Upon hearing her story of a love too old, the snake led her to a secret place in the woods whereupon she found a sleeping Prince."

"Don't tell me. She roused him with a single kiss?"

"That is the right formula. Can you guess his name?"

"Charming."

"One and the same," she said before closing her eyes to embrace him.

And they all lived happily ever after.

THE END

Note

1. After TrueHeart vanquished Rich in Wisdom with his unforeseen questions and saved the Kingdom, the King offered Brigid a four-year consulting contract to teach the King and his Court the principles of Unrational Leadership™. Her first piece of advice was for the King to relinquish the Ninth Habit. He accepted readily.

Appendix A
Unrational Leadership™ Effectiveness Survey

Name: _____

Measurement Key:

5 = Excellent; 4 = Above Average; 3 = Average; 2 = Below Average; 1 = Poor

Wise Leader Activities					
• Makes excellent decisions—more right than wrong	5	4	3	2	1
Comments:					
• Defines/articulates and defends norms, values, rules, etc.	5	4	3	2	1
Comments:					
• Discovers/makes essential meaning for oneself/team: "Why are we really doing this?"	5	4	3	2	1
Comments:					
• Organizes and develops a strong team	5	4	3	2	1
Comments:					
• Identifies and develops successors	5	4	3	2	1
Comments:					
• Rewards team for good performance—shares the treasure!	5	4	3	2	1
Comments:					
• Creates sense that he/she is worth following—can take a person to a better place	5	4	3	2	1
Comments:					
• Communicates company story, status, etc.	5	4	3	2	1
Comments:					

Committed Manager Activities					
• Develops solid strategies and plans	5	4	3	2	1
Comments:					
• Delivers the goods and makes the numbers—has a bias for action	5	4	3	2	1
Comments:					
• Chooses the two or three things that matter and disciplines the organization to accomplish them	5	4	3	2	1
Comments:					
• Sees and responds courageously to brutal realities	5	4	3	2	1
Comments:					
• Able to sustain/endure suffering over long time in order to achieve objectives	5	4	3	2	1
Comments:					
• Manages his/her team effectively	5	4	3	2	1
Comments:					
• Manages stakeholders: customers/suppliers/investors effectively	5	4	3	2	1
Comments:					

Walking Through the Clouds of the Unknown

• Walks own talk—follows own rules	5	4	3	2	1

Comments:

• Looks at own shadow—can tolerate criticism	5	4	3	2	1

Comments:

• Asks for help when he/she is lost	5	4	3	2	1

Comments:

• Changes structure and process as needed	5	4	3	2	1

Comments:

• Avoids blaming others for bad situations	5	4	3	2	1

Comments:

• Avoids relying on "chosen few" for advice	5	4	3	2	1

Comments:

• Shares critical information throughout the organization	5	4	3	2	1

Comments:

• Doesn't get overwhelmed with a sense of power	5	4	3	2	1

Comments:

Creative Facilitator Activities					
• Brings creativity to all problem-solving processes	5	4	3	2	1
Comments:					
• Can get a "hunch" and track it—despite "facts" to the contrary	5	4	3	2	1
Comments:					
• Has deep sensitivity and intuition—can read people easily	5	4	3	2	1
Comments:					
• Easily sees relationships and connectedness between different people /groups/partners	5	4	3	2	1
Comments:					
• Facilitates resolution of conflicts	5	4	3	2	1
Comments:					
• Creates open atmosphere—feeling of empowerment	5	4	3	2	1
Comments:					
• Displays sense of humor—can lift the troops with it!	5	4	3	2	1
Comments:					
• Colors the world around—makes it "come alive" through décor, fun, sound, etc. for employees	5	4	3	2	1
Comments:					

Organizational Visionary Activities					
• Defines/articulates a compelling, clear, concise vision	5	4	3	2	1
Comments:					
• Possesses consummate technical knowledge of business core competencies	5	4	3	2	1
Comments:					
• Capable of applying technical/knowledge in creative ways—has delivered the product or process homerun	5	4	3	2	1
Comments:					
• Routinely selects, develops and initiates younger people	5	4	3	2	1
Comments:					
• Protects organization appropriately (secrets, risks, betrayal, etc.)	5	4	3	2	1
Comments:					
• Unleashes technical or process change with wisdom—is aware of and protects against "meltdowns"	5	4	3	2	1
Comments:					
• Detached and calm in a legal/process/technical crisis . . . able to think through problems clearly	5	4	3	2	1
Comments:					

Appendix B

Detailed Comparison of Rational and Unrational Leadership™ Problem Solving

Saving the Great Lakes

This problem concerns two countries, several native tribes, millions of people and the greatest fresh water ecosystem in the world. Currently, overdevelopment, pollution, invasive species, climatic change, and water withdrawals from other regions of the country threaten the Great Lakes. Although many groups have been formed to watch over the lakes, no single group has the authority to ensure that the lakes survive as a viable source for drinking water, fishing, recreation, and travel. For example, a comprehensive process to assess and monitor the health of the lakes does not exist. Invasive species are wiping out the fish; mercury continues to accumulate in the wildlife; farm and industry pollutants continue to pour into the water; and development eats up more and more shoreline. Although many helpful programs exist, there is no comprehensive approach for saving the Great Lakes.

Strategy for Saving the Great Lakes:
Confront and Partner with the Unconscious

The critical challenge in a project like saving the Great Lakes is getting the important constituencies on the same page at the same time. This level of unity generally occurs only when there is a crisis, as when the Cuyahoga River caught on fire or Lake Erie almost died. In so-called normal times, the times when the crisis is building, rational leaders try to build consensus through education, communication, political deals, etc. These consensus-building efforts take a long time (if they work at all) on problems that defy reason because the rational leader ignores the unconscious drives, fantasies, emotions that fragment and derail unified approaches. In other words, he only works with the tip of the iceberg. To shorten the problem solving cycle, the unrational leader concentrates on partnering with the unconscious energy. Then, he or she educates the participants about the power of the unconscious and helps them prepare plans to address the inevitable resistance that will emerge as a plan unfolds. The rational leader will often resist this strategy, saying: "It takes too much time." But, in the long run, confronting and integrating the unconscious fragments saves time and dramatically increases the chances of success. Remember: When the unconscious drives emerge early, the group can deal with them. When they emerge late in the process, they are viewed as betrayals.

Saving the Great Lakes:
Rational and Unrational Leadership™ Approaches

Phase	Rational Leadership	Unrational Leadership™
Organize	• Find the powerful political sponsor(s). • Identify the key players that need to be involved. • Form a committee(s) to study the problem. • Hire technical experts to collect and analyze data. • Hire facilitator(s) to run efficient and relatively conflict free meetings.	(Everything the rational leader does, plus) • Researches ancestral visions of the Great Lakes. • Connects with and listens to the inner voices of all participants. • Conducts extensive dialogue sessions until common meaning is achieved on *"Why should we save the Great Lakes?"* • Depicts powerful ideas and emotions in a mandala picture. • Establishes a team to prepare a 500-year vision for the Great Lakes.

Phase	Rational Leadership	Unrational Leadership™
Plan	• Based on the study, the problem is divided into different functional domains. • Unconsciously agree to not raise any issues that involve personal change or intractable political or international conflicts. • Sub-committees are formed to develop action plans. • The action plans are presented to the sponsors. • Tentative agreements are reached, pending endorsement by various agencies, governmental bodies, etc.	(Everything the rational leader does—except the second bullet—plus) • Teaches the participants about the impact of the unconscious on the planning process. • Teaches the participants creative activities that stimulate the intuitive mind (poetry, singing or drawing). • Conducts community-planning sessions throughout the Great Lakes that tap the unconscious • Develops a plan that directly addresses the irrational forces in the community that will derail any significant change.

A Tired Information Technology Company

An information technology company has an old and entrenched management team that has failed to groom the next generation for corporate leadership. This management team doesn't have energy for mentoring or coaching. In the past five years, turnover has risen to triple the industry average and several key leaders have joined competitors or formed their own companies. Formerly, the marketplace used the company as the benchmark, but the firm's reputation is declining. In the last two years, layoffs reduced the staff by 25 percent. The management team changes the organization annually and some people have worked for five managers in five years. The management team wants to sell the company, but global competition (especially from India) is driving valuation prices into the cellar.

Strategy for Rousing a Tired Company: Increase Energy

The unrational leader sees this problem as an energy shortage and taps the unconscious for energy. The rational leader plans to accomplish the job with hard facts and disciplined planning. In the process he plays to the logical, analytical strength of his management team. He doesn't know that rationality is wearing out in Comfortopia. He also doesn't know that when his personality wears out, it turns into a weakness. A strategic plan will be created, but this tired management team will not implement it effectively. Then, they will place the responsibility for failure on the shoulders of the next generation. They will say: "They don't have the same fires that we had when we were young."

A Tired Information Technology Company:
Rational and Unrational Leadership™ Approaches

Phase	Rational Leadership	Unrational Leadership™
Organize	• The CEO gathers the management team and informs them about the problem and shares pertinent data—trends and forecasts. • Seeks feedback on analysis, gauges team's readiness to face the brutal reality. • The team brainstorms components of the problem, which are then prioritized and classified by function. • Functional sub-teams are formed for data collection. • The teams debate how much to share with the people. The HR voice carries the day.	(Everything the rational leader does, plus) • The CEO presents the concept of the heroic adventure and says the greatest monsters lie within—shows movie to stimulate emotions/unconscious. • Presents The Individual and Organizational Path to Discovery™ (IOPD) and uses it to help the team see that the company can't change without individual change. • The team identifies dominant personality couplings and paths to personal growth. • Forms team of corporate elders to intuit a vision for the next 100 years.

A Tired Information Technology Company: con't

Phase	Rational Leadership	Unrational Leadership™
Plan	• A strategic planning offsite is conducted to analyze data and to develop five-year goals and action plans. • Corporate mission, value and vision statements are reassessed and changed to reflect the future vision. • Sub-teams form in the organization with leaders assigned as champions. • Identify and remove roadblocks to productivity. • Form a team to discuss culture/training issues. • Prepare/publish detailed five-year action plan and integrate into incentive plans.	(Everything the rational leader does, plus) • The CEO presents information on stages of life. • Helps leaders understand the prime directive of the second half of life—giving back to the next generation. • Encourages team leaders to document their dreams and conducts a series of dream circles to identify powerful symbols that will catalyze the rejuvenation of the company. • Assigns leaders to the most energetic people in the company—gets them involved in the heroic journey. They plot the company's path to a new land, using the heroic journey as the model.

A CEO's First Failure

This struggling manufacturing company went through two CEOs in five years, so the Board exhausted itself in hiring the third, a rising star in the sector with an unblemished resume. She sold the Board on her ability to turn around the company in one year. She started the transition quickly by bringing in her own management team. At the six-month mark, she confidently told the Board that the turnaround was in sight. But, by the end of the first year, not a single indicator had improved on the company's balanced scorecard. Under intense questioning, the CEO admitted she had underestimated the depth of the problem, and predicted the light at the end of tunnel was only six months away. After the CEO left the meeting, the Chairman of the Board (COB) revealed that he had reports that the CEO had lost the confidence of her management team and that she frequently blew up at meetings. In his view, she had made two gross hiring mistakes, one in Sales, the other in Engineering. The Board concluded its meeting by agreeing that it did not want to bring in another CEO.

Strategy for Dealing with CEO Failure: Take Personal Responsibility

In general, the more successful a rational leader is, the less likely she is to question herself when a significant failure occurs in her organization. During the past decade, we watched the directors of large corporations sit passively as CEOs ran their companies into the ground and cost investors billions of dollars. In this case of the CEO's First Failure, the directors will turn their guns on the CEO and begin a series of rational defensive actions. But the COB pursues a strategy of personal responsibility by asking: "What role have we played in this drama in view of the fact that we have repeated it twice in the last five years?" And he doesn't stop at the tip of the iceberg; he goes below the surface and asks everyone to look how his or her unconscious contributed to the problem.

A CEO's First Failure:
Rational and Unrational Leadership™ Approaches

Phase	Rational Leadership	Unrational Leadership™
Organize	• The COB conducts discrete conversations with key executives, investors, including the Corporate Counsel. • The HR VP reviews compensation plans for irregularities and assesses the possibility of harassment lawsuits. • The CFO reviews the financials and prepares worst-case scenarios. • Conversations are initiated with a recruiter. • The Board asks the CEO to prepare presentation on the Strategic Plan.	(Everything the rational leader does, plus) • The COB examines his own actions in the hiring process, and leads the Board to do the same. • The COB presents the concept of corporate shadow and how a corporation can make scapegoats of its leaders. • The Board conducts dialogue: Do we turn our CEOs into scapegoats? • The Board considers and decides what changes are needed to promote better performance by the Office of the CEO.
Plan	• The COB informs the CEO that the Board is exploring options. • Based on findings, the COB considers replacing the CEO, hiring a coach for the CEO, dividing the CEO/President role into two positions. • The CEO presents the Strategic Plan to the Board. • In private session the Board decides on CEO's future.	(Everything the rational leader does, plus) • The COB meets with the CEO and discusses concept of personal shadow. • The COB directs the CEO to do 360° evaluations with the Unrational Leadership™ Effectiveness Survey. • The COB gives the CEO heroic quest: To use results of survey to identify her personal shadow and how it impacts her and her people. • The CEO develops a plan for deep personal change.

References

Chapter 1
1. Gregg Michael Levoy, *Callings: Finding and Following an Authentic Life*, part 5, page 272 (Harmony Books 1997).

Chapter 2
1. Marcus Buckingham & Curt Coffman, *First, Break all the Rules: What the World's Greatest Managers Do Differently*, chapter 3, pages 71–78 (Simon & Schuster 1999).
2. Peter M. Senge, *The Fifth Discipline: The Art & Practice of The Learning Organization*, part 1, page 10 (Doubleday & Company, Incorporated 1990).

Chapter 3
1. Stephen R. Covey, *The 7 Habits of Highly Effective People* (Free Press 1989).
2. Juliet B. Schor, *The Overworked American: The Unexpected Decline of Leisure*, chapter 2, pages 17–41 (Basic Books 1957).

Chapter 5
1. Roger Harrison & Herb Stokes, Workbook *Diagnosing Organizational Culture* (Bass/Pfeiffer 1992).
2. Susanne F. Fincher, Foreword by Robert A. Johnson, *Creating Mandalas For Insight, Healing, and Self-Expression*, chapter 1, page 2 (Shambhala Publications, Inc. 1991).
3. Carl Jung, *Memories, Dreams, Reflections*, chapter VI, pages 195–196 (Random House, Inc. 1961).
4. Robert L. Moore & Douglas Gillette, *King, Warrior, Magician, Lover: Rediscovering the Archetypes of the Mature Masculine*, part II, pages 47–141 (HarperCollins Publishers Inc. 1990).

Chapter 6
1. Brothers Grimm, Translated by Jack Zipes, *The Complete Fairy Tales of the Brothers Grimm*, chapter 53, page 204 (Bantam Books 1987).

Chapter 7

1. Carl Jung, *Psychological Types (The Collected Works of C.G. Jung), Vol. 6*, introduction, page 6 (Princeton University Press 1976).
2. Katharine D. Myers & Isabel Briggs Myers, The *Myers-Briggs Type Indicator® (MBTI)* was first developed by Isabel Briggs Myers (1897–1979) in collaboration with her mother, Katharine Cook Briggs.
3. John L. Giannini, *Compass of the Soul: Typology's Four Archetypal Directions as Guides to a Fuller Life* (Center for Applications of Psychological Type, Inc. 2004).
4. Renee Baron, *What Type Am I? Discover Who You Really Are*, page 167 (Penguin 1998).
5. Richard Florida, *The Rise of the Creative Class: And How It's Transforming Work, Leisure, Community, and Everyday Life*, chapter 5, pages 85–101 (Basic Books 2002).

Chapter 8

1. Carl Jung, *Aion*, page 8 (Ediciones Paidas Ibcrica 1993).

Chapter 9

1. Stephen R. Covey, *The 7 Habits of Highly Effective People*, part 2, habit 3, pages 153–154 (Free Press 1989).
2. Artemidorus, Robert J. White (Translator) *Oneirocritica; Interpretation of Dreams by Artemidorus* (Original Books, 1990).
3. Robert McCarly & J. Allan Hobson, (Activation-Syntheses Model) Article *Dreams: Disguise of Forbidden Wishes or Transparent Reflections of a Distinct Brain* (Annals of New York Academy of Science 1998).
4. Carl Jung, *Man and His Symbols*, introduction, pages v–xii (Dell Publishing Company, Inc. 1964).
5. Ad de Vries, *Dictionary of Symbols and Imagery* (Elsevier Science Publishers B.V. 1984).
6. Carl Jung, *Psychological Reflections: A New Anthology of His Writings, 1905–1961*, pages 53–77 (Bollingen Foundation Inc., 1953).

Chapter 11

1. Carl Jung, *The Development of Personality, (Collected Works of C.G. Jung Vol. 17)* page 179 (Princeton University Press, 1954).
2. Roger Herman & Joyce Gioia, Article *Teens Shun Fastest Growing Careers* (Herman Trend Alert 2004).
3. David H. Maister, Charles H. Green & Robert M. Galford, *The Trusted Advisor,* part one, page 8 (Free Press 2000).

Chapter 13

1. Carl Jung, *Memories, Dreams and Reflections,* chapter XII, page 345 (Random House, Inc. 1961).
2. Richard Wilhelm; rendered into English by Cary F. Baynes, *The I Ching: Or, Book of Changes* (Princeton University Press 1950).

Chapter 14

1. Heinrich R. Zimmer, *The King and the Corpse,* part I, pages 202–235 (Princeton University Press, 1948).

Chapter 15

1. Margaret J. Wheatly, *Leadership and the New Science: Discovering Order in a Chaotic World* (Berrett-Koehler Publishers, Inc. 2001).

Index

ORDERING INFORMATION

Individual sales:

Special discounts are available on quantity purchases by corporations, associations, and others. For details, contact the "Special Sales
Department" at the Right Brain Books address below or visit our
website www.rightbrainbooks.us

Orders for college textbook/course adoption use:

Please contact Right Brain Books at the address below or visit our
website www.rightbrainbooks.us

Right Brain Books, LLC
22000 Springbrook Ave. Ste. 106
Farmington Hills, MI 48336

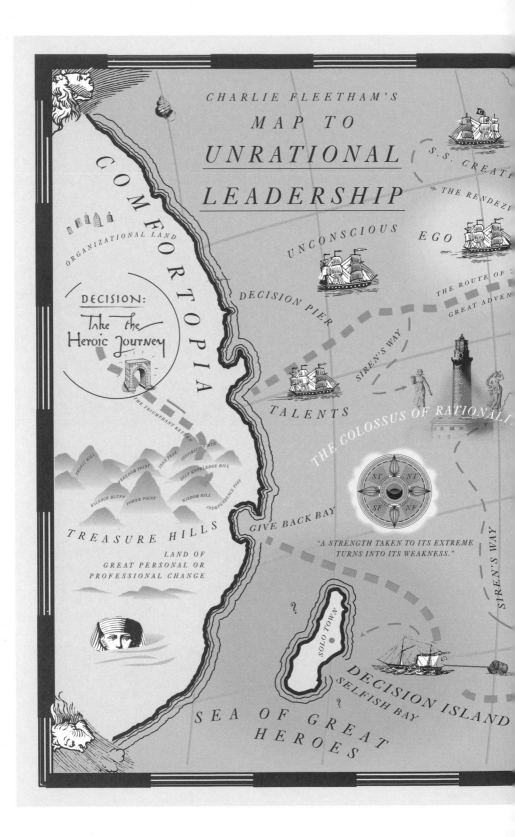